Working Skin

ASIA PACIFIC MODERN

Takashi Fujitani, Series Editor

Working Skin

MAKING LEATHER, MAKING A MULTICULTURAL JAPAN

Joseph D. Hankins

UNIVERSITY OF CALIFORNIA PRESS

University of California Press, one of the most distinguished university presses in the United States, enriches lives around the world by advancing scholarship in the humanities, social sciences, and natural sciences. Its activities are supported by the UC Press Foundation and by philanthropic contributions from individuals and institutions. For more information, visit www.ucpress.edu.

University of California Press
Oakland, California

Library of Congress Cataloging-in-Publication Data

Hankins, Joseph D.
    Working skin : making leather, making a multicultural Japan / Joseph D. Hankins.
        pages   cm. — (Asia Pacific modern ; 13)
    Includes bibliographical references and index.
    ISBN 978-0-520-28328-2 (cloth : alk. paper)
    ISBN 978-0-520-28329-9 (pbk. : alk. paper)
        1. Buraku people—Social conditions.   2. Buraku people—Government policy.   3. Multiculturalism—Japan.   4. Labor—Japan.   5. Working class—Japan.   6. Japan—Social conditions.   7. Japan—Politics and government.   I. Title.
    HT725.J3H255   2014
    305.5'680952—dc23

                                            2014005898

Manufactured in the United States of America

23   22   21   20   19   18   17   16   15   14
10   9   8   7   6   5   4   3   2   1

In keeping with a commitment to support environmentally responsible and sustainable printing practices, UC Press has printed this book on Natures Natural, a fiber that contains 30% post-consumer waste and meets the minimum requirements of ANSI/NISO z39.48-1992 (R 1997) (*Permanence of Paper*).

人の世に熱あれ
人間に光りあれ

CONTENTS

ILLUSTRATIONS

Hailing from Texas

TEXAS IS AN OCCASIONAL but persistent part of the story this book tells. Much of the rawhide produced in West Texas in the last half of the twentieth century was sent to Japan to be processed into leather there. Chapter 2, "Ushimatsu Left for Texas," touches on the ways in which Texas has lived in a Buraku[1] imaginary as a place that values rather than stigmatizes human involvement in meat production. And, finally, I too am from West Texas and have been well served by that romantic imaginary in conducting my research on the leather industry in Japan.

To begin this book I would like to relate a story explaining how I came to this project, an account more personal than a similar examination that happens in the conclusion. My reasons and motivations for engaging in this research are more diffuse, contingent, and motivated than this one story might indicate. However, this story serves as a convenient shorthand to open the central issues of my research.

When I entered my PhD program in anthropology in 2001, I intended to research language use, gender, and sexuality in Japan. In my second year I moved from Chicago to Yokohama for language study and had the good fortune of joining a "Minority Research Group" at the University of Tokyo. Led by sociology professor Fukuoka Yasunori, this group met monthly to discuss the research of graduate students and faculty working on minority-related projects. After a few months, Fukuoka invited me to accompany him and a handful of his students to a leather tannery in Tochigi Prefecture, north of Tokyo, to tour the facility and conduct interviews over a weekend. It was to be a brief study tour of Buraku-related issues. At that time I was aware of Buraku issues. I knew they were a group of stigmatized people in Japan, but I thought of myself as studying something very different. However, one

FIGURE 1. Cattle in a feedlot outside of Lubbock, Texas.

of my advisers in graduate school, Danilyn Rutherford, had repeatedly stressed the methodological value of accepting all invitations. In that spirit, I headed north with Fukuoka and a handful of his students.

When we arrived at the tannery in Tochigi, we were ushered into the main office to meet with the owner and manager. We went around the room introducing ourselves, and I could sense the curiosity building as my turn approached. Who was this obvious foreigner—white, redheaded, and six foot two—and why was he present? When my turn came, I introduced myself to the group as a graduate student in anthropology from the University of Chicago, and also as a native of Lubbock, Texas. At that point the manager of the tannery stopped me and said, "Lubbock? It's flat and dry and ugly there." While that is arguably the case,[2] I was surprised that these men from a small town north of Tokyo would be at all familiar with an equally sized town in West Texas. I responded, "Well, yes, Lubbock is flat and dry and ugly, but how do you know that?"

It turned out that the majority of the rawhide used at this tannery came, in salted crates, from my hometown, shipped through Los Angeles to Tokyo and then up by train to Tochigi, to be tanned into leather there, 7,000 miles away from where it had started. A small group of the tannery management had traveled to Lubbock several years prior to tour ranches, feedlots, and slaughterhouses in the Texas Panhandle; they knew Lubbock was flat, dry, and ugly because they had been there. I was stunned by this information. Growing up in Lubbock, I had always been aware that the ranching and meat processing industry was large—anyone with a working nose is aware of the cattle, and the ranching heritage center around the corner from my house was a frequent destination on school field trips—but I had not anticipated that parts of the cattle in the feedlots outside my hometown, feedlots where high school friends of mine worked, might end up on the other side of the planet where I too then lived.

I typically narrate this moment as one of epiphany, a paradigm shift for my project: I decided to take contingency as a sign of providence, discard an examination of language use and gender, and instead take up a study of Buraku issues as they connected to global commodity circuits reaching as far back as Lubbock, Texas. "Providence," however, is a gloss that deserves some unpacking; the ethical and political impulses it encompasses are deeply entangled with the ethical impulses that are part of the subject matter of this book.

Moving to graduate school from living in Seattle, where I had been part of the political protests against the World Trade Organization in 1999 and had worked with AmeriCorps VISTA and an anarchist collective, I had arrived convinced that I *should*—ethically and politically—be studying something related to myself rather than studying "the Other." Social justice should be less about helping someone less fortunate than about transforming a larger social system that privileges some at the expense of others; understanding one's own position, particularly for someone relatively privileged, was a means of thinking about issues systematically and dismantling a system that entailed both oppression and privilege. My commitment to this belief, however, was reliant on a version of politics that over-valued individual experience as a primary source of knowledge production. The danger here would be entrapment in direct experience, that is, an insistence that a subject only has the authority to speak about their[3] direct experience and nothing beyond that. As much as this position might grant the silenced a voice, it does so by confining that marked or marginalized voice. For me at the time, this position was more of a reaction against what I saw as anthropology's (and, more broadly, any unmarked subject position's) tendency to monopolize the discourse of others, that is, in more vulgar terms, the tendency for white people in the United States to speak for people of color, straights to speak for queers, or anthropologists to speak for "natives." My reaction against this tendency was instead to (attempt to) turn the anthropological gaze on myself, but in so doing I had only gotten as far as queer sexuality, still in Japan. What the tannery offered, then, was a way for me to take up an object of investigation that pushed the question of what it meant for me to be related to my object of study, perhaps breaking free of the trap of direct experience. Here was an industry tied to an economy that supported the town where I grew up.

This set of desires to study something "close to home" corresponds broadly with the expanding currency of ethnicity and locatedness that this book tracks but transposed to an unmarked white middle class in the United States—a desire for the unmarked to, in some capacity, mark themselves as regionally and perhaps economically, though rarely racially, rooted. In much the same way that it is currently appealing for my demographic to track our food from farm to table or to partake in the locavore or, more broadly, "locanomic" movement, the rawhide connection between Lubbock, Texas, and stigmatized industries in Japan held too much of an appeal for me to pass by. I found myself, as a particular type of anthropological researcher, part of the same shifts in global capital and political representation that have made Buraku issues obtrude as an international political and ethical object of intervention. For reasons similar, they obtruded for me as an object of anthropological investigation.

In this book I do not dwell on this reflexive question from a vantage point of personal experience. I instead offer it as a way of thinking through the conditions that enable and shape my own disciplinary practices. In many ways, this consideration, along with the conclusion that considers at greater length the role a book like this has in Buraku politics, is meant as an explicit response to a challenge that, though decades old, has shaped my work as an anthropologist.

In his 1991 article, "Anthropology and the Savage Slot," Michel Rolph Trouillot contends that anthropology grew out of a five hundred-year-long political, ethical, and economic process reliant on a notion of progress based across polities in the North Atlantic. The process frequently hails by the geographic moniker "the West" but, Trouillot argues, is more productively understood as a project of management and imagination rather than a geographical location. In order to propagate itself, this project of "the West" required both an idea of savagery against which to mark its own progress and an idea of expanded human potential to project a utopic future. Between

the late 1800s and 1950, anthropology coalesced as the discipline of the no-
ble savage, placed in a privileged position to deliver unto the project of the
West precisely this type of knowledge—the knowledge of Others, commen-
surated within the West either as savage signs of the West's past or as indica-
tors of utopic human possibility toward which that West could aspire. In
either case, however, the Other that anthropology examined served primarily as evidence in an argument that the West was having with itself. Anthropology served as a vehicle for this geography of imagination, with little
attention, Trouillot argues, to the ways in which it relied on a simultaneous
geography of management, that is, with little attention to how these other
places and people, frequently taken as bounded, discrete locales, were already
connected to a Western project of economic, racial, and military domination of which anthropology was a part. Trouillot's contention is that while
these enabling conditions of anthropology have transformed, the discipline
conducts itself as if these conditions were still the case—perennially rein-
scribing the savage slot and doggedly digging the hole of its own irrelevance.
Trouillot leaves his anthropologist readers with a challenge: to break free of
the savage slot.

To be sure, the conditions Trouillot describes have shifted. Anthropologists have found renewed public relevance as reporters on the plight of marginalized groups subjected to economic, social, and physical risk. The overtly
colonial aspect of the "Western" project, which justified its propulsion with
a civilizing narrative, has shifted to a more liberal one, which justifies itself
with a narrative of attending to those it wounds through misrecognition.[4]
These shifts have significant ramifications for how social difference is
managed: the status of "wounded," for example, is very different from that of
"savage." However, a fundamental logic animates both moments: in order
for this project to sustain itself, it requires knowledge of those at its margins,
knowledge that then is used in the pursuit of perfectibility, or at least self-
improvement. As I elaborate throughout this book, the project of liberal
modernity finds itself, in part, in the production of suffering subjects to
serve as evidence in an argument it is having with itself. Anthropologists,
here, are recruited to the role of what the philosopher Richard Rorty calls
"agents of love," tasked with portraying in intricate emotive detail different
modes of being human so that liberalism can learn to be not simply more
loving but more just.[5] In this second moment, Trouillot's challenge for anthropology, then, is to disrupt that reiterated logic of the savage slot instead
of serving as a conduit by which liberal modernity learns its own limits.

In his article, Trouillot does not offer a resolution to this challenge, other than understanding the specificities of other peoples: to make them a lowercase other rather than reducing them all to the "Other" whose primary life is as evidence in the anthropologist's argument. In his book *Global Transformations*, however, he offers the beginning of a solution, fundamental to which is understanding how the geography of imagination that an anthropologist might trace is always already connected with a geography of management.[6] He urges anthropologists to perform an anthropology that does not take other people as disconnected, bounded units but that instead demonstrates the connections among the imperatives faced by the anthropologist and the object of anthropological inquiry alike. He pushes, for instance, for an anthropology that would not merely understand bride wealth in Plateau State in comparison to bride wealth in, say, New Britain but that would take as essential to that understanding the fact that Plateau State is located in Nigeria and New Britain in Papua New Guinea, both set within imperial and economic transformations global in scope and intimately tied to the relevance of the anthropological gaze.[7] Such an insistence, Trouillot argues, would challenge the empiricist tendency in anthropology to reduce the object of study to the thing observed; it would show the practices that create that thing. It would also necessitate addressing the epistemological status of the native voice, for anthropologist and "native" are always already interrelated. This is an anthropology that highlights connection or, as the anthropologist and cultural theorist Elizabeth Povinelli puts it, "co-substantiation."[8] In the mode of the suffering slot, then, it is an anthropology that does not merely ask its reader to step into the experience of the wounded but, rather, shows how the lived worlds of the reader and the wounded are already intertwined.

Working Skin is fundamentally inspired by this challenge. This is an ethnography of the contemporary situation of the Buraku people. However, the project proceeds by pulling apart the practices, global in scope, that constitute that situation and render it available, tractable, and even pleasurable as an object of anthropological inquiry. This book is an examination of the labor involved in identifying, dismantling, and reproducing the contemporary Buraku situation; it is also an examination of the labor involved in overcoming this repeated refrain. Ethical orientations and economic relations are being formed and reformed in the tanneries of Tokyo, the offices of human rights workers, and the practices of Western ethnographers, all in ways that are linked together across geographical distance. This labor is part and parcel of transformations in the project of the West that are global in impetus and effect and that sit alongside the transformations in international Buraku recognition and political solvency that are the subject of this book. This is not a book that simply demonstrates that Japan is multicultural. Instead, I analyze how the incitement to multiculturalism disciplines both those who produce representations of social difference in Japan and those who are summoned as evidence in such a project. I show how the demands of liberal modernity arise in the work of Buraku laborers and the governmental and nongovernmental organizations that represent them. This is an attempt to trace the conditions that reproduce the logic of the suffering/savage slot, even as I position my own work within those conditions.

Most broadly, then, *Working Skin* is an examination of ongoing changes in global capitalism and styles of political representations, that is, in the geographies of management and imagination that, among other things, have enabled practices of anthropology such as my own. The conclusion, as I have said, returns to a more robust examination of the conditions of this book's production and its role in Buraku politics. With this prologue, however, I want to seed questions regarding these enabling conditions. How is it that at the same moment that Buraku issues become a recognizable object of international human rights and multicultural concern they have also become a renewed object of anthropological inquiry? How might radical transformations that are happening in the economic structure of stigmatized industries and nongovernmental political organizations relate to the sudden appearance of international funding for a scholarly project about stigmatized minorities in Japan, even in the midst of a larger decline in funding for "Western" projects that take Japan as their object of study? How is it that both Texan leather and Texan anthropologist ended up at the same tannery north of Tokyo?

I have several aspirations for this book. I hope that it will serve as an analysis of multiculturalism from the inside—of what grants purchase to this mode of producing and managing difference, of what possibilities it opens, and of what it might foreclose. This book is not normative in the sense that it provides a road map to some other alternative, but I do hope that a close read of the practices of multiculturalism and its relation to particular economic imperatives will serve as a useful tool for others to take up in their work toward other social arrangements. This book is the result of several years of working on and thinking about these issues, particularly motivated by a connection to the industries of my hometown. I hope my perspective and analysis can enter into conversation with other people who struggle for Buraku liberation on a day-to-day basis and who have spent the majority of their lives working on and thinking about these issues.

I also hope in doing this that my book might respond to Trouillot's challenge. Trouillot taught me my first class in anthropology in 2001. Shortly after that course ended, he suffered a debilitating set of aneurysms that left him incapacitated until he passed away in 2012. My attention to the savage slot is as personal as is my connection to Texas. This book is meant as a tribute to the challenges Trouillot posed to us in that class and the ways in which they have shaped my work as an ethnographer, scholar, and antiracist.

ACKNOWLEDGMENTS

SUPPORT FOR THIS PROJECT has come from many directions and in many forms, and, mentioned here or not, thanks are due to all of them.

My greatest debt is to those alongside whom I have worked and studied over the past decade: the people who work in leather factories in Japan, who face Buraku discrimination on a regular basis, and who work to dismantle this and other systems of subjection. Thank you for sharing your lives and thoughts, and for sharing mine with me. Special thanks to my coworkers and friends at the International Movement Against All Forms of Discrimination and Racism (IMADR), through the Tokyo Toren, and at the tannery—to Malaya Ileto, Nozomoi Bando, Ogasawara Sumie, Arai Setsuko, Komori Megumi, Morihara Hideki, Hara Yuriko, Mizuno Matsuo, Caroline Ezhil, and to all of those at the tannery and otherwise whose names I cannot give. You were and have been great companions, teachers, and friends. Thank you for putting up with me when I got in the way more than I helped, and for opening doors to me that have transformed my life. Thanks too to the incredible staff at the Buraku Liberation and Human Rights Research Institute, to the board of IMADR, to the friends I made in the Buraku Liberation League headquarters, and to all the other activists I met in Japan and beyond through this work. Here in particular I express thanks to Tomonaga Kenzō, whose hospitality, intellect, and political commitments continue to inspire me; similarly to Mushakoji Kinhide—your commitment to social justice sparks something in all who meet you, and I count myself fortunate to have been able to work alongside you; and to Kumisaka Shigeyuki for your generosity and in tribute to your passion for your work. I hope this book serves in some way as a useful tool in the work that all of you do. Thanks also to all those along the chain of leather production—from my high school friend Reagan Anders to John Hochstein at Cargill to the owners of the different tanneries I visited—for opening your doors to me.

So many people provided me with feedback as I formulated this project, carried out my research, and wrote this book. Thank you to Sakurai Atsushi and Fukuoka Yasunori, whose support as I started this project did much to inspire its direction. Thank you to Uchizawa Junko for endless hours of conversation, adventure, and friendship, to Nakajo for sharing meals, baths, laundry, time, and stories, and to Kadooka Nobuhiko for key insights and introductions. Thank you to my advisers, to Susan Gal, Danilyn Rutherford, Norma Field, and Beth Povinelli, for reading drafts, encouraging me, and provoking me at all the right moments. Michel Rolph Trouillot and Michael Silverstein also had profound effects on my thinking, and I am and always will be in their debt. A special thanks to Shimizu Yuri, Dennis Washburn, Otake Hiroko, and Noto Hiroyoshi, who spent countless hours pushing and pulling me into the Japanese language. Thanks as well to David Slater, who provided tremendous help and feedback during my fieldwork and beyond. I also thank my colleagues and students at the University of California, San Diego (UCSD), who read versions of some of the contents here and did much to foster my growth as a scholar. Nancy Postero, David Pedersen, Rupert Stasch, Kathryn Woolard, Joel Robbins, Esra Özyürek, John Haviland, Roshanak Kheshti, Patrick Anderson, Elana Zilberg, Christo Sims, and Martha Lampland, thank you all; similarly, thanks to Esin Duzel, Raquel Pacheco, Brendan Thornton, and Kara Wentworth. I feel extremely lucky to have you as friends, students, and colleagues. A special thanks here to Michael Berman for all that you have taught me as my first student, for your feedback on the manuscript, and for your help in bringing this book into being. I also appreciate all of the critique that portions of this manuscript received at talks, conferences, and from various editors and reviewers over the past many years. Thank you to all who offered critical engagement, in particular to Miyako Inoue, Michael Fisch, Marilyn Ivy, David Novak, Lorraine Plourde, Tomomi Yamaguchi, Nancy Abelmann, Takashi Fujitani, Nathanial Smith, Marie Abe, Carolyn Stevens, Tak Watanabe, Jun Mizukawa, Gabi Lukacs, Allison Alexy, Anne Allison, Jennifer Robertson, Tessa Morris-Suzuki, ann-elise lewallen, Christopher Nelson, John Davis, Kurokawa Midori, Lisa Yoneyama, Christopher Bondy, Tomonaga Yugo, Lily Chumley, Ritu Birla, Francis Cody, and Nicholas Harkness. Thanks also to the colleagues and friends I made at the Institute for Advanced Study who provided invaluable feedback at a crucial final moment, to Didier Fassin, Danielle Allen, Joan Scott, Nikhil Anand, Elizabeth Davis, Joe Masco, Ramah McKay, Omar Dewachi, Noah Salomon, Cristina Beltrán, Jeff Flynn, Nitsan Chorev, and Ellen Stroud. Thanks in particular to the friends, cohort-mates, and now colleagues without whose support at every step of this academic ride none of this would have happened, and with whose support every bit of this became that much more delightful. Thanks to Catherine Fennell, Kabir Tambar, Kelda Jamison, Sarah Muir, Rocío Magaña, and Rihan Yeh. So much of this book emerges out of our conversations over the past thirteen years, and I am thrilled and honored to have done this with you as my friends and colleagues.

A special thanks to Anne Chi'en for providing me and all in the Department of Anthropology at Chicago with years of guidance and support. My thanks to everyone at the University of California Press—working with you to bring this book into being has been a pleasure. Thanks to my family— Larry, Sally, Emily, and Katie—for not once getting up, coming across the room, and slapping me in the face, no matter how much you may have wanted to. It has been that much more fun getting to include y'all in this. A huge thanks as well to the group of friends who made my life outside of writing that much richer along the way, who stood with me across joys and sorrows. I have a lot of love for you all. Particular thanks to Bryan Sykora, Amanda Green, Amanda Gordon, Julie Hollar, Rebecca Steinfeld, Andrew Sloat, Frampton Tolbert, Jim Gaylord, Sarah Bendit, Katerli Bounds, Hattori Kou, Kimura Narihiro, Bettina Ortmann, Mark Pendleton, Dan Vaughn, Nelson Stauffer, Jack Meyers, David Franklin, Scott Winn, and Eric Husketh. Thanks also to Scott Ballum for what you shared with me and helped me carry, for your support and love over years of me writing. A huge thanks to my faethren and family in Los Angeles and beyond—to Steven Schweickart, Nick Austin, Tyler Daly, Harpal Sodhi, Jol Devitro, Aram Kirakosian, Devan McGrath, Gavy Kessler, Jeremy Mikush, Timothy Power, A. J. Goodrich, David Rasmussen, Daniel Aston, Adam Pogue, Johnny Follin, Michael Svoboda, Brighid, Mike Dimpfl, and so many others—you caught me at just the right time, and I cannot wait for more. Special thanks too to Seth Holmes—your work and support at key moments have served as pretty stunning inspiration for what anthropology, scholarship, and friendship can be. And, at last, to Kevin—a plusher friend I cannot imagine.

My appreciation, finally, to the institutions whose funding has made my research possible—the University of Chicago, the National Science Foundation, the Japan Foundation, the Social Science Research Council, the Charlotte W. Newcombe Foundation, UCSD, the Hellman Foundation, and the Institute for Advanced Study. Resources from all of these institutions have allowed me to spend most of the past thirteen years devoted to doing something I love.

Introduction

THE LABOR OF MULTICULTURALISM

RECOGNIZING THE BURAKU

In 2001 Mika and her husband, Isamu, moved from a small town north of Tokyo into an inexpensive neighborhood in the eastern part of the metropolis. They both quickly started applying for jobs but had little luck. They noted that when they wrote down their new home address, their interviewer's demeanor tended to change, grow colder, and that follow-up calls were rarely forthcoming. One day Mika mentioned this lack of luck to one of her neighbors, who was not at all surprised. She explained to Mika that the neighborhood was a Buraku, and that the employers, seeing the address, had probably thought that Mika and Isamu were Burakumin, despite the fact that neither of them had any family connection to Buraku industries.[1]

Yuko met Keisuke in college. They started dating and after five years decided to get married. However, when Keisuke told his parents of their intention, they hired a private detective to investigate Yuko's family background. When they received the results of the investigation, they opposed the marriage and forbade Keisuke to marry a woman from a Buraku family. Respecting his parents' wishes, Keisuke broke the engagement and told Yuko why. Yuko was shocked. She had learned a little about Burakumin in history classes in junior high but always as something that had existed in the past and that had disappeared along with Japan's feudal period in 1868. She had no idea that she or her family was Buraku. Devastated at losing Keisuke, she asked her parents about what he had told her, and they reluctantly admitted that their family was Buraku. They had never told her because they didn't want to worry her; they had hoped that discrimination would be gone by the time Yuko was an adult.

Satō-san first went to India when he was seven years old. He went with his father, a prominent Buraku activist and historian. Satō-san's father researched the history of caste systems throughout Asia and over the course of his research had made friends with a Dalit (a word meaning "crushed," which refers to outcastes) scholar from India. The Dalit activist had a daughter a bit younger than Satō-san, and he, as did Satō-san's father, hoped that the children would grow up friends. Satō-san and Sareeta did just that. By the time they were fifty, they had visited each other close to thirty times and had co-organized Buraku study and solidarity tours to India. Satō-san had grown up very much thinking that he and Sareeta faced a similar kind of discrimination, as Buraku and as Dalit, and that there was a lot each group could learn from the other.

Misato's father owned a leather tannery in the central city of Himeji. He had inherited this tannery from his father, who had inherited it from his, who had inherited it from his, back four generations. Misato's parents were heavily involved in the neighborhood liberation movement, and from a young age Misato followed her parents' example. In Buraku summer camps and liberation classes in school, she developed strong ties with other kids from their Buraku neighborhood. When Misato turned fifteen, however, her father pulled her aside one evening and explained to her that the family was not actually Burakumin. Despite living in a Buraku, despite participating in liberation activities, and despite having worked in a traditional Buraku industry for over four generations, her ancestors were originally, Misato's father explained, clothiers and had made kimonos. Misato was shocked and ashamed, and even twenty years later, still living and working at the tannery, she had not told a single one of her childhood friends that she was not Buraku, for fear of being shunned.

Tanimoto-san was sixty-one years old and had spent the prior five years jumping through four different manual labor jobs in Tokyo, not keeping any of them long because of his temper and his tendency to show up slightly late and inebriated. Out of options and money, he went to the unemployment office and was introduced to a job in a leather tannery. He had never worked in a tannery or a slaughterhouse before but knew that the people who worked there were Burakumin and were supposed to be the lowest of the low. He wanted nothing to do with them or with their dirty, smelly work. However, lacking money, he didn't have much of a choice and took the tannery job, with its relatively high hourly wage. But he took care not to talk to the other workers. He maintained his distance while working and during breaks, not wanting anyone to think that he was the same as *them*.

These are not aberrant individual experiences. Each of these anecdotes highlights some aspects of a group of people in contemporary Japan. The word "Burakumin"[2] literally means "people of the neighborhood," where *min* refers to "people" and *buraku* "neighborhood." It is a euphemism, however, for a group identified by an occupational, a spatial, or a genealogical relationship to historically stigmatized labor such as meat and leather production. It is a group whose members, like the aforementioned Satō-san, sometimes know they are classified as Buraku and at other times, like Yuko, have no idea. It is a contagious category, capable of traveling along any of its defining characteristics: by change of job (e.g., Tanimoto-san's case), by residence (e.g., Mika and Isamu's situation), or by marriage (e.g., Yuko and Keisuke's situation). And it is a categorization that is hard to shake completely once one has contracted it. As the previous examples indicate, it is a category capable of marshaling avoidance, embarrassment, disgust, affiliation, and pride. These strong emotions animate the day-to-day aspects of life, steering decisions about where to live, where to send one's children to school, whom to date, and where to work.

Recognizing someone as Buraku can be a tricky matter. The stakes are high, the evidence shifting, and not everyone who might be recognized as Buraku understands themselves as Buraku. This is not a form of social difference that consistently calls out physical or linguistic qualities to mark itself, as does race or sex.[3] Instead, it relies on family registries, labor and residential records, family stories, and workplace and neighborhood gossip.[4] Each of these sources of evidence has its own legal and social underpinnings, its own material trappings, its own history, and its own regional idiosyncrasies. Over the past forty years in particular, each of these has shifted as traditionally stigmatized industries such as leather tanning have left Japan for more lucrative shores and family and residential registries have become less publicly accessible and track back fewer generations. With these shifts the number of those unaware of themselves as perceived Buraku has grown, and the ability for anyone to recognize someone as Buraku has diminished. The trick of recognition, then, is not simply being able to marshal evidence that someone is Buraku. It is also getting people like Yuko, Mika, Isamu, and Tanimoto-san to respond to the hail of that identification as much as Satō-san or Misato might. To recognize someone as Buraku, to assert that any individual, family, or neighborhood is stigmatized in this way, means relying on shifting sources of evidence as much as it levies formative expectations on who might be considered Buraku.

There are patterns to recognition. The Japanese government estimates the number of Buraku people at almost 1.2 million; the premier Buraku political organization, the Buraku Liberation League (BLL), estimates that number at close to 3 million. The government only counts people who are residents of Buraku neighborhoods that registered with the government in the latter

half of the twentieth century; the BLL extrapolates a number from historical records, tracing lineages of "outcastes" from the Tokugawa period.[5] The
government's metric is based on residence and sits within imperatives to
show that it is proactively addressing Buraku issues, a set of imperatives born,
in part, of a long history of political organizing on the part of Buraku organizations. The BLL's standard is one of lineage and residence and sits within
the imperatives of liberation, the contours of which have changed over the
century of Buraku organizing as the political organization revises its understanding of subjection alongside its solidarity work with, for example, labor
movements, ethnic Korean and Chinese political organizations, and international human rights organizations. Inasmuch, then, that recognizing
someone as Buraku makes demands of those recognized and the materials
used to render judgment, it also has implications for those doing the recognizing. It calls on political, ethical, and economic imperatives and is grounded
in the day-to-day activities of people such as government officials and BLL
activists whose job it is to produce representations of the Buraku situation
in Japan.

This book examines the formative labor of this recognition—its conditions, its demands, and its possibilities. Situated always in between—between
those recognizing and those recognized, between people and their ethical
commitments and economic dependencies, between a stigmatized people and
those objects summoned as evidence of that stigma—recognition is a practice
of forging relationships, and it is a practice intimately intertwined with the
distribution of psychological and physical well-being, economic vitality, political viability, and ethical obligation. This book examines one particular pattern of recognition, one particular mode of inscribing and managing social
difference, which I refer to as "multiculturalism."

Multiculturalism has become a buzzword of sorts in millennial Japan, for
state programs and social commentators on Japan alike. In the past decade
the Japanese government has made strong efforts to support *tabunka kyōsei*
(multicultural coexistence), a phrase that typically refers to social difference
on the basis of citizenship and national status. In 2006 the Ministry of
Internal Affairs proposed the "Plan for *Tabunka Kyōsei* Promotion in Local
Communities," and as of April 2010, it reported that 96 percent of prefectural governments, 100 percent of the governments of specifically targeted
cities, and 41 percent of all cities had implemented such a plan for fostering
the inclusion of "foreigners."[6] This program does not include those who
might already hold Japanese citizenship, such as the Buraku or the indige-

nous Ainu; nor does it clearly include such populations as resident Korean or Chinese people. In scholarly arenas there has been a burgeoning discussion of multiculturalism in Japan,[7] and there is an expanding set of social scientific literature in English that examines the status of minority groups in Japan.[8] These academic investigations of difference include more than the *tabunka kyōsei* state programs, typically extending their analysis to the Buraku people, the indigenous Ainu, resident Koreans and Chinese people, and beyond. Several characteristics are apparent across these depictions and analyses of multiculturalism, namely a tendency to examine the situations of multiple groups alongside each other, commensurate as minorities; an attention to groups potentially overlooked; and an understanding of these groups as centered around some authentic cultural core and as wounded. It is this particular style of governing difference, its deepening entrenchment in Japanese politics and daily life, that I take as my object of study, more than the use of any particular word.

This burgeoning interest in multiculturalism in Japan might seem odd, given the country's much-touted homogeneity. Following centuries of *sakoku* (national seclusion, 1633–1853), this small island country has maintained stringent immigration and citizenship laws. Japanese nationals make up 98.5 percent of the population of the country; it is a *jus sanguinis* state in which it is difficult for non-nationals to gain permanent resident status and even more difficult for them to naturalize. However, in recent years, scholars have argued that the image of Japan as homogenous did not gain popular purchase until after the Asia-Pacific War.[9] Prior to that period, during Japan's imperial conquest and rule of the region, the dominant discourse had been one stressing the unity of all Asian people. Japan's empire accommodated social difference, even while it used race and racism as techniques for governing that difference.[10] Following Japan's defeat in the war, however, scholars and public figures on the left and on the right both fell back on an idea of Japan being a nation-state of a single, homogenous people.

Claims that Japan is multicultural fit within this history, posed as resistance to the strong purchase of the narrative of homogeneity. In a 2007 *Japan Times* article entitled " 'Multicultural Japan' Remains a Pipe Dream," scholar Chris Burgess quotes two government officials commenting on Japan's homogeneity. In February 2007, Bunmei Ibuki, then minister of education, called Japan "an extremely homogenous country"; similarly, in 2005, Taro Aso, who was at the time foreign minister and later served as prime minister of Japan, described the country as having "one nation, one civilization, one language, one culture, and one race."[11] These comments, Burgess notes, met with little controversy and received little attention in the mainstream Japanese press. In this context, it is by no means self-evident that Japan is a multicultural nation-state, either in terms of sheer numbers of racial or ethnic others or in terms of how difference is managed in government policy. It is precisely in this context, pitted against a hegemonic discourse of homogeneity, that claims of multiculturalism as both a state of affairs and an aspiration make sense.

In some ways multiculturalism can serve as an avenue for groups such as the Buraku to demand recognition and resources. Describing themselves as one of several minority groups in Japan allows the Buraku to make demands on UN actors and domestic and foreign scholars, for example. In other ways, this new multiculturalism boom reinscribes Buraku invisibility: the government's *tabunka kyōsei* programs, which see difference through the lens of national affiliation, leave little room for groups like the Buraku to assert themselves. Indeed, these programs have come about only after the end of a set of laws that directed government funds to registered Buraku neighborhoods and organizations, an end that the government justified in 2002 by declaring that Buraku discrimination was over. Taking advantage of such *tabunka* programs would take enormous work on the part of Buraku political organizations to rework definitions of difference to include so-called internal minorities like the Buraku or resident Koreans.

In either case, claiming and critically engaging the tools of multiculturalism require disrupting standard patterns of recognition and instating new ones. It takes challenging the established procedures for the management, regulation, support, or neglect of human life and establishing new imperatives in their place. This uphill struggle requires much more labor as the signs that mark people as Buraku become more elusive and the numbers of people unaware that they might be perceived as Buraku grow.[12] The labor to transform the bases of recognition has a reciprocal effect: it simultaneously transforms those who undertake it and those who might be recognized as evidence of difference. In the Buraku situation, the nongovernmental organization (NGO) worker and the tannery worker alike are recast in the struggle to represent a multicultural Japan. As Buraku political organizations attempt to render Buraku issues legible and pressing on national and international stages, they apply themselves to a labor that requires devotion and ethical commitment. That labor also requires particular habits of work, leisure, concern, and intimacy. At the same time, as these actors frame Buraku issues in new contexts, they rely and make demands on those who would appear as Buraku, those with purported connections to labor considered unclean. This tension, between the labor of representation and the labor represented—a tension I refer to throughout the book as "the labor of multiculturalism"—shapes the lives, aspirations, and prospects of those who stand on either side. In these moves, this labor gives shape to a Japan that is modern and multicultural.

MAKING LEATHER, MAKING
A MULTICULTURAL JAPAN

In the preface I described how a visit to a tannery north of Tokyo that uses rawhide from my hometown in Texas prompted my study of Buraku issues. Following that tour, the sociologist who had organized the event invited me along to a set of oral history interviews he was conducting with Buraku activists and residents in a town in Chiba prefecture, east of Tokyo. Over the next several months, Professor Fukuoka Yasunori and his collaborator, Professor Sakurai Atsushi, generously let me sit in on their interviews, to learn from them and their interviewees, and to ask the occasional question. One pattern to people's histories immediately became clear: many people from this Buraku neighborhood were raised not knowing that they could be considered Buraku. Furthermore, many of these people, even people active in the local branch of the political movement, had never told their children that they too could be considered Buraku. Here were people potentially marginalized by others but unaware that they belonged to a stigmatized group. Many of the interviewees had been harassed in elementary and middle schools by classmates whose parents had told their children not to play with kids from this Buraku neighborhood. The interviewees faced this harassment thinking that they were facing it alone, with no knowledge that they were connected to a group of people scattered across the archipelago and with a centuries-long history.

This tendency is not limited to the residents of a neighborhood in Chiba. In the ten years since those initial interviews, I have conducted over twenty-eight months of fieldwork, spent a year and a half working as an intern with an international NGO founded by the BLL, the International Movement Against All Forms of Discrimination and Racism (IMADR), and six months as an apprentice in a small tannery in eastern Tokyo that occasionally uses rawhide from my hometown in Texas. Across those venues and across the past decade, I have encountered numerous people who, like Yuko in the vignette that opened the chapter, spent many years not knowing that other people perceived them as Buraku. It is a tendency with which the political movement has struggled for the past century, and it is one that is heightened by recent changes.

This widespread tendency, which I found so striking in the early months of my research, highlights a deepening conundrum of the contemporary Buraku situation. Across the same span of time that the genealogical, spatial, and occupational markers that point out people as connected to stigmatized industries have, on the whole, become more elusive and opaque, the imperatives of multiculturalism in Japan have intensified. A multicultural mode of managing difference has become almost given, gaining force as a commonsense rebuttal of the myth of Japanese homogeneity. Buraku political actors, then, find themselves balancing the possibility of renewed traction through multicultural representation even as their constituency is less interested in and less capable of recognizing itself as Buraku.

People like Yuko, Isamu, Mika, and Tanimoto-san, as well as Satō-san and Misato, are all invested, whether they like it or not, in being Buraku. Satō-san and Misato have known themselves as Buraku since they were children, and they have learned to hold that identity with some pride, though Misato now worries that it is not hers to hold. Tanimoto-san, forced to work in a Buraku occupation and therefore potentially thought of as Buraku, does his best to keep that identification at bay. Yuko must deal with being told that she is and always has been from a stigmatized group. Suddenly, whatever she may have learned in school about Buraku issues, or more likely about the Tokugawa period caste system, is supposed to be somehow relevant to her. Similarly, Mika and Isamu must deal with their new status as Buraku, not as something that was there without their knowing all along but as something more recent and, they might hope, more expungeable from their record. As these vignettes indicate, some people actively choose to take up their social positioning, others might seek to disavow it, and still others have no idea of it at all. Faced with this constituency, the political problem for organizations like the BLL becomes, in part, how to cultivate interest and affiliation among a group of people who understand themselves as Buraku in no uniform manner, if they understand themselves as Buraku at all. How might one cultivate volitional individuals equipped with the knowledge, interest, and ethical commitment to choose to hold tightly to this investment?

And how does one do that so such a commitment arrives in the form of authentic choice rather than coercion?

This staging of ethical obligation, authenticity, and volition is not simply directed at a Buraku constituency. Buraku political organizations also seek to transform public perceptions of Buraku and other stigmatized groups. To do so, they must equip that public with both the knowledge and the desire to engage actively with these issues, a task made that much more difficult as the markers that point people out as Buraku become increasingly intangible. The public must be taught to be aware of and concerned by discrimination against a people who are becoming harder to track, and that concern also must appear authentic rather than imposed. This type of work requires a lot from those political activists who undertake it. It requires long hours at work, specialized skills, and substantial financial resources; it requires networks with other NGOs domestically and abroad, and connections to politicians and journalists; and it requires an ethical resolve to continue to labor in the face of increasingly difficult odds. "The labor of multiculturalism" entails all of these potential transformations—of the Buraku constituency, of a broader public, and of those who labor for Buraku liberation. It is the labor directed at securing a Buraku position within multicultural Japan, even as the conditions that capacitate such a position, in some regard, fall apart.

This conundrum sits at the intersection of transformations in global capital and political argument. The changes in each are not coincidental. They both rely on an increasing emphasis on individuals as self-determining. The opening of the Japanese leather market to international trade expresses an increasing prioritization of market exchange among individuals understood as free. Restricted access to family and residential records that now track back fewer generations similarly emphasizes the priority of an individual as self-determining rather than subject to the constraints of family or residence. The turn to multiculturalism requires the cultivation of authentic, volitional individuals empowered to choose their associations. This convergence of transformations serves as the condition of possibility for the problems of the contemporary Buraku situation. At the same time, the labor required to face this conundrum calls on and reworks these conditions: it allows for particular understandings of economic and political shifts as much as it relies on them.

The tension between political argument and economic organization is not the only guise this tension takes. The labor of multiculturalism sits nestled between the work of representation and work represented. Located in between, it drives the relationship between the two, creating meaningful distinctions and relations across this proposed divide. Such a division occurs in multiple forms, which I explore throughout the book. The economic sits against the political here, as we saw earlier. Similarly, factory labor stands against the labor of NGOs, material labor is pit against an immaterial labor of care, and each side is gendered, the factory labor cast as masculine, the NGO labor cast as feminine. There is also a temporal divide in which Buraku issues might be seen as a holdover from a purported feudal period, standing in contrast to the minority issues of today. On a smaller historical scale, the industrial capitalism of the factory sits against a postindustrial capitalism of the NGO work, and political tactics such as denunciation are felt as anachronistic compared to more recently developed human rights seminars.[13] Similarly, constraint is set up against freedom, the former thought to be characteristic of a feudal past, the latter of a modern present or future.

Different contrastive relations such as these run throughout the contemporary Buraku situation, sometimes mapping neatly onto each other and other times not. These divisions are simultaneously the conditions that capacitate the labor of multiculturalism, and they are divisions called on, accentuated, muted, or transformed by this labor. The relationship across these divides is never given ahead of time; it is not one of neat causality. Rather, in the labor of multiculturalism, the relationship is worked and reworked, granting form and content to that which stands on either side: what counts as economic, masculine, material, anachronistic, or constraining is given shape in this labor. The task of *Working Skin* is to provide an ethnographic exploration of this tension, in all of its guises, between the making of leather and the making of a multicultural Japan.

HISTORY OF THE BURAKU PRESENT

Working Skin both relies on and enables a particular understanding of the long, intertwining relationships among political and economic forces in the Buraku situation. These forces have been in the making at least since the beginning of the Meiji period (1868) and have undergone significant transformation during that time. These changes have reached a peak in the decades since the late 1970s, in turn radically transforming the stakes of what it means to be Buraku and what it means, for Japan, to have a Buraku minority population.

The Buraku population is managed as a minority group in Japan not simply through techniques of race or ethnicity—though at times these are used—but instead through associations with particular types of labor. As the vignettes that open this chapter indicate, the Buraku population is amorphous beyond any direct lineage back to the *senmin* (abject classes) of the Tokugawa period. With the promulgation of an edict in 1871 the new Meiji government officially abolished these groups, rendering them, at least on paper, the same as any other *heimin,* or "commoner."[14] Since then, the contours of this group have grown increasingly blurry, even as the variety in the types of stigmatized jobs across regions within Japan has decreased. Police, street performers, or bamboo artisans, all professions that in parts of Japan were at one time stigmatized, have lost that stigma. Instead, over the past century, leather tanning and meat production have become the gravitational center of this category of person, even as, formally, this group lost both its monopoly on these trades and the economic security that that monopoly provided.[15] That centripetal pull has resulted in Buraku lives characterized not only by economic hardship and social discrimination but also by employment that overlays acute immediate danger, for example, the threat of fingers lost to sharpened blades or skin burned by caustic chemicals, with long-term chronic hazards of breaking physical labor and chemical exposure. It has also left those inheritors of now-peripheral stigmatized trades such as bamboo work less susceptible to both the hazards and the potential joys of being recognized as Buraku.

Working in a stigmatized industry has never been the sole means by which a person might be constituted as Buraku. Living in neighborhoods that housed stigmatized industries, or being related to someone who fell into these categories, likewise rendered someone potentially recognizable as Buraku.[16] The examples at the beginning of this chapter illustrate each of these possibilities: forced to work in a tannery, Tanimoto-san takes great care to guard against being seen as Buraku; Mika and Isamu are refused employment because they, unwittingly, live in a neighborhood stigmatized as Buraku; Keisuke's family forbids his marriage to Yuko because they believe her family is Buraku. These types of employment, residence, and kin relations subject Buraku people to heightened risks—physically, emotionally, and economically. Managing the hazards of one's stigma, then, has meant managing one's occupation, residence, and kinship ties, as much as it has meant managing the information and reaction surrounding those relations. Conversely, protecting oneself from the contagion of this stigma has meant fearing, and resisting, proximity with Buraku people, especially as coworkers, neighbors, and family members.

Since the late 1970s the contours of the Buraku condition have changed dramatically. Occupations such as leather and meat production have steadily decreased in number in Japan, coming to a head in the first decade of the twenty-first century. In 2005 the World Trade Organization (WTO) met in Hong Kong. One of the outcomes of its meeting was the intensification of pressure on the Japanese government to remove domestic regulations protecting commodities associated with the tanning industry. This industry has enjoyed relative immunity to the increasing liberalization of the Japanese economy since the 1960s.[17] Until the late decades of the twentieth century, factories remained small and specialized, foreign workers scarce, and the leather largely domestic. This immunity was in large part due to late 1960s legislation—the Special Measures Law—that aimed to ameliorate the effects of discrimination against this and other stigmatized industries. In 2002 the legislation protecting stigmatized industries expired, leaving the Japanese Ministry of Economy, Trade, and Industry (METI) amenable to the demands of the WTO in a way that it had not been before. The end of this act also cut funds to Buraku organizations across the country, leaving them less capable of organizing around these issues. Around the same time (2003–5), the Japanese Environment Ministry, in coordination with the U.S. Environmental Protection Agency, raised standards for wastewater effluvia. These changes, combined with METI's removal of regulations protecting the leather industry, have dramatically decreased the viability of leather production in Japan.

During the same time period, political and legal shifts in Japan reformed attachments between people and the neighborhoods in which they resided, which made it harder to recognize a person as Buraku by the location of their residence. Concurrently, reforms in family law have reflected and promoted an increased emphasis on the nuclear family, even as public access to government information about family lineage has been restricted. In total, this set of changes—in industrial labor, family residence, and family registration—has radically reconfigured the conditions and hazards that make people recognizable, to others or to themselves, as Buraku. The first Buraku-led political organization, the Suiheisha (1922), defined Burakumin primarily by genealogical ties. As of 1997 the BLL granted membership to those who lived in or were raised in a Buraku neighborhood. There is a shift here from genealogy to residence, but in all cases these ties have become harder to ascertain.[18] In more extreme cases, formerly trackable indications have given way to no markers whatsoever, except for the act of labeling itself. It is here that gossip and hearsay gain purchase. These changes perhaps herald the end of residence, kinship, and occupation as primary determinants of Buraku identity, and instead experiences of discrimination, and I would argue, pride, come to serve as the basis for Buraku identity.[19]

With these global and national transformations, the hazards facing Buraku people are undergoing a sea change. For some, the physical dangers of factory work have faded, thereby putting into greater relief the violence of systematic economic hardship, exacerbated by the disappearance of these jobs. For others, however, no longer visibly marked by the scars that come with hazardous factory labor, it suddenly becomes much easier to "pass" as non-Buraku. The possibility of escape from stigma and discrimination opens up before them.[20] Buraku individuals then are presented with dramatically different ways of being Buraku: not visibly marked, they find themselves able to make different decisions about where to send their children to school, where to work, whom to marry, and in what communities to live. While they might still be identifiable as Buraku by their official family registry (koseki) or the location of their ancestral homes (honseki), these people see the possibility of a life untainted both by the danger of arduous labor and the violence of discrimination. For them, however, this possibility is attainable on one condition: the surrender of their Buraku identity.[21]

That surrender comes at a political cost. At the same time that Japan's leather industry is liberalizing, Buraku political organizations have met with recent and unprecedented international success. Their founding aim is to eliminate structures of discrimination against Buraku people and thereby dismantle the balancing act that Buraku individuals must navigate—that is, to make it possible to simultaneously live a life free of violence and physical harm *and* claim a Buraku identity. Indeed, the political organization considers the denial of Buraku identity to Buraku people a form of violence. This balancing act is compounded by the post–Asia-Pacific War ideologies of a homogenous Japan that stress the similarities among Japanese citizens and deny the presence of ethnic, racial, and other minority groups in Japan. BLL strategies in this struggle for Buraku identity are manifold but recently have been channeled into two tracks: first, garner the support of international human rights organizations and mechanisms as a means of putting pressure on the Japanese government to enact antidiscrimination legislation (something Japan has never had); second, cultivate and celebrate a Buraku cultural identity that would challenge the stigma associated with this category of person.[22] In pressing this agenda, the Buraku liberation movement also creates an image of a multicultural Japan, poised in political and ethical juxtaposition against the image of a homogenous Japan.

Aware of the impending end of special legislation supporting Buraku communities and industries, and aware too that this would herald the end of municipal and national funding, the BLL succeeded in 2002 in having the United Nations introduce a new category of discrimination, "Discrimination Based on Work and Descent." What exactly this discrimination is, how it should be investigated, and how it might be addressed have been topics of heated debate within the United Nations and among affected communities such as the Buraku and the Dalit of South Asia.[23] This category breaks new historical ground in establishing a framework in which the Buraku, defined by labor more than by ethnicity or race, are recognizable as a minority on an international level. This change sets the Buraku firmly on the international stage alongside other minority groups and allows them to enter into discussions, in newfound ways, of discrimination, violence, and subjection with racial, ethnic, indigenous, and gendered groups.[24] Put differently, labor, as described under "Discrimination Based on Work and Descent," is becoming an identity category. It is becoming recognizable in the same terms as race, ethnicity, indigeneity, and other categories tangled up in the cultural politics of multicultural recognition. As a result, the possibilities for solidarity and for marshaling international support have expanded exponentially, and Buraku political organizations have found new allies in their struggle against systematically being refused marriage, employment, and education, and being vilified in graffiti and on the Internet.

In a similar vein, the BLL has experienced recent successes in mobilizing the category of race to their advantage.[25] In 2005 it helped coordinate the visit to Japan of the UN special rapporteur on contemporary forms of racism, racial discrimination, xenophobia, and related intolerance. This visit culminated with the release in February 2006 of the first report on the cultural status of minority groups, racism, and xenophobia in Japan. The Buraku feature prominently in this report: their history is charted, their cultural specificity is investigated, and their characteristics are compared and contrasted with the indigenous Ainu, resident Koreans, and Okinawans. This is a more standard multicultural framework, and, working in concert with "Discrimination Based on Work and Descent," it establishes labor as a social category and as a potential indicator of authentic culture, that is, of a bounded group with characteristic patterns of behavior. Forms of leatherwork and meat processing are increasingly claimed as evidence of such a Buraku culture, when requested by UN and other foreign visitors. These UN-level moves—the creation of a new category of discrimination and the release of the special rapporteur on racism's cultural report—are but two of several indications, at many levels domestic and international, of the entrenchment of multicultural recognition in a previously "homogenous" Japan.[26]

As the Buraku have garnered increasing international attention as a labor-based "minority group" among other minorities in Japan, Buraku politics have shifted. A new set of ethical imperatives and new strategies for the management of discrimination and violence have been established, granting content to Japanese multiculturalism. Both individuals and Buraku organizations accept more and more as a matter of course that Buraku difference ought to be recognized and characterized as minority difference, and that other minority groups ought to be accepted and worked with as potential allies. Furthermore, with this entrenchment of multiculturalism, the Buraku group, as a minority, comes to need an authentic and a historically demonstrable cultural center, and those demands for authenticity arrive naturalized under the guise of simply recognizing facts on the ground. These ethical obligations provide an avenue for insisting that Burakumin need not shy away from shameful scars or stigmatized labor. Instead, they can claim those characteristics with pride, to be shown off as they attend festivals highlighting traditional Buraku culinary forays into intestinal soup or artisanal showcasings of drum-making and cobblery, alongside corresponding Korean and Ainu displays. These strategies for dismantling structural discrimination and ameliorating attendant psychological violence are both indicative of a new moment for the Buraku liberation movement and productive of new possibilities for the elimination of structural subjection. However, their effectiveness hinges precisely on a set of dangerous labor practices that are now disappearing.

Taken together, these two interrelated sets of changes—in the contours of the Buraku people and in their political representation—are giving new shape to the stakes of the contemporary Buraku moment. The vitality of transnational categories of discrimination, the well-being of individuals and groups, and the cultural capital commanded by modern, liberal nation-states are all affected by this tension between the increased solvency of political argument regarding labor and the waning presence of such stigmatized labor. On a first level, as signs of being Buraku fall away from Buraku individuals, discursive norms and legal codes on both the international and national levels hang in the balance. The work of Buraku political organizations, the possibilities of national antidiscrimination legislation, and the efficacy of solidarity movements all consist in the changing movements and aspirations of Buraku subjects. Similarly, the categories of race, caste, and culture are all made and remade in the daily actions and political movements of Buraku people.

On a second level, people themselves—whether they are leather workers or political organizers (Mika, Tanimoto-san, or Satō-san)—are placed at risk within these global transformations. The ability of leather workers to care for and support themselves and each other frequently relies on jobs that bring to them and their families the risk of physical harm and unwanted social pressures. In turn, Buraku political organizations rely on the workers to perform these jobs as a sign of culture, and at the same time they hope to enact legislation that might alleviate the economic and social woes accompanying such occupations. The financial stability and ethical fulfillment of these political organizations and their ability to employ their workers depend on their capacity to do this work effectively.

On a third level, the status of Japan as a multicultural nation-state also hangs in the balance. The work involved in asserting Japan's multicultural status requires that Buraku political actors produce signs of a Buraku minority meant to sway national and international actors and to fulfill what they see as their own ethical commitments. In doing this, those actors create the grounds for international audiences such as the United Nations, foreign scholars and activists, and funding agencies to recognize Japan as a nation-state equipped with the trappings of multiculturalism. These framings group Buraku people both alongside other "minorities" in Japan, for example, resident Koreans, Okinawans, or the Ainu, and alongside other groups internationally, for example, the Dalit of South Asia, the "caste" people of Kenya, or caste workers in Yemen. Inasmuch as these groupings introduce new (and perhaps contrasting) obligations of similarity and solidarity, they also characterize Japan as a multicultural nation of a kind with other multicultural nations. The currency of this multicultural status depends on the production of convincing representations of groups like the Buraku as minority populations.

Working Skin uses "the labor of multiculturalism" to understand these broad-ranging stakes across individuals, organizations, and governments. Focusing on the interaction of the circulation of political argument with economic transformation, I investigate the distributions of care, vulnerability, trepidation, shame, and pride that characterize the current Buraku situation. I do this in the hope of showing how multiculturalism disciplines and dominates the lives of people both at the margins and at the center of the nation-state, and in examining this, I perhaps provide fodder for alternatives.

THE LABOR OF MULTICULTURALISM

My argument about "the labor of multiculturalism" unfolds in this book across three thematic sections. These sections are meant to build a set of interlocking arguments, namely: (1) that the labor required to produce convincing signs—whether they are arguments, cultural artifacts, moral judgments, or even types of people—always has a reciprocal effect of transforming those who labor; (2) that multicultural recognition is a particular liberal mode of governing social difference centered on a staged tension between freedom and obligation; and (3) that globalization can be productively understood through the embodied practices that allow for movement and commensuration across arenas of action. Each of the sections examines a particular moment in the labor of multiculturalism—from the concrete work of the tannery and NGO, to the political strategizing in domestic arenas, to the labor required to produce an internationally recognizable minority group commensurate with other groups around the world. My first argument serves as the basis for the following two. The global circulation of styles of political argument and economic forms is a product of human labor that renders such arguments and forms meaningful and powerful in context.

Labor and the Willfulness of Things

The premise of my investigation is simple: the production of convincing signs—whether they are arguments, cultural artifacts, moral judgments, or even types of people—takes labor, and that that labor transforms its object and subject alike. I place particular emphasis on the form that labor takes. In order to make money, Tanimoto-san is placed in a position where he must apply himself to tanning leather under factory conditions. He moves raw skins from pallet to barrels filled with tanning chemicals and back out. He must chart the path of the skins, keeping track of the timing along the way. Over time he develops an eye for how the skins are oriented, and his body acquires a muscle memory, allowing him to grab the tail end of the skins and sling them with more and more fluidity. He becomes more familiar with recording times and gains an intuition for how long is too long for a skin to sit in a chromium bath, calibrated against the temperature of the day. This disciplined labor, this work, leaves marks on his body. Particular muscles and abilities are emphasized and developed while others are not required for the tasks at all. Furthermore, he risks losing a finger or splashing caustic chemicals into his eyes, as well as other hazards such as the long-term effects of exposure to known carcinogens. Commuting to and from the tannery, venturing out into surrounding neighborhoods for lunch, he travels paths that could indicate to onlookers his status as stigmatized. Beyond his body proper, working at a leather factory leaves traces on his record of employment, which might enable other people to track him as Buraku, and it also rewrites his relationships with these others. As he makes leather, Tanimoto-san transforms himself, but not necessarily under conditions of his choosing and not always in ways of which he is immediately aware or initially intended.

This process is not limited to the immediately concrete task of producing leather. Buraku political organizations such as IMADR are concerned with creating signs of the presence and vulnerability of minority populations in Japan. They maintain networks with these different populations, track their numbers and instances of discrimination, and generate reports to the Japanese government, to UN representatives, and to the Japanese public. In order to do so they must become familiar with interviewing techniques, develop writing skills for multiple audiences and language skills beyond Japanese, and potentially sit long hours at a computer or spend sleepless nights frantically preparing for a press conference, worrying that they might not be doing quite enough to combat discrimination. In so doing they transform their skill sets and their bodily habits, exercise and cultivate an ethical orientation, and render themselves recognizable to people in other positions, for example, a UN special rapporteur, as NGO workers. Again, like Tanimoto-san, the IMADR employee transforms herself in the work of representing minority groups in Japan, also not always under conditions of her own choosing and not always in ways of which she is immediately aware or initially intended. Each of these laborers sets out to make a particular thing, whether it is leather or a description of Buraku discrimination, and in the process they make themselves. The transformative power of labor in these two examples, which I explore in greater detail in chapter 1, is not limited to the making of individuals. Through the actions of its workers, IMADR itself becomes recognizable as a kind of organization; likewise, the tannery becomes evidence of a Buraku minority or Japan becomes a multicultural nation-state.

My approach to labor here, which undergirds my analysis throughout the book and which I elaborate on in much more detail in chapters 1 and 2, speaks to two divergent strands within social theory that examine the productivity of human action. On the one hand, I draw from insights of the performance theory and linguistic anthropology, that language use accomplishes things in the world, only one of which is conveying referential content. Consider the distinction between the person who offers an "excuse me" as they accidentally bump into you on the bus and the person who shoves by with a gruff "get out of my way." The first is legible as polite, the second as rude. In using language, constructed under conditions not of their choosing, people make and remake themselves, transforming their relations with other people and qualitatively building who they are. This insight need not be limited to language use; indeed, that shove alone might be enough to signal that the shover is rude, though perhaps less rude than the one who combines the shove with the gruff command. Throughout this book I pay close attention to differences in the specific tools that actors use to create things and through which they transform themselves.

Here I speak to a different lineage of social theory, that of the study of value in conversation with the work of Marx. Marx masterfully demonstrates the transformative powers of human labor, its sensuous material force, and its relation to social relations, using capitalism as his analytic crucible. He distinguishes humans from other animals in their capacity to envision in advance a product they seek to create. His canonical example here is the architect and the bee, with the architect first setting out a design of a building and then working to produce it, and the bee simply working and in the process of that work creating a hive.[27] However, humans produce more than simply the object they seek to create. As we have seen, they also produce themselves, embedded in a web of relations with others. In laboring, in establishing a durative relationship with an object, they also create something that they need not, and arguable could not entirely, have envisioned in advance—themselves.[28]

In this fuller range of productivity, we can see a "willfulness of things." There has been much recent work in English examining the qualities and agency of material things.[29] An iconic example here comes from cultural theorist Bruno Latour's examination of a sheepherder's fence.[30] Sheepherder and dog are tasked with keeping sheep together, fed, and safe. In building a fence to enclose the sheep, the herder cedes to the fence an agency directed toward that objective. The herder also becomes subject to and makes demands on the qualities of that fence. It must be durable and hard. It must be able to withstand weather changes and occasional butts by unruly sheep. Whatever material the herder uses to build the fence, these qualities are the ones called on to complete the task.[31] But the fence will have other qualities too; if it is made of wood, it might splinter or rot. Or, if it is made, say, of old railroad ties, it might contain creosote, a substance that could leak into the ground, harm the grass in the fenced-in area, and in turn hurt the sheep, potentially costing the herder their job and reputation. Any one quality only comes bundled with others, which could come into effect in unanticipated ways.[32] While things may not have a will or purpose on their own, which in no way prevents them from being ascribed will and related to as if they had a will,[33] they do have a certain willfulness, a capacity to act back in relation. This is a point that goes beyond concrete objects alone. In relating, anything—whether a piece of rawhide or a description of Buraku issues or a scar on the body or a set of muscle memories—meets with demands that call out particular qualities, but at the same time that thing also acts back, bundled with other qualities, with effects that exceed the anticipated. Someone might take up one object to work on another and then be transformed by entering into relations with willful objects, in ways they never imagined.

The labor of multiculturalism is a mode of orchestrating and adjudicating these kinds of formative, coproductive relationships among humans and nonhumans alike. Certain relationships become durative, certain modes of demanding qualities last longer than others, and some labor becomes habituated into conduct or disciplined into patterned forms of work. In investigating the formative effects of human labor, I am attentive to the conditions under which the labor of multiculturalism has enduring effects, regularly exacting from objects and humans alike particular arrangements, qualities, and dispositions. None of the actors I previously described works under conditions of their own making; rather, social institutions, themselves accreted products of human action, guide and shape the labor, bolster some forms of labor into habituated conduct, shove others into occasional contingency, and outright preclude other forms altogether. Chapter 1, "Of Skins and Workers," examines the labor on the part of the NGO and tannery workers that goes into producing convincing signs of being Buraku. Chapter 2, "Ushimatsu Left for Texas," serves as a counterpoint, examining the political and social life of the *non*production of such signs, with a particular focus on how stigma constrains and allows forms of life—particularly realized in relations of kin, space, and occupation—for people who pass much of their lives unrecognized as Buraku.

The Governance of Multiculturalism

The 1871 promulgation of what would come to be known as the Emancipation Edict abolished formal distinctions between the "abject classes" *(senmin)* of society and "commoners" *(heimin)*. In so doing, it liberated the *senmin* from their status as abject, from the restrictions on their clothing and use of public space, from their tax-exempt status, and from their occupational designations (and security). This formal dismantling of social hierarchy, then, was a trade-off: the erstwhile *senmin* achieved formal equality as citizens with an attendant loss of economic security. Despite this formal assertion of equality, however, the problem of their difference persisted. In some places, rather than being designated as *heimin* in family and residential records, these people were marked as *shin-heimin* (new commoners), or *kyū-eta* (former eta, one of the "abject classes"), and were still tracked as different. Similarly, while the law abolished formal distinctions, social norms and mores were slower to change, on the part of erstwhile *senmin* and nonabject people alike. This group difference persisted alongside the promulgation of a formal, legal principle of individual equality, seeding one of the foundational tensions of the liberal, modern nation-state.[34]

Historian Kurokawa Midori traces this tension between the principle of equality and the politics of difference through Buraku political history in her 1999 book, *Ika to Dōka no Aida: Hisabetsu Buraku Ninshiki no Kiseki (Between Dissimilation and Assimilation: The Trajectory of Buraku Recognition)*. She demonstrates how the management of Buraku difference informed the development of modern citizenship, with particular attention to how that management is complicated by the ambiguities of the Buraku category.[35] She points out that while this tension has been part of Buraku history since the Meiji restoration, it, in line with the history I traced earlier, has become particularly inflected by identity and cultural authenticity since the 1980s. It is in these decades that the tension in rights, between equality and difference, takes on cultural stakes. Not only, then, can recognition potentially fail, but its failure can constitute a blow to one's own authentic self, striking, as the political theorist Charles Taylor puts it, a "grievous wound."[36]

Multiculturalism is a form of governance that aims to ameliorate these wounds.[37] It seeks to provide to groups cast as different the recognition they seem to properly deserve. This governance consists of disposing of the relationships among people and things in a manner deemed correct and ethical. This is the formative labor I examine. It involves the distribution of resources, but it is framed in terms of recognition.[38] Part of the quandary of multiculturalism, as inheritor of this tension between difference and equality, is to ever maintain a respect for individual authenticity even while working to shape groups—in the case of minorities, into recognizable populations centered on an authentic cultural core; in the case of the nation, into a collective where citizens are concerned by those wounded by misrecognition or exclusion and choose to work to ameliorate those wounds. This tension, between freedom and obligation, runs through Buraku politics as its leaders seek to cultivate a constituency able and willing to recognize itself as Buraku as well as a broader public that is attentive to and actively working against discrimination. In these political tasks, they must cultivate authentic individuals whose desires and ethical commitments must appear to stand prior to any such cultivation.

Across the book I work through specifics of the Buraku situation to portray the traction of multiculturalism in Japan; here, let me provide a quick gloss. In Japan, multiculturalism has arisen as a tool in a struggle against the specter of homogeneity that has haunted Japan since the Asia-Pacific War. It consists of a cultural politics organized around two related tensions: one, that between social relations that are read as constraint and social relations that are read as freedom; and two, that between individual equality and group specificity. Multiculturalism recognizes groups that can demonstrate both a cultural core and social harm. Multiculturalism demands vigilance. To be properly multicultural requires being on the lookout for new groups to recruit to the list, and always anxious that some groups are left out. It is a never-ending process, perpetually looking for another group whose wounds will be assessed and remedied. In short, it maintains a flow of groups through a suffering slot, all in an attempt to improve itself.[39] In looking for these groups, however, this vigilance rarely examines the group cast as the norm, the forces that regulate and police the boundaries and habits of that default group, instead looking to those positioned on the margins. Building from my argument about labor, I contend that multiculturalism, as a historical technique of managing social difference, disciplines and transforms the groups it includes as much as it might the groups that it excludes.

My approach here complements and diverges from the preexisting literature on minorities in Japan. Over the past three decades, there has been a noticeable increase in English-language literature on minority populations in Japan. Much of this work voices the projects in terms of shattering the myth of Japanese homogeneity.[40] As I asserted previously, the idea of Japan as being an ethnically homogenous nation-state only gained institutional purchase following the war, amidst postwar assertions of Japanese-ness.[41] The project of resistance inherent in the majority of the work on minorities in Japan can only make sense in this historical and social context. The literature on minorities in Japan, however, tends to elide its historical conditions of possibility and to assume an ahistorical fixity in their object of argument, that is, "minorities."[42] Sociologist John Lie even goes so far as to assert that "Japan has always been multiethnic."[43] In these analyses, there is little attention paid to why it is possible or even necessary now to explain difference in Japan in terms of serial, distinct, and equilibrated (and arguably homogenized) minority groups; how culture and woundedness, with its attendant sympathetic attention, has become the standard of minority authenticity; or how an additive model of identity, or "multiple discriminations," can be seen as an appropriate analytic for people who "belong" to several different minority categories simultaneously. In fact, the naturalized analysis of this minority literature perforce precludes an examination of the enabling historical conditions of its own categories of thought, and in so doing renders itself incapable of, and disinterested in, analyzing the effects of this particular conceptualization of difference.[44]

This academic literature is clearly and instructively parallel to changes within Buraku political argument. As the Buraku political movement experiences greater levels of success in obtaining recognition on an international level, it does not merely create new political, ethical, and material conditions for the Buraku people or for those who work in its name. It also creates a narrative of the Japanese nation-state as a multicultural one. International recognition of the Buraku minority, either through categories of race, ethnicity, or class, or newer categories of labor, enables the recognition of Japan as multicultural. This situation is partially ironic. As my conclusion elaborates in more detail, in these political venues, the Buraku people are being reconstituted not simply as a source of shame but instead as evidence of the status of Japan as a modern and multicultural nation-state. Recent academic literature reliant on a definition of multiculturalism based on the serial arrangement and recognition of minority identity is as much a symptom of this shift as it is an analysis of it. It creates it even as it reflects on it.[45]

The stated objective of the BLL is to liberate the Buraku subject, that is, to stage an engagement with Buraku identity as an individual choice: a Buraku person should be able to choose how to make being Buraku relevant to their own life, relieved of the threat of discrimination or labor hazards. Key to this process of staging liberation is an understanding of how the essence of Buraku is located. Chapter 3, "Locating the Buraku," examines the primacy of ties of kinship, occupation, and residence in determining who is Buraku and who knows themselves as such, the way those ties have changed over time, and how these ties distinguish Buraku stigma from racial stigma. I elaborate on this argument by looking at two forces affecting the locations of Buraku: an environmental critique of Buraku industries that furthers their disappearance and the spatial marginalization of Buraku communities, and a private detective industry that attempts to capture those fading signs for paying clients. I trace the conflicting ethical orientations at the heart of this struggle for a Buraku subject choosing to be such. Chapter 4, "A Sleeping Public," shifts the emphasis to Buraku political strategies for a concerned public composed of individuals who choose to be attentive in a clearly delineated manner. Two tactics in this process are the "denunciation session," a public verbal shaming of those who discriminate against Buraku people, and the "human rights seminar," a public forum organized to advertise and discuss the importance of human rights and respect for minorities. Tracing out the connections between these two forms of politics, I show how multiculturalism and human rights, as abstract universal ideals, are made and remade in concrete settings.

Movement, Solidarity, Sympathy

In 2006 a small group of Japanese sanitation workers and Buraku activists traveled from Tokyo to Chennai, India, to meet with a group it saw as a potential comrade, the Dalit.[46] During a seven-day period, the Buraku contingent toured leather factories and slaughterhouses, met sanitation workers, visited Dalit homes and communities, and exchanged stories of discrimination, hardship, and struggle. It was the second solidarity trip in as many years, and it would hopefully lead to many more in the future.[47] The final section of this book explores the politics of international solidarity among the Buraku and minority groups in other countries such as the Dalit. This solidarity requires the movement of people and money and an ethical commitment. Chapter 5, "Demanding a Standard," focuses on the recently established UN category, "Discrimination Based on Work and Descent," and examines the labor necessary to create a new and convincing standard of discrimination effective across disparate populations. Chapter 6, "Wounded Futures," complements this focus on UN-level solidarity strategies by looking at groups that do not have the resources or relative political status vis-à-vis the United Nations to be in Geneva but that create for themselves other possibilities of commensurability and international solidarity. I follow in this chapter the Tokyo sanitation and tannery workers on their study tour to Tamil Nadu, and examine the role that pain, both physical and psychological, serves in building a politics of solidarity and transnational sympathy.

Standing behind the contemporary Buraku situation is a politics of movement. This is a movement not simply of people—as they travel from Japan to Geneva or South Asia, or the reverse—but a movement of commodities such as rawhide and leather, of styles of political argument, and of ethical commitments. A vast amount of labor is required for any of these things to move. First and most fundamental in this process is the commensuration of value; these things must be judged the same thing across different arenas of action. This judgment takes labor, requires backing standards of authority, and is subject to faltering and failure.[48] In order for the leaders of the Buraku political movement to achieve the goal of liberation, they must get more people—domestically and internationally—aware of, concerned by, and willing to act to combat Buraku discrimination. Likewise, they must maintain a robust constituency that knows and claims itself as Buraku. These maneuvers require laying a foundation for their ideas and ethical commitments to travel; they require establishing ethical and political standards that can judge, for example, Buraku discrimination as a violation of human rights or Buraku pain equivalent to Dalit pain, as examples of "Discrimination Based on Work and Descent."[49]

Part of "the labor of multiculturalism" is the laying of this foundation of movement. Over the past decades, there has been a tremendous amount of scholarship arguing that contemporary globalization is marked by an increased rate and prevalence of circulation and exchange,[50] and anthropologists have increasingly turned their attention to the problematics of transnational circulation, how to understand the long-standing analytical bifurcation between economy and culture, and how to think about boundaries within a globalized framework.[51] In the midst of this profusion of academic literature, the materialist, pragmatic bent of "the labor of multiculturalism" offers a concrete methodology to think about movement and its codification into more systematic circulation. Attending specifically to the movement of discursive activity, recent scholars of linguistic anthropology have cautioned against the temptation to view the movement of a text as a simple matter of production, transmission, and reception, arguing that such a line of thought tends to reify both text and context.[52] Instead, they pursue an alternative line of inquiry that is attentive to how actors frame one text as related to another. As linguistic anthropologist Susan Gal argues, what we perceive as movement is "more precisely a repetition or imitation of forms that are framed, *reflexively and in retrospect*, as being 'the same thing again' or as instantiations of an ideal, a genre: a sonnet, a wedding."[53] In this model, the movement of ideas, words, or organizational forms can be understood as the outcome of activity that frames discursive events as repetition or instantiation.

The work of Marx provides a strong reminder that these insights need not be left to the negotiation of discursive signification alone. Gal's analysis of circulation focuses solely on the movement of what she calls "discursive activity." Her argument rests on an initial separation of such discursive activity from other such things as people and objects: "Persons may circulate by moving bodily from place to place, as at a party or in migration. Objects may circulate by being moved or exchanged from person to person, as gift, commodity or entitlement. But signs, messages and practices—discursive activity—only *seem* to move in this way."[54] Having singled out discursive activity, Gal then proceeds to develop the argument that the circulation of discursive activity is always an achievement that requires semiotic labor. I contend, however, that similar commensurating labor is as necessary in the case of people and objects as it is in the case of discursive activity, and her analysis of linguistic phenomena is equally instructive when it comes to people and objects. In moving, people engage in different types of activity, creating themselves and being interpreted in newfound ways.

The final two chapters of this book examine transnational solidarity projects as a way of ethnographically grounding and developing this argument about the movement of people, words, and things across national, economic, and racial boundaries. In particular I focus on solidarity as a project of cultivating sympathy: a feeling *with* rather than a feeling *for*.[55] I investigate the standards that allow for the Buraku to feel alongside the Dalit and, likewise, the abstract ideals called on as UN representatives and other actors at a distance respond to the Buraku situation with concern or anger. In these projects, such standards are asserted, questioned, and refashioned. At times they are even placed in jeopardy. My approach provides an immanent view of social structures and institutions created in movement. Rather than bifurcating social life between a macro plane of broad significance, such as capitalism, bureaucracy, or neoliberalism, and a micro plane of interaction, I argue that such scales of social life are themselves products of the framing labor of creating texts and contexts, an orientation that crucially guides the methodological orientation of this book.

Across these three interlocking sections of the book, I slowly build my analysis of "the labor of multiculturalism." As an analytical insight, "the labor of multiculturalism" frames changes in the category of labor over the past three decades. As a methodological entry point, "the labor of multiculturalism" directs one's attention to the material and symbolic processes through which categories of identity, convincing political arguments, and ethical commitments are simultaneously codified and vivified. As an ensemble, "the labor of multiculturalism" serves as a practice-focused intervention for understanding how changes in global circulations of capital intersect with circulations of political mobilization to create and mitigate the possibilities and risks of the contemporary Buraku situation.

The experiences, anxieties, and desires of people like Mika, Yuko, Tanimoto-san, or even Satō-san and Misako are not aberrant. Nor are the experiences and political and ethical priorities of the IMADR NGO worker, the BLL activist, the UN representative, or the foreign researcher. All of these orientations, grounded and material in lived lives, are tied to each other across borders that traverse bodies, neighborhoods, and nations. The ethical and affective orientations spanning these lives are tied to each other, at times delicately and at times robustly, in a transnational web that constitutes contemporary Buraku issues. *Working Skin* traverses that web, delving into the lives of people who live as Buraku and people who work in the name of Buraku, and shows how, as they work through the dual skins of leather and multiculturalism, they grant force to categories of life and difference, with transformative effects for themselves, for their communities, for Japan, and beyond.

PART ONE

Recognizing Buraku Difference

ONE

Of Skins and Workers

PRODUCING THE BURAKU

FRAMING DISCRIMINATION

In July 2005, Doudou Diène, United Nations (UN) special rapporteur on contemporary racism, officially visited Japan to examine the socioeconomic and cultural status of minority groups in Japan. Among the groups he visited on his nine-day trip were the Buraku people. Diène met with leaders of Buraku political organizations and visited Buraku neighborhoods. He was warmly welcomed with emblematic displays of Buraku ways of life: he attended a drum-making workshop, visited a tannery, and was guest of honor at a dinner that featured *motsu nabe* (offal stew) and local dances.

Diène's office used these visits, along with historical and contextual research, as the basis for a report later submitted to the United Nations that provided recommendations for the Japanese government as to how it might improve the situation of domestic minorities. Throughout this process—of arranging and conducting Diène's visit, of searching out contextual information, and of scripting and revising the report—Diène's offices leaned heavily on support from the International Movement Against All Forms of Discrimination and Racism (IMADR), founded in 1988 by the Buraku Liberation League (BLL) as a conduit for internationalizing the BLL's mission to eliminate discrimination. IMADR has close relations with other Japanese minority organizations and populations, but its primary constituency remains the Buraku people.

In partnership with Amnesty International Japan, IMADR handled the minutiae of Diène's visits and provided assistance with drafting, revising, and circulating his report. IMADR staff members helped establish Diène's itinerary, using their network through the BLL to set up meetings with

FIGURE 2. Doudou Diène, United Nations Special Rapporteur on contemporary forms of racism, racial discrimination, xenophobia, and related intolerance (2002–2008), on a mission to Japan.

national and local leaders of the organization and to arrange visits to the variety of Buraku and other minority cultural events Diène attended across Japan; they also organized the interpretation between Japanese and English, and sometimes Japanese and French, for Diène's entire mission to Japan. Effectively, IMADR created and maintained the logistical and linguistic framework through which Diène was able to experience and understand the situation of minorities in Japan; conversely, it created the framework through which Japanese minority groups, including the Buraku, achieved international representation.

This work of creating and maintaining the relationship between organizations such as IMADR and its Buraku constituency has formative effects on all involved. Organizations such as IMADR seek to create politically solvent representations of marginalized populations in Japan. They speak in the language of rights, culture, and identity; they maintain the company of like-minded organizations, both domestic and international; and they collaborate across the boundaries of the marginalized to effect political solidarity and to combat discrimination. In so doing, they make themselves recognizable as particular kinds of political and ethical actors. On the other side of this rhetorical frame stand populations that serve as evidence in arguments about the enduring presence of social marginalization. In the Buraku situation, this includes tannery and slaughterhouse workers; it includes people who might not work in a traditionally Buraku industry but who were raised by Buraku parents or in a Buraku district; and it, at times, includes people who might not have the inclination or the tools to recognize themselves as Buraku. Even as the nongovernmental organization (NGO) workers develop and fulfill desires, aspirations, and selves in their labor, so too do the people who lead lives taken up as evidence of the Buraku minority.

Between 2005 and 2007 I spent several months working in each of these kinds of venues. I served as an intern at IMADR for a year and a half and apprenticed in a tannery for half a year. I worked the trades that I was simultaneously studying, subjecting my body and time to the demands that these workplaces foist on those they employ. One of the tasks I collaborated on at IMADR was building a website that would represent Buraku and other minority issues to international audiences. I spent my time at the factory learning how to make leather, from utterly raw and still bloody hide to a finished sheet of tanned and dyed leather. My time in each of these locations was relatively brief, and my financial and emotional support came from other locations; in no way does my experience equal a lifetime spent slinging skin or preparing reports in the name of dismantling discrimination. However, devoting myself to the production of website and leather gave me a sense of the rhythms, demands, pleasures, and challenges operative in each situation.

These venues articulate two different regimes of labor and value, each associated with a particular historical moment, a complementary political formation, and each taking on a gendered aspect. The masculinized labor of the factory floor sits against the Internet-savvy, feminized care of the liberal, multicultural office work; Fordism is set against post-Fordism; the politics of labor and unions contrasts with the politics of identity and human rights. The work of this framing happens within these boundaries, simultaneously asserting them, policing who might be feminized and who masculinized, what might count as Fordist and what might count as beyond that moment. This is a work that cuts across any neat divide between the material and the immaterial.[1] Both the knowledge-producer, who spends most of her day seated, typing at a desk, and the tannery worker, who spends his day hefting wet hide, must use their bodies in particular ways to produce artifacts that can circulate beyond them.

The uneven coupling of these trajectories—for the production of a website is always framing the production of leather, even as it depends on it—opens a window into the formative labor of multiculturalism, into the types of people and organizations, the ethical orientations and forms of life that are required in the labor of representing stigmatized labor. It also opens a window into the staging of the aforementioned contrasts—of a Fordist moment of factory labor against a moment of liberal care—so key in the staging of Japan's modernity.

This chapter sets the scene for the remainder of the book. It is a first pass at understanding the myriad, sometimes conflicting and sometimes complementary, ways in which ethical commitments, political aims, and a system of categorizing people are achieved, sustained, and transformed in quotidian, patterned action; the ways in which obligation and choice intertwine in action; and the ways in which those dances of demand and effort circulate transnationally. These themes resonate throughout the book.

Let me invite you, then, into the skin of things.

DESCRIPTION

In the summer of 2006 IMADR posted the following description of the Buraku minority group on its English website:

The Buraku Issue

Buraku people are a Japanese social minority group, ethnically and linguistically indistinguishable from other Japanese people. They face discrimination in Japan because of an association with work once considered impure, such as butchering animals or tanning leather. In particular, they often have trouble finding marriage partners or employment.

Brief Historical Context

During the Tokugawa feudal period (1603–1867), what is now called "Buraku discrimination" was officially structured in a caste system that dominated society at that time. This system formalized a division of labor that associated people with their jobs, and society was stratified into four primary castes: warriors, farmers, artisans, and merchants, with a portion of the population falling outside of this basic caste structure. These outcasts held jobs that the rest of the population refused (frequently on the grounds of ritual and religious impurity) such as working in slaughterhouses, tanning leather, and performing executions. Furthermore, their social habits—their clothing, where they could walk, to whom they could speak, where they could live—were all regulated by various laws in a way that set outcastes apart from the rest of the population. Some historians trace a preceding informal version of this system, which provided a basis for treating different kinds of people differently in social settings, back to the Heian period (794–1185).

Modern Forms of Discrimination

The Tokugawa feudal system set the grounds for how Buraku discrimination functions in modern-day Japan, but does not fully explain the current manifestations of discrimination. Those facing discrimination are not limited to descendants of Tokugawa outcastes. The original meaning of the word *Buraku* is "neighborhood" or "community," but it has become shorthand for *tokushu buraku*, or "special communities," a euphemistic designation for the neighborhoods in which descendants of outcastes have historically lived. While these neighborhoods were relatively stable during the Tokugawa period, after the Meiji Restoration (1868), populations became more mobile, with events such as earthquakes, wars, and economic growth leading, over the next century, to the massive relocation of people throughout Japan. As a result, people who were not descendants of outcasts moved into neighborhoods formerly designated as outcast, and boundaries of these neighborhoods shifted. Despite these changes, these Buraku neighborhoods are still known, tracked formally in governmental registers and informally in daily conversations that people have about their own neighborhoods and hometowns.

Present-day Buraku discrimination is primarily based on whether a person lives in a Buraku neighborhood, or whether her or his parents are from such a neighborhood. This means that it is possible for people with no connection to the Tokugawa outcaste status to be labeled as Buraku and face anti-Buraku discrimination. It is even possible for a family to unknowingly move into an historically Buraku neighborhood and, unbeknownst to them, become Buraku. The stigmatized category of Buraku, which is based first and foremost on an individual's family lineage and occupation, has come also to depend on one's family address.

The largest Buraku political organization, the Buraku Liberation League (BLL), estimates that there are over 3 million Buraku people nation-wide. The BLL produces annual reports that track the hundreds of cases of discrimination that happen throughout Japan every year, cases which include harassment and refusal of marriage or employment. The political movement's efforts have resulted in great improvements in the quality of life in Buraku neighborhoods, the elimination of physical violence against Buraku people, and a continuing reduction in other forms of discrimination as well. However, anti-Buraku prejudice is still prevalent throughout the country, and discrimination remains a key issue.[2]

This description frames Buraku issues for IMADR's Internet readership, with the hope that it might have explanatory traction beyond the boundaries of Japan. It is but one page of a larger website overhaul that IMADR conducted while I interned there, but a key page on that website. This is the point, in English, where IMADR hopes to make Buraku issues—the contemporary situation and historical underpinnings—legible and gripping for an audience potentially global in scope.

IMADR was founded in 1988 with precisely this mission: to internationalize the Buraku mandate of eliminating discrimination. It was formed with support both from the BLL and the then-named Buraku Liberation Research Institute (now Buraku Liberation and Human Rights Research Institute, or BLHRRI), under the direction of Mushakoji Kinhide, a well-known scholar and activist. IMADR's formation marked a change in strategy within the Buraku political movement, heralding the institutionalization of a broad focus on human rights issues, both within Japan and internationally. In its broadest articulation, IMADR's primary three goals are to eliminate discrimination and racism worldwide; to forge international solidarity among minority groups; and to advance the international human rights system across the globe. Other leftist groups in Japan during the 1970s, 1980s, and 1990s had critiqued the BLL for its almost exclusive focus on Buraku issues and its relative neglect of international human rights mechanisms.[3] IMADR's founding was aimed in part at addressing these critiques. Over the year and a half that I interned with IMADR, the six-member staff of its Tokyo office, all women except for the secretary general and me, addressed issues that cut across minority experiences in Japan and worked hard to forge ties among minorities that extended beyond the boundaries of the state. This they did with regular contact and discussion with the BLL leadership.

IMADR maintains both an international secretariat, which coordinates activities with partner organizations across the globe, and a Japan Committee, which focuses on issues within Japan. Both of these organizations are managed by the same permanent office staff and share the same headquarter space in the Tokyo office. During my fieldwork with IMADR, six office staff members, one intern, and a host of irregular and regular volunteers would help with such activities as mailings. In addition to its Tokyo office, IMADR also maintains an office and a staff member in Geneva and then titularly maintains offices and connections in North America, South Asia, Central America, and Europe, though this last set of offices receives only the most minimal funds needed for paired-down mailings and has no devoted office space. In addition to the permanent staff, there is also a governing board of directors, headed by Nimalka Fernando, a prominent lawyer and activist from Sri Lanka, which consists of the leaders of the BLL, BLHRRI, one representative from Nigeria, another from Nepal, and six European and United Nations–based dignitaries, including Theo van Boven. This board of directors meets once a year to talk about long-term strategic planning; the office staff, in contrast, works daily to enact these larger plans and to appear accountable to them.

The internationalist aspiration of IMADR, both of utilizing and refining international human rights mechanisms and of strengthening connections among minority groups across the globe, has gained momentum since the mid-1990s. There have been more trips to Geneva to work with UN special rapporteurs on racism and related forms of discrimination, more visits by international activists to domestic minority communities and organizations, and more trips to such places as India to conduct research into the United Nations' newly established category "Discrimination Based on Work and Descent," under which fall Japanese Buraku and South Asian Dalits. IMADR coordinates all of these activities, serving as a bureaucratic, economic, and linguistic conduit between international and domestic actors. All IMADR officers are proficient in English as well as Japanese, some have a command of other languages, and the organization actively recruits multilingual and frequently non-Japanese individuals as its interns to assist in negotiating its role as conduit to the international community.

I served an extended term as an IMADR intern, working with the organization from September 2005 through the early spring of 2007. I spent three days a week working in IMADR's Tokyo office, translating documents among Japanese, English, and occasionally Spanish and French, interpreting for Anglophone visitors, and accompanying IMADR and BLL officers on their trips to Osaka, Geneva, and Okinawa. As had interns prior to me and as would interns after me, I also attended to more bureaucratic tasks: the maintenance of membership lists and mailing labels, the organization of incoming mail from other NGOs, and the taking of minutes at organizational meetings. One task unique to my internship, however, was revamping the organization's English website.

In 2002 the UN Sub-Commission on Human Rights formally recognized "Discrimination Based on Work and Descent." The addition of a new category of discrimination was the result of years of lobbying on the part of IMADR, BLL, BLHRRI, and partner Dalit organizations to have the United Nations create a formal structure of recognition for caste-based discrimination issues. Since then, IMADR has been particularly engaged in increasing its visibility, an engagement further strengthened by Diène's mission to Japan. With these changes, IMADR devoted more time and money to the development of its web presence, in Japanese and English alike. It looked for someone bilingual to coordinate this process and in 2005 hired a communications officer, part of whose job would be to direct the expansion and revision of the website. I entered IMADR as an intern one month after Malaya began her job. Two years prior, she and I had been classmates and friends at Stanford's Japanese language school in Yokohama, a school for academics and professionals whose work would require the regular use of Japanese. Malaya, who had a master's degree in international relations, with a focus on human rights, from Columbia University, had been working with a fair-trade NGO in Tokyo since we finished language school. Prior to that she had worked as an interpreter with Peace Boat, a global NGO based in Japan that fostered international connections as a means of promoting peace, human rights, and sustainable development.

The IMADR staff had decided to redevelop the website prior to hiring Malaya, and it became her license then to oversee the process. Every member of the office was involved. Malaya established a time line and then worked back from that to generate tasks. Members there already had their own area of expertise and took the portions of the website that most closely coincided with their job focus, whether it was working on solidarity issues with Ainu groups, working on gender issues, working on Roma issues, or working on "Discrimination Based on Work and Descent." Work at IMADR was typically shared. The overall content of the website was discussed in the weekly staff meetings, and tasks were assigned. Each person drafted a version of their assigned portion, in either Japanese or English, and then the group worked on revising that statement and translating it into the other language, with formal weekly check-ins along with the day-to-day informal check-ins that happened as we all worked together.

Malaya recruited me to work on the general introduction to Buraku issues in English, and also on a description of the ongoing legal case, known as the Sayama Case, against a Buraku man accused of murdering a young woman. Three days after a full staff meeting on the website, Malaya met with me to discuss the time line of this portion of the project. That morning she had asked me, speaking across the room in the basement of the BLL, where IMADR was headquartered, whether I had time after lunch to meet about the web project, maybe around 2 P.M. I did. We continued at our computers working on other things, eventually went to a 1 P.M. group lunch at a nearby Korean restaurant, and then headed back to the office to meet.

My conversations with Malaya, in general, were primarily in English, with Japanese words and phrases liberally peppered in throughout, sometimes at random, sometimes marking a Japanese word that had no quick English equivalent, or perhaps a word such as *eki* (train station) that we were accustomed to saying even while speaking English. This type of speech, the back and forth of English and Japanese, characterized most of our interactions; whenever it was just the two of us, this was the language we used. It was less a code-switching than a code unto itself, indexing a familiarity with each other and each other's linguistic abilities, and indexing the fact that our friendship had come about because of and in the Japanese language. While the back and forth between languages happened in all of our one-on-one interactions, it did differ according to the perceived level of the formality of our setting. In two-person meetings, versus over lunch, the random Japanese words and the new unusual words we had recently added to our vocabulary meant to impress and provoke a laugh were strained out, and the softening term *to omou* (I think), tacked onto our otherwise English sentences, was clipped off. The number of such linguistic flourishes decreased in formal settings, while the words with no quick English equivalent and the set Japanese phrases remained untouched. Our code switched not so much from Japanese to English but from informal to formal English with Japanese, marking the beginning and the ending of the meeting, as well as carving out space for informality within the formal, allowing us another mechanism to play with our registers, and to simultaneously characterize our dual relationship as friends and as colleagues.

Back at the office after lunch, everyone else returned to their desks. Malaya and I gathered notebooks and pens from our desks and sat ourselves at the meeting table facing each other. I made us tea, we opened our books in a self-aware show of readiness and anticipated formality, a grin shared between us, and then we started to talk about the project at hand—the production of an English-language description of Buraku issues. We discussed what this description should do, by whom it would be read, and what textual life it might have. In addition to being on the web, available for the audience I sketched earlier, it might also be used for a general English-language pamphlet explaining the Buraku situation to people who happen to wander into the IMADR offices, or to classes we were occasionally called on to teach at international schools in the city. With this range of audience in mind, we lightly touched on content—a description of current conditions and the basis of the identity, a brief history, and a description of discrimination. These topics were thrown back and forth rapidly, a partnered brainstorming, before the writing license was handed entirely over to me. With the brainstorming finished, the content of the description became my charge. We had three weeks before the content was to be sent to the designer and decided that I should have a draft to Malaya in a week and a half, three days of which I would be interning at IMADR.

What was required of me in finishing this description dovetailed neatly with what many academics typically do with their time: research, read, write, and revise. I broke my larger task into constituent parts, drafted a to-do list, and set to it. I first sought out other standard descriptions of Buraku issues in Japanese and English on the Internet and in the small library that IMADR maintained. I went through the websites of all of the organizations that work on Buraku issues: the BLL, BLHRRI, the now-defunct Communist-affiliated Zenkairen, the Tokyo branch of the BLL, government websites describing the issue, and online encyclopedias. All of these sites maintained descriptions in Japanese of Buraku issues; some had descriptions in English, always briefer and typically rough translations of the Japanese original. I then went back through notes I had already compiled on English-language social science literature that discussed Buraku issues: the published work of Ian Neary, George de Vos, Frank Upham, Emily Reber, Timothy Amos, Chris Burgess, Michael Weiner, and John Lie and the dissertations of John Davis and Christopher Bondy. I supplemented the notes I already had with a perusal of IMADR's bookshelf and then, that evening, with a perusal of my own. Finally, this first task took me to literature from Buraku community centers and human rights museums, samples of which were either saved on IMADR's server or filed in its stock of pamphlets, or which I had in previous e-mail exchanges with these different organizations.

Reading across these different materials, printed and digital, book and pamphlet, website and note, and constantly dodging the distractions of the office, I culled what seemed to be typical features of the literature's explanation of Buraku issues: foremost, a focus on discrimination, followed by an explanation of work- and neighborhood-based identities and the fact that Buraku people are not linguistically, ethnically, or religiously different from the majority of Japanese people. I got a sense of the regnant genre of description, which content was expected, and what was commonplace. My initial to-do list task, interspersed with other demands from other projects I was working on simultaneously, took the rest of that day and another full day. It demanded of me nimble hands and fingers, computer, linguistic, and research literacy, an ability to stay seated and focused, and concentration through other conversations, phone calls, and random visitors at the door, all of which constantly bombard the IMADR working environment.

My next step, after this research, was to draft my own description that was legible within this genre and push beyond whatever critiques I might have of other descriptions. I jotted down guidelines: "specify forms of discrimination, specify how present-day discrimination is different from 'feudal-period' discrimination, avoid anachronistic projection of Buraku identity into the past, demonstrate variety of theories of historical depth, show history as political argument." The demand of writing required focus and the direction of attention away from, again, the low-level conversations in the office, the phone calls, the delivery man, and an impromptu visit from Kumisaka Shigeyuki, the BLL secretary general, as well as attention away from e-mail, the telecomforts of Skype and my family and friends within quick virtual touch, and online newspapers and blogs. With the draft eventually done, I read through it to correct typographical mistakes and then sent it to Malaya.

My next day back at IMADR, three days later, Malaya had suggestions for revision. First, I had not mentioned recent changes within the UN structure to accommodate and recognize this form of discrimination. Since one of IMADR's primary goals was to enhance international human rights mechanisms for the elimination of discrimination, it seemed appropriate, she argued, that these changes be included. At the same time, however, since such matters are typically considered dry and distanced from actual grassroots organizing, which was the primary constituency we were trying to address, it was best to put such a description at the end. Her second point concerned word choice. I had used the term "Buraku people" rather than "Burakumin." "Burakumin" is standard in English-language activist and scholarly literature on the topic; however, this word was a locus of argument within the Japanese-speaking political movement and within Buraku communities. The word held discriminatory overtones, and some argued that it should be avoided in official documents in order to avoid replication of those overtones; others argued that it should be used in order to confront and dispel that discriminatory edge. Malaya, working as an editor and as a representative for a minority constituency, was torn: she knew the overtones of "Burakumin," but it was standard, and she wanted to make sure that our usage was consistent across the entire website. She consulted with another staff member here, someone who identified as Buraku (a *tōjisha,* or "person directly concerned"), and the group decided that IMADR as an organization had the authority to make the change and potentially establish a new convention in English. We circulated the revision to another of IMADR's program officers who had a few minimal suggestions that I incorporated quickly. I then had for Malaya a final draft, in English, right on schedule to be sent to the designer.

INSCRIPTION

The process I detail here, which happened over the course of a month and entailed a large number of e-mails with attached edited documents, resulted in the description of the Buraku situation I quoted at length previously. This is a description that uses the language of minorities, of rights, of discrimination, and of political agitation in a form intended to make sense across different contexts, to speak to people with no direct connection to Buraku issues in Japan. It provides a basic explanation of the history and present conditions of the Buraku minority population, intended to be legible to as wide of an Anglophone audience as possible. The process of its production included an explicit discussion of the various types of audiences to which this text needed to speak. The discussions questioned which words might most effectively be used and which form of narrative might best suit this context. In these discussions, however, other assumptions were unquestioned, perhaps not even recognized. In the process of drafting the previous description, it was tacitly assumed that groups working on justice and minority issues throughout the world, if not any person of the Anglophone world, would have an understanding of the basic parts of the description. For example, the term "discrimination" only ever receives a brief explanation; its content and its ethical status as something reprehensible were assumed to be self-explanatory. Assumptions regarding the precarious status of minority groups worldwide were likewise assumed and reproduced. IMADR uses such sets of tacit assumptions as a base from which to launch its further strategic discussions concerning, for example, the explanation and consolidation of "Discrimination Based on Work and Descent," which as a new category is not nearly as widely recognizable.

The process of producing this description is bureaucratic, detail oriented, and familiar to the eyes of an academic. Indeed, all labor of NGO care is largely bureaucratic. These are bureaucratic processes, however, that reveal and assert something beyond the ins and outs of the Tokugawa social system, the etymology of the word *Buraku*, or the persistence of both discrimination and political movement. This English-language Internet page is a claim that IMADR sees itself speaking to an international audience, and that the imagined international audience can read English and not Japanese (or French or Spanish or Russian, for that matter). It indicates that IMADR has the resources necessary to create a web presence and the resources necessary to do so in native English. IMADR sees itself and asserts itself as authorized to represent Buraku people to this international English-speaking audience. It reveals and portrays an IMADR that is concerned about discrimination against Buraku people and is convinced that this is a problem worthy of international attention, and it reveals and portrays an IMADR that is invested in garnering international attention.

In addition to producing this description, the process described earlier also produces a host of other objects—types of people, ethical stances, and interorganizational relations. The person who can step up to these demands is one whose personal biography—friendships and birthdays—can potentially form a basis of work. These ties helped me get hired as an intern, but they also came into play and were intensified over the course of my Japanese/English linguistic exchanges with Malaya. This is also a person who can afford to take on a job that is relatively low paying, and who might be expected to operate as a translator for the BLL's cause.[4] This figure is a gendered one, feminized in contrast to the offices of the BLL, and recruiting more women as employees. As I mentioned previously, aside from the secretary general and me, all IMADR employees were women. Over the course of IMADR's existence, the vast majority of its employees have been women; as of the writing of this book, all employees and interns are women. The leadership of the BLL, in contrast, is consistently male, and men are overwhelmingly recruited to positions of influence within the organization. Likewise, the person here created and sustained is also one of an age and economic and educational background sufficient to make one not simply familiar with computer technology but intimately involved in it.

The actions of IMADR, of which the creation of the website is but one example, expected and demanded that the individuals that conduct it be equipped with relevant but separate private lives that serve as the basis for judging who these people are. From that basis they are cast as relatively autonomous. Take, for example, the genre of the "to-do list" and what it says about the people who create such lists. The broadest items on the to-do list are decided on in meetings in which each staff member has input. The tasks then are apportioned off to individuals, who structure their own terms of accountability, refining their to-do lists according to their time and work constraints. These individuals all get to play a role in establishing the tasks that they are then obliged to do, and in the completion of those tasks they actively acquiesce to and affirm the tasks' obligatory authority. The constant presence of distractions in the office underscores the ways in which the tasks on the to-do list operate as choices, and in which these biographical individuals are affirmed as autonomous determiners of their own obligations.

Simultaneously, however, the to-do list illuminates aspects of the interplay between equality and hierarchy within the office and also gives light to the complications of individual autonomy. When the group meets to decide the broadest tasks, Morihara, the secretary general, has the final say and final accountability. However, the actual discussion is conducted *as if* each person had equal say and equal right of veto and operates in such a manner unless a conflict or mistake arises. Similarly, though Malaya, program officer, formally outranks me, intern, and thus has final accountability, we decide on and share the actual tasks *as if* we were equals. She never orders me to do anything, just as Morihara would only very rarely order anyone to do anything. Rather, we collectively decide what we each will do in fulfillment of a broader task that also is collectively determined. The furniture arrangement in the office underscores this interplay between formal, and gendered, hierarchy and ideological equality: there are no cubicle walls—each person sits at the same level and has visual and auditory access to every other person's space. At the same time, however, Morihara's seat is farthest from the door and the potential distractions it allows; the intern's desk is closest to the door.

Producing the description of the Buraku situation, as much as it calls upon and consolidates types of people, also consolidates ethical and affec-

FIGURE 3. Worker in an east Tokyo tannery loading hides into a tanning barrel.

tive stances. Malaya is compelled in her work by the desire to do something for the benefit of IMADR in its struggle to end discrimination. The stresses of the job are counterbalanced by the sense of potential ethical fulfillment. This obligation operates on the level of the ethical and the personal as much as it does on the level of interoffice dynamics. Malaya, as an individual who is independent of IMADR, is presupposed in the actions of IMADR to have similar ethical orientations to those of the organization—ethics of care and social justice.

I linger on this quotidian and commonplace scene to highlight the emergent political subject: someone nestled in a formal hierarchy but permitted and expected to breach that hierarchy by virtue of a biographical individuality, tied to bonds of friendship and a supposed camaraderie with other staff members, and with a presumably equally shared ethical stance toward social discrimination. These individuals are entailed in the activities of IMADR even as they themselves perform those actions. And, in doing so, this assemblage of people assumes a countenance of a human rights NGO, potentially recognizable by the UN special rapporteur and the factory worker alike.

The second trajectory I examine is of a very different type, that of animal hide becoming leather. There is a neighborhood in east Tokyo known officially as "Higashi Sumida," and known more affectionately by its residents and by the political movement by its previous name, "Kinegawa."[5] For the past century, it has been the epicenter of leather processing in metropolitan Tokyo. In 2006 this neighborhood, which is less than one square kilometer, housed thirty-one animal-part processing plants—tanneries, raw-skin dealers, lard processors, independent leather shavers and dryers, and soap makers. It is an out-of-the-way east Tokyo neighborhood with no subway access and, compared to the more fashionable west or central portions of the city where IMADR is located, only the occasional bus. It is a neighborhood comprised primarily of leather-related factories, spotted with a few public housing buildings, even fewer individual homes, an abandoned elementary school, and a small handful of gravel-covered public parks, each large enough to hold a swing set and a slide.

The building material of economic choice for the factories is corrugated tin, mostly in shades of blue, gray, and green. The material provides the three-meter-wide streets with an eerie-sounding board for the clanks of forklifts, gushes of water running from tanning barrels, and caws of the *karasu*[6] that dominate the airspace. None of the companies in Kinegawa has more than fifty employees, and most focus on one or two steps of the tanning process and employ only four or five people. In many ways this entire neighborhood, with its sounds, its running water, and its frenetic movement of workers and skin, is one large leather factory. Moving from company to company as much as hand to hand, the skins carve out a peculiar industrial neighborhood space on their journey toward becoming a profitable commodity.

For six months in 2006 I apprenticed at one of the larger factories in Kinegawa. This factory, unlike the majority of others in the area, handles all the stages of leather production, from raw pig and occasional cowhide to fully tanned, dyed, and sometimes even printed-on sheets of leather. It is a family owned and operated business and has been in the same location, with the same family, for the past four generations. The owner, his wife, his younger brother, and daughter, each with his or her own specialty, oversee the twenty-two hourly employees and attend to financial matters and maintain client relationships; the younger brother's son works on the factory floor. Each of the men of the family has worked along the factory line, and the wife and the daughter have intimate knowledge, based on daily contact and ongoing familial conversation, of each of the steps. The owner and his wife raised their children here, in a house adjacent to the factory. Though their three children now live elsewhere, the owner and his wife continue to live in this same home, close enough to the factory to hear the sound of the tanning drums rotating through the night.

A similar long leather engagement also characterizes the lives of most of the factory's employees, all but three of whom are male. The majority of these employees were born, raised, and still live in Kinegawa, and some grew up knowing this factory as their fathers' workplace. Other employees live in adjacent neighborhoods, having more recently come into the leather business, driven here by the demand for work and directed over by the unemployment office. Still other employees come from farther away, from Bangladesh and Ghana, to work for higher wages in Japan than what they could receive at home. The factory maintains a small dormitory for its workers, tucked behind the owner's home, and three of the four full-time foreign workers live here. All workers except the owners make an hourly wage, which ranges from approximately 7 to 14 U.S. dollars, depending on the particular job and how long a person has been there. The workers on the floor maintain time cards that track their arrivals and departures, eight hours a day, six days a week.

Despite being a foreign worker, I did not live in the factory dormitory, nor did I work out of economic necessity. I worked for free, paid not by the factory but by the Japan Foundation, and paid not to produce leather but to research the ways in which this factory setting might be related to the social and political category of Buraku—a question particularly salient in Tokyo because, as I discuss in greater detail in chapters 2 and 3, there are no officially registered Buraku districts in the Tokyo metropolitan area. Here in particular, what counts as Buraku can be a matter of rumor, hearsay, and debate. Allegations and assertions of Buraku-ness rely on authorities other than the state for social traction. I lived in a neighborhood adjacent to Kinegawa that was not home to the leather industry but that was nevertheless impacted by it, marked both by lower rents and, if the wind hit just right, the pungent odor of tanning chemicals. I positioned myself there in part to see how Kinegawa was discussed by its immediate neighbors and in part because I was only a short ten-minute bike ride to the factory, where I had to be every morning by 8 A.M. to help receive the incoming skins.

FIGURE 4. Pig hide as it arrives at Higashi Sumida tanneries fresh from the slaughter facility in Shinagawa.

The skins come in by the hundreds. They come in wire mesh containers, approximately one hundred per bundle. Some of the skins are sent from far away—from the northern reaches of Honshu, Akita prefecture—and some from even farther, such as Lubbock, Texas, my hometown. The long-journeying skins are salted to prevent rot and pressed tightly into each other, seeping down into salted puddles of blood and fat pressed out of the skins. Other skins arrive fresh, unsalted. They come directly, day-by-day, the same day, from slaughterhouses in other parts of Tokyo or from neighboring prefectures, from Tochigi or Chiba. The freshly harvested skins move against each other and against the bare hand, like human flesh does, the hair still attached on one side, the flip side coated with newly congealed blood and lingering adipose tissue, with globules of fat and blood making each individual skin slippery to the human hand and at the same time each skin sticking to the next. Each of these 2,100 per week salted and unsalted skins is the skin from a full pig, weighing in at 8 to 10 kilograms. Gathering the gourmandizing gaze of *karasu*, skins enter the factories constrained in wire mesh cages. Their 10,000-plus kilogram weight has fomented a proliferation of miniature forklifts on the small roads of Kinegawa's back streets. Their movement demands drivers with a visual attentiveness to small spaces and to directions forward and behind, with manual adroitness and coordination. Simultaneously this dermal movement requires of bystanders, even those in "safer" spaces not occupied by large rolling drums or caustic chemicals, a visual and aural alertness to these forklifts that whip around corners, the sharp forks carrying containers of hides.

Assisted by the forklifts, the caged skins enter the tannery and take their places in front of large wooden drums that will roll them through caustic chemicals on their journey to becoming leather. Their travel along this path toward a profit-garnering commodity requires of the workers and surrounding machines vigilance, timing, regularity, and attentiveness to environmental conditions, such as ambient heat and humidity. This attentiveness, subjected to a need for replication beyond any individual workers, sediments itself into the books, charts, and graphs that litter a wooden bench in the midst of the rolling drums, intermixed with workers' lunch boxes and tea, at the ready for reference. These charts, provided by the owners and modified by the floor manager, provide a guiding map for the course and duration of the skins as they make their way into and out of and into again the large rolling drums and across the steps that facilitate their metamorphosis from rot-susceptible, fragile raw skin to durable, rot-resistant leather.

Once in the factory, the skins must first have the hair removed. Except for the very occasional buffalo or cowhide, the majority of these skins are from pigs. Porcine hair is thick, thicker than human hair or bovine hair, and requires a lengthy engagement with a lime and water mixture to melt away entirely. Because of its thickness, simply soaking the hair would take up to ten hours to dissolve it, and the proteins in the skin itself would start to loosen, which would adversely affect profits. Instead, pushed by a demand to speed up the process, the owners have built drums that rotate, which shortens the immersion time to approximately six hours, depending on the ambient temperature—the factory is open to outside air, as hair and straggling fat disappear into an alkaline solution. Into the drums the skins go, calling on the workers to, one by one, set their bodies working against the weight and adhesion of coagulated, bloody skin to skin to shuttle one hundred, two hundred, seven hundred skins into the wooden drum vats filled with a carefully measured mixture of lime and water. This movement demands from the workers glove-shielded hands, arms with strength, hearty backs, and pivotal spines. Occasionally two hides go drumside together, but typically their weight and sticky slipperiness prevent the workers from lifting more than one at a time. Once rolled through these chemicals, the skins must be immediately removed from the drums, which calls for precision in the timing of the drums and an awareness on the part of the workers as to what constitutes "finished." The workers then pour the contents of the drums out onto the floor, with caustic chemicals washing into the wastewater system and skins piling up on the floor.

This skin, hairless and tumid with water, is at this limed point too thick for quality leather making. To secure the best prices, it needs to be thinned out and scudded so only its outermost dermal layer is left. Here at this factory, four people scud full time, working on a scudding machine equipped with a dangerously sharp blade. Workers feed the skins through the machine, separating top from bottom, *ginmen* from *toko*. With the *toko* shaved off and sent to the gelatin factory, the *ginmen* top side then must be taken back to the drums, stacked in piles on pallets and moved by forklift. The occasional worker is missing parts of fingers, palpable reminders of the need for vigilance while performing this dangerous task.

With a splish and a splash that send caustic chemicals flying, the *ginmen* skins are thrown back into the drums, on the verge of unraveling, their wobbling thinness coupled with residual liminess. Next they are subjected to a careful mixture of corrosive vitriolic acid and water, a low pH to counterbalance the alkaline height of the lime. After a good three-hour spin that slowly, with mechanical and proletariat assistance, neutralizes the lime, the workers dilute the mixture, slowly bringing it to plain water, at which point they replace the drum seal with a wooden grate that keeps skins in but lets water out. Water here is needed in great quantities—liters and liters run over the skins, washing recalcitrant skin flaps, chemicals, and the water itself down the tannery drains.

Washed clean of this acidic bulk, the skins sit ready for their last chemical bath on the way to being tanned. Workers again fill the drums with water and then carefully stir in a preblended mixture of bluish chromium and catalytic enzymes. Seven hours later the end of the process is in sight, and the workers spill the skins out of the large drums and onto a prepared, protective blue tarp, piled in heaps of wrinkled blue hide amidst runny rivers of heavy metal effluvia. The demands on the workers now shift from following the charts that dictate the times of each step to a more back-breaking physical labor: piling skins in organized stacks. In preparation for the next steps, drying and shaving, the presently wadded-up bluish mass of identically square, wet skins must be sorted from the tangled weave into individual skins and then piled one on top of another onto a pallet, with tops up and hindquarters all headed in the same direction. The skins' orienting clues are at this point scarce: almost completely square, these bluish wet rags of skin have subtle follicle markings on one side, not the other, and the texture of the surface is slightly different top to bottom. Lengthwise, the skin gains an extra millimeter in thickness in the move from forequarters to hindquarters; there is usually a slight wrinkled nub in the center back of the hindquarters, where the tail was, and occasionally there are remnants of nipples demarcating the sides of the hide. Into this disorienting fray, the skins, now fixed against rot, summon the workers for the swift completion of their appointed stacking.

Workers with the acquired ease of twenty, thirty, or more years at this job step up to the skins' summons and, in the interest of keeping this job, let their arms, legs, and backs take over. Skins that are to be stacked in an oriented slap-slop call less for active engagement than conscious release. A pile of seven hundred skins, three a day, most every day of the year, demands the regulated moves of bodies, rendered automatic time after time. The skins' scarce visual cues and subtly graded thickness, haunches to head, shove away visual engagement in favor of feel; they summon hands and forearms, clad in thick rubber chemical-resistant gloves, into a reflexive knowing of hind end from front end, simply from the change in thickness, the change in wet, wobbly weight from head to tail. Skins pick up eyes at the beginning, as they are initially grabbed, and then discard those eyes to command more useful backs, hands, and arms—bend down, extend back and legs, and with the right hand grab a skin at a point offered to the eyes as a promising tail point; then raise the skin with the right hand, slide the left hand down the wet length of the square skin, and brush the right rubber-encased thumb across the surface of the wetly blue hide to determine its inside from its outside. Next, straighten the back and shake the right hand once to determine the spread of thickness, send the left hand grabbing at the thinner corner of the skin, wobble and shake and know the orientation, up and then down, head to haunches. Finally, extend the hands out, each to a corner, grasp the skin at the hind haunches, topside up now, and with an unfurling spin throw those forearms outward, releasing the hands on time to send the hide wetly slapping across, spun, down-oriented on top of its mates on the pallet, all in time and rhythm with the two others working on a pallet.

The skins, arriving in bulk, summon to this task anywhere from one to five sets of hands, arms, legs, backs, and eyes. These bodies work together in co-ordinated rhythmic ease, stepping back, grabbing, straightening, twisting, and unfurling in a punctuated effectiveness of skin movement. The process uses these men simply for their bodies; who they are matters less than their ability to get the job done. At the same time, however, this reduction of self only summons certain kinds of people. The job is dirty, dangerous, and difficult *(kitanai, kiken, kitsui)*.[7] Economic necessity and lack of other options motivate most of the workers to come to this job each day. At the same time this dehumanizing labor draws from the chronically underemployed, it also potentially marks those people—their bodies, their employment records—as a certain kind of people, as Buraku. In the midst of these demands, however, the process also gives workers space to talk to each other, as long as they release into the habituated action of slinging skins. With hands, arms, legs, and backs released into this task, the men can pull their consciousness away from working and to other tasks, such as talking about Ootake-san's rotating set of girlfriends or gently harassing the inept though eager foreigner in their midst—a quasi-worker whose body is new to this task. While I worked there, the other tanners alternately harassed and consoled me about my inability to slap down a properly oriented skin with any speed or accuracy. These conversations that the men have over their working parts do not frame their bodily engagements but, rather, sit alongside them, perhaps at most slowing the pace to make room for an occasional laugh.

The habituated reflexive action demanded of each worker's body parts became readily apparent the second I, the researcher, I, the graduate student, who had not worked a wage-labor job, much less a physically demanding one, in years, stepped into the fray in response to the waiting skins' summons. The floor manager, Mizuguchi-kun, glossed over the procedure for me, gave me pointers for recognizing up from down, head from tail, and showed me how to hold my arms and rotate my torso to get the best fling. Taking in my instructions, I stepped up to the task, eager to not be any more of a nuisance than I always already was.

The task was daunting, though perhaps less daunting because in my case it was not mediated by necessity. I could find other field sites, other ways of getting to the questions that motivate my research. The stakes of the workers' stepping up were different. Frequently pushed into this job as the last possibility or as the only option visible, they worked six days a week, as (vocally) compared to my five, to make enough money to support themselves and sometimes wives, children, and parents. They struggled to habituate themselves, motivated in part by the fearful weight of the equation of a job well done, a dependable income, and an ability to support a family.

Unencumbered by that weight, I stepped up to the task and was confronted with another encumbrance, something that any first-timer must feel: my entire self. Surrounded by bodies rapidly hurling six skins a minute, I struggled to pick up hides slippery with blood and fat or with chromium or lime, to find the head versus the tail, and to unfurl the skin onto the stack in rhythm with my coworkers. Wearing two layers of gloves—an inner rubber set to protect the hands from the heavy metal and enzymatic remnants, an outer set of cotton cloth, supposedly there to improve the grip on the hide but decidedly resistant to staying where it was against slippery wet rubber—I fumbled and slipped, dropped hides, and got in the way of other workers. I struggled to focus, unable to partake in the sweep of conversation as my consciousness strove to overtake what the bodily bits around me were doing with such rapidity. Even at my best, after weeks of working there, I could only unfurl one hide every minute, in stark contrast to the six-per-minute pace of the professionals around me. At that point I found that I could pull my attention back from the task ever so slightly and that my body worked better without direct supervision. Like playing the piano or riding my bike, I eventually experienced the slightest hint of this task becoming second nature, entrenched in muscle memory. I learned to peel away my reflective sense of self as a person working from the task, ease into the conversation about that day's hot topic (frequently a Japan versus the United States topic prompted by my presence), and surrender my hands, forearms, legs, and back to do the work commanded by the skins in motion.

Across the steps of tanning—hair removal, scudding, deliming, tanning, and stacking—the skins move in and out of the drums, in batches of seven hundred, one at a time, and undergo fixation: they slowly change consistency, elasticity, and durability as their molecular structure becomes fixed and made less susceptible to rot. At the same time, the movement demanded for their fixation slings burning liquids and stinging fumes across workers' arms, faces, noses, and eyes, bringing a sharp focus to these parts of their bodies. Eight men work this initial part of the leather. Day after day, year after year, and occasionally generation after generation, they respond to the call of the skins and surrender hands, arms, legs, backs, eyes, and ears to the obligations of the skin-to-leather transition. They move the skins from cage to leather, all the while dripping and splattering chemicals across their own bodies and the bodies of the men working next to them. Vitriolic acid, chromium, lime, neutralizing enzymes, sodium—all of these are slung across the men's bodies as skins are slapped down one by one on pallets; they splash back onto the bodies as the skins are thrown into the wooden drums, and they creep into the workers' eyes, noses, and mouths as the chemicals are freshly mixed.

These moments of contact accumulate in the men's bodies, and there they encounter things beyond the bodies. Working alongside the workers, my own eyes burning, my own nose hair beating a swiftly dissolving retreat up my nostrils, I point out scars, the sharp bite of skin-flung chemical against my body, the acrid sting that clots the breath and blurs the eyes. I ask about back pain, about regular chronic visits to the hospital, and about the lack of eye protection, the lack of masks, barriers that might run interference against the slosh of causticity—about all sorts of signs not simply of critical, immediate risk but of slow, steady health collapse. These concerns are defenestrated with casual mentions of professionalism: *"Orera ha puro-da. Masuku ka go-guru ha tada no jama. Hora, Ootake-san wo mite. Mou, zutto kore wo yatte kita yo. Go jū go nen kan. Kareha masuku wo tsukawanai"* ("We are pros. Masks and goggles only get in the way. Look at Ootake-san. He has been doing this his entire life. Fifty-five years. You don't see him wearing a mask"). Or, these concerns are thrown out with equally casual hints of a masculinity, eschewing intimations of a body prostrate to the penetrating perniciousness of chemicals, characterizing themselves in opposition to another sex: *"Oreraha tsuyoiyo. Mizuguchi-kun no ude wo mite, okii darou. Kore wo sukoshi yattara, Jo-, jimu ni ikanakutemo ii. Josei ga dekiru shigoto janai yo"* ("We're strong. Look at Mizuguchi-kun with his massive arms. After a few days of this, Joe, you won't need to go to the gym anymore. This isn't a job for women"). At the intersection of these professionalized, masculinized bodies, the immediate and long-term harm of the chemical-carrying skins is, at least here in the factory, in front of me and in front of the other guys, valorized. Around the guys, keloids are something to be eased into; they are less emblems of a stigmatized Buraku-ness than they are signs of a gnarled but firm virility or the smooth operation of expert ability attained after years of trial and error.

A case in point—one of the eight men working on the initial stages of tanning was new when I was there; he had only been working in the factory for six months, entering three months before I did. Tanimoto-san had found the job at the *haro- wa-ku* (literally "Hello, work," an unemployment office), and this was his first time to work in skin. He was a newcomer to the factory and to the industry, and possibly to the Buraku social stigma. This latter newcomerness, that to the possibility of stigmatized identity, was never mentioned by the other workers; indeed, never once did the workers as a group discuss this stigma that marks them in their labor. However, they did quickly assess this newcomer's past work experience, determined his status, and summarily assigned him the most onerous task of mixing chemicals to be added to the rolling drums. Pinned low on the scale of professionalism, he was constantly at the center of an aerobic swirl of caustic, skin-tanning chemicals.

This man was quiet and meticulous in his self-care—head cleanly and daily shaven, hands washed time and time again, and mouth rinsed out (twice) before taking a sip of the tea. He struggled to let none of the industry's debris adhere to his person. He was the first to point out to me the parts of the body affected, which he did with a wide and self-abandoned smile—stinging eyes, calloused hands, and nose hairs missing from only weeks of inhaling the powdered lime. He alone wore a mask and goggles, which he did at his own expense. The goggles you can get through the factory, he explained, but it takes time and paperwork; it is easier to buy your own. Masks, on the other hand, are only there if you get them yourself. I saw this man as somewhat aloof, bound to the ineluctable need to make money at an advanced age with few options—a redoubtable yet resigned worker.

However, in the mouths of the other men, in their conversation as they slapped hides stained chromium blue onto their pallets, this newcomer was *a-gu,* which, after a confused and confusing linguistic dance, was revealed to me as English, used for my benefit, for "argue," meant to mean the man is *herikutsu*—a quibbler and a whiner. These other men, with longer histories of engagement with this stigmatized industry, disparaged the newcomer, his self-ministrations and concern for masks and goggles, and they cast his future in the factory in units of weeks or months, not years or decades. Clearly this man will never become a professional; he was not man enough for the job. Here in their characterization of Tanimoto-san, they neatly tie the objects of their work, the skin and the chemicals, to each other and to themselves as men and as professionals.

Stinging, burning, and scarring those bodies into the sharp obviousness of a working class, and even more specifically into a pungent sign of Buraku stigma, these skins and these chemicals, splashing together, mark certain people as certain kinds of people. Encountering at the nexus of the body socially circulating notions of meaningful identity and stigma, the animal-skin-delivered chemicals inscribe on the skins of these eight men indexible identity, an identity potentially seen and voiced as Buraku outside of the factory and outside of the neighborhood. There they might be pieces for embarrassing barroom conversation—for askance glances, for silent acknowledgment and avoidance, for aghast and hidden shame. But here they are valorized as assertions of masculinity and professional ability.

The movement of skins through the hands of the workers demands a physical adroitness and offers a ground for the elaboration of a ruggedly scarred masculinity and long-term tempered professionalism. It requires a habituation of the body and a charting precision of the chemical process of dermal transformation, and at the same time it leads to the steady collapse of those bodies over long periods of time. Being Buraku gains purchase here in the masculinity of workers, in hurt backs, in an economic dependence on a corrosive job, in the subjection of one's time and labor power to the owner's press to make surplus value, and in the detachment of one's person from bodily work. Here parts of the body—hands, arms, backs, and legs—are rendered exchangeable; people are exchangeable, as long as they get the job done.

MATTERS CATEGORIZED, SUBJECTS RECOGNIZED

In his short essay, "Postscript on the Societies of Control," Gilles Deleuze juxtaposes Foucault's notion of discipline with a newer regime of control.[8] Discipline is characterized by sites of enclosure, each with its own laws, through which subjects travel, moving seamlessly from one to the next: from family to school to barracks to factory, with occasional visits to the hospital, or, potentially, prison. Within any one of these enclosures, there functions a regime of discipline that concentrates and distributes in space; that orders in time; and that composes individual forces within that space-time with a greater gestalt effect. Deleuze claims, however, that the societies of discipline are crumbling and instead knocking on the door are *societies of control*. In contrast to discipline, which operates within the molds of enclosure, control operates as a *modulation* that changes from point to point. Here Deleuze argues that the corporation has replaced the factory, perpetual training the school, and floating rates of exchange instead of gold as a numerical standard. He ends this essay by speculating on the coming forms of and resistances to the society of control, remarking that "many young people strangely boast of being 'motivated'; they re-request apprenticeships and perpetual training. It's up to them to discover what they are being made to serve, just as their elders discovered, not without difficulty, the telos of discipline."[9]

Such a break, between control and discipline, resonates across the IMADR/ tannery divide. In both arenas, Buraku issues come to matter within material and symbolic quotidian action. They orient political and ethical aspirations, set a pace to daily life, and call forth characteristics from the people and bodies that engage in that action, an action pinioned between the demands of the process and the workers' attempts to meet those demands. This action both subtends and links both arenas, calling forth dramatically different yet intimately related forms of life in the NGO and the tannery.

For IMADR, the creation of a description of Buraku issues for a website makes use of motivated individuals. Those individuals are called on to complete a task—the writing of a description—but the individuals themselves are granted some range of autonomy in deciding the task as well as the steps leading up to its fruition. They are given license to set the tempo and direction of their work. They are pushed by their ethical obligations to work in an industry chronically underfunded, with a high turnover and burnout rate, and with long hours sitting at computers and evaluating the actual social justice impact of their efforts. Under that umbrella, their specific tasks are multiple and changing, built on their prioritizations, personal interests, and individual histories. It is here that we can see a serpent of control, nestled in a self-guiding motivation, responsive to an obligation to *care*, and manifest in a pursuit of political and social change.

On the factory floor, Buraku comes to matter, or not, in a contrasting way. Here biographical individuals are not a necessity or even an allowance; what is needed are workers motivated, primarily by necessity but sometimes buttressed by a romanticized notion of masculine Buraku familial labor, to take up a job that reduces them as human. Poverty, economic and social hardship, and family attachment guide people to these jobs but are allowed into the enclosure of the job site only to the extent that they do not interfere with the production of leather. Producing skin disciplines strong hands, backs, legs, attentive eyes, and inured noses. It eschews innovation on the part of the individual and does not bend to attempts to change the pace of production. Here individuals are molded; they have little ability to alter the overall process of production, or to shape how the demands come to their bodies. Instead, they must simply succumb and internalize the discipline, release their bodily capacities in exchange for money and for the praises of masculinity and professionalism. It is, instead, the chemicals, the skin, the weather and ambient temperature, the push and pull of negotiations with clients and providers, and the limits of the bare body itself that set the time line of leather production. Here the accountability of individuals is to make skin, to take care of one's family, wife, children, mother, or father, and this accountability can only be discharged in surrendering oneself to the demands of the skin.

The distinction between societies of discipline and societies of control is not the only historical periodization that resonates across the IMADR/tannery divide. Each of these arenas of action is marked by proper forms of politics—that of human rights and antidiscrimination versus labor unions and strikes—as well as a proper ethical orientation—toward the equality of all versus the resettlement of the means of production under the workers themselves. Outside of the factory, in the realm of exchange, the baseline presumption is of equality. Just as all actors are presumed equally able to sell their labor power on the market, so too is there a presumption that formal differences in the distribution of resources (i.e., discrimination) are abhorrent. In the NGO all workers are presumably there of their own freedom of choice, obligated not by economic necessity but by ethical orientation. Here thrives a politics that seeks to manage and dismantle inequalities across populations, tracking them statistically, set in tension with a formal equality of individuals. In producing descriptions such as the aforementioned, the IMADR staff also creates itself as a proper interlocutor with similar NGOs and with the United Nations. Enclosed within the factory, in the realm of production, there is a foregone split between the workers and the owners, with workers subjecting themselves to the demands of the work process and owners constantly seeking to maximize the surplus value of that production process. At the same time, however, all—floor worker and owner alike—are potentially seen as Buraku. More traditional forms of exploited labor here, however, are treated by IMADR and similar organizations as examples of discrimination rather than exploitation. Class action stands in tension with the politics of identity.

The connection between these two arenas of action requires labor to maintain. It requires labor to link them, and labor to show their differences. This is a labor that creates these differences—in type of person, politics, risk, and ethics—as much as it calls on them. As workers in each of these arenas produce signs that can index Buraku identity, whether descriptions with international range or marks on the body and employment records, they also produce themselves as linked to the NGO and the factory in an uneven relationship of material representation. This productive labor, in which the NGO worker and the tanner engage, also has a complement that has been a thorn in the side of the Buraku movement since its inception: the active *non*production of such signs. It is that to which I turn next.

TWO

"*Ushimatsu Left for Texas*"

PASSING THE BURAKU

NOT WITH KIN, BUT THROUGH KIN

Hoping to prompt a conversation about Buraku affirmative action, I leaned over to my closest dinner companion, Oguma-san, and told him, "I am 1/32nd Native American. Comanche."

We had just finished the group English lesson I taught every other Monday and had moved on to Watami, the chain restaurant that we frequented after class. Several months prior, the twelve people in the class, mostly self-identified Burakumin and all between forty and eighty years old, had planned a study trip to India for late 2006.[1] They wanted to tour slaughterhouses and tanneries and, above all, meet with Dalits—outcastes they saw as comrades in the fight against caste-based discrimination. They wanted to learn some English to prepare for the trip, and had met Malaya and me a handful of times as their work overlapped with that of the International Movement Against All Forms of Discrimination and Racism (IMADR). We were both native English speakers with a command of Japanese and with an understanding of contemporary Buraku issues. I was both available and interested, and they swiftly recruited me to teach their class.

My conversation companion at Watami that evening, Oguma-san, was a Buraku man in his fifties, originally from Niigata and now living in Tokyo. He was a regular participant in both the class and the post-lesson meal. He struggled with English but seemed to enjoy that struggle, and he also seemed to enjoy the rare opportunity to talk to a foreigner. He frequently did his best to walk next to me from the class to dinner and always positioned himself next to me during the meal. He asked lots of questions about English, about Texas, and about other countries I had visited.

That evening I wanted to talk to him about affirmative action, lineage, and minority group identity, so while the others were engaged in various other conversations I continued speaking to him, in Japanese: "It was five generations ago, a woman on my mother's mother's side. Apparently qualifies me for special minority scholarships, but I have never applied for them, didn't feel right. My gleamingly white face and bright-red hair have, thoroughly and consistently throughout my thirty-one years of life, entitled me to the social privileges of the American white...."

Oguma-san finished a drink of his beer and cut into my blathering to say, *"Nihon ha chigau yo"* ("It's different here in Japan"). While somewhat relieved that he stopped the sentence I had gotten myself into, I cringed at his statement—yet again, Japan is different. It is not the foreign country that is different, it is Japan that is different. It is Japan versus the rest, and he is Japanese, and I am not and never can be. The lines were drawn. I also cringed because I thought I had an idea of the kind of thing a man like Oguma-san, a man who had not been part of the student movement in the 1960s and who had little contact with foreigners, might say next—that such ethnic or racial mixing does not happen in Japan; national difference and Japan's uniqueness would be built around the notion of *kissui* (purity) and pitted against a *konketsu* (mixed-blood) other. Buraku stigma made no sense, because Buraku people were Japanese just like other Japanese. I blurted out some rush of words trying to forestall such a continuation but was interrupted again with another *"chigau."* But this time it was not a *"chigau"* of "Japan is different" but a *"chigau"* of "Joe, hold on. You're getting me wrong."

He continued with a statement that I misunderstood as a question: "You talk to your parents." I was caught off guard, did not know quite what he was talking about, what this shift was, and I answered "yes." Again, *"chigau."* (It had been a statement, Joe, not a question.) "Your parents have told you; their parents told them," he said, as he pointed to the Hankins genealogy I had hastily scribbled on a napkin. I was beginning to catch on and scrambled to recover from my rhetorical comeuppance and follow the shift in footing as he continued: "My parents never told me that I was a Burakumin. Their parents certainly didn't tell them. And I have worked with the Buraku Liberation League [BLL] for over thirty years but have never mentioned any of this to my children. But you, your parents are the ones who told you you are part Native American, right?" "Right." "Hard to imagine from a Japanese perspective."[2]

"Japan as different" was still being brought into play here, but this category of exclusive nationality (Japan, not others), to which the Buraku, by default, belonged, entextualized a relationship between kinship and stigma different from what I had imagined. I had anticipated that we would talk about how a stigma based on descent brings family members closer together in the struggle for governmental support. Instead, however, I found us talking about how hereditary stigma can actually serve as a blockage to intergenerational communication. My misunderstanding, and Oguma-san's correction, proved unexpectedly productive.

Oguma-san's story indicates two aspects of Buraku life that trouble the present-day Buraku political movement. First, that there exist realms of life in which people who might otherwise be thought Buraku do not produce signs of that social identity but instead merely produce signs of relatively unmarked social categories. Second, that that nonproduction leads to generations of people not knowing that they might be considered Buraku. While the previous chapter examined the labor of tannery and nongovernmental organization workers involved in creating Buraku as politically intelligible, this chapter focuses on a complementary set of practices, namely, the nonproduction of signs of being Buraku, and it examines how this nonproduction troubles the Buraku political movement.

It is an unsurprising fact that there are situations in which people otherwise identifiable as Buraku do not produce signs of this marked category, instead falling back on a presupposed backdrop against which sit contestations over Buraku identity: Japanese national belonging. It is equally unsurprising that this nonproduction is, by and large, unproblematic. Even the most Buraku-appearing individual in Japan—for example, Kumisaka Shigeyuki, secretary general of the Buraku liberation movement, son of leather tanners, from a Buraku neighborhood outside of Fukuoka—even this man in his sixties, who frequently appears in public as Buraku, does not in all social situations produce indexes of being Buraku, intentionally or otherwise. Nor does he feel the need to.

Though most of this nonproduction passes without notice or censure, evocative of no anxiety, there are types of nonproduction that function as sites of contestation, drawing both notice and censure, and provoking anxieties for the political movement. There are times when the political organization sees nonproduction as counter to their political aims, viewing it as a sign of secrecy, of actively hiding an identity that *should* be there. The tenor of their objection is not merely strategic and practical; it operates on an ethical and affective level, provoking commitments and attachments across the actors who act in the name of Buraku. In turn, these commitments seed the ground for individual worries about the correct and consistent production of signs of being Buraku, and for shame in "succumbing" to the desire to "hide" that given identity. Oguma-san had not told his children, he explained, in the optimistic hope that discrimination would not be an issue by the time they were old enough to experience it. But as he told me this, he did so with embarrassment as well as resignation. He knew he *should* have told them. It just never happened.

THE UNKNOWING AND THE KNOWING: DISTRIBUTING THE ANXIETIES AND ASPIRATIONS OF BEING BURAKU

Commitments to visibility are not limited to the political commitments of Buraku activists. The imperative to appear as Buraku, while initiated and funded by the liberation movement, also lives in the simple desire to belong and to be accepted by peers, outside of realms explicitly framed as political. These desires to belong, here to a stigmatized minority, at times extend beyond those who might be considered Buraku. Examining a particular instance of this tendency, a complement to Oguma's situation, highlights the stakes of appearing or not appearing Buraku.

Toward the end of my fieldwork in 2006, I went with the Tokyo Leather Guild to a hot spring resort west of Tokyo. The money for the trip was put forth, in part, by the Tokyo branch of the BLL in hopes of fostering more cooperation among Buraku industries in the Tokyo area. I was invited partially because the organizers knew I was researching leather, and partially because the boss of the tannery where I did fieldwork was going along too. The trip was for Burakumin (plus Joe), and funds were secured for what the liberation league referred to as an "empowerment activity." All the participant families were owners of leather-related companies and had been so for generations. The trip included, just after the visit to the winery and right before the dip in the hot spring, a tour of a leather wallet factory—the cultural Buraku punch amidst the more standard Japanese sightseeing.

A week after this event I went out for coffee with one of the people I had met on the trip. She was in her late thirties, the fourth generation in her family to work in a leather factory. She was born and raised in a Buraku neighborhood, right next door to the family factory and its sounds and smells; and she had had difficulty getting married. One partner had turned away at the urging of his family, and she ended up marrying in her mid-thirties. Even now, her father closes the factory doors in light embarrassment whenever the in-laws come to visit. This is a woman recognizable—by potential marriage partners, by the liberation movement, and by me—as Burakumin, which is why her words that day, a week after the Buraku field trip, took me by surprise. As we settled into our conversation over coffee, Misato eventually paused for a second, looked around the room, and then, leaning in, told me in a low voice that her great-great-grandfather had owned a kimono weaving and dyeing mill. Her family, counted back through the male line four generations, had not, originally, been involved in a Buraku industry. It was the 1/32nd rule, with valuation flipped (and taken down a generation). She confided in me, in a manner very similar to people who drop their voices in public to talk of being Buraku, that she was perhaps not really Burakumin. She has never told any of the people who went on the Buraku field trip, none of the people with whom she grew up in her neighborhood, and she was terrified by the prospect of having them know. "They might no longer respect me. They would look at me differently."

Her father had explained to her when she reached junior high school what Burakumin were, and he had explained to her, with a slight defensiveness, that despite generations of working in a Buraku industry and despite being born and raised in a Buraku neighborhood, they were not, deep down, Burakumin themselves. They were simply, he said, "regular Japanese" (*futsū no nihonjin*). Despite this difference, however, she was raised going to summer camps for the neighborhood children and spent most of her free time with those children. She realized with her father's explanation that all her friends were Buraku and that probably, if they knew what that was, they assumed her to be the same. But she was not the same. She was struck with anxiety that her friends might find out, and that is an anxiety she still carries. Unlike Oguma-san, this is a difference that she learned about through her parents, and it is an anxiety that she can and does voice to her family.

Like Oguma-san, however, Misato's story is indicative of the allures and stakes of appearing or not appearing Buraku. For this woman, the politically motivated empowerment activities of the liberation movement have translated into opportunities to cultivate friends and business partners; she worries about being discovered in this circle as non-Buraku and losing these affective and economic connections. She also enjoys a sense of distance from the stigma, believing that if hard-pressed, she could show herself to be other than Buraku. Her case is not an anomaly but demonstrates one of the many ways in which people invest in this category, despite and because of its stigma. Her situation points to the possibility of being nostalgic for a disappearing stigma, just as it points out the range of contexts, that is, with her "Burakumin" peers, in which such a nostalgia might be most pertinent. At the same time, however, that this case demonstrates the appeal of the category, it also demonstrates its stakes. Her father still closes the factory doors when the in-laws come to visit. She lowers her voice and leans in whenever we talk about her family business in a public setting that is not predominantly Buraku. Even while they seek to hide their stigma, they also hold to it with affection, particularly so, perhaps, as it vanishes.

Oguma-san's story sets into relief a further characteristic of this situation. Signs of Buraku identity are not simply not being produced in relatively public arenas of employment or political activity; they are also not being produced in the more intimate setting of the family. Oguma-san did not learn that he was Buraku from his parents, and he did not raise his own children thinking they were Buraku. This widespread phenomenon has created an increasingly large group of people—those who are not actively "hiding" their Buraku identity and passing as non-Buraku people. Instead, these people simply do not know that they are Buraku or that other people might think them so. They do not imagine that this category of person, which they might hear about occasionally in school or on the news, has any personal relation to them. Faced with parental silence, some of these people are instead told they are Buraku by the local political movement, some are told by a direct act of discrimination, and some are never told at all, instead leading their lives as "regular Japanese." This fact has large implications for the ways in which the anxieties and aspirations associated with being Buraku are distributed across a potentially Buraku population. At the same time that the potential shame of knowing about their stigma is unavailable, so too are the potential affective ties to it and to friends through it, all without their awareness.

In his study of stigma, the sociologist Erving Goffman suggests that the social life of stigma involves two different kinds of parties: stigmatized and nonstigmatized.[3] Any one person might occupy either role, depending on the context. In the Buraku situation, exemplified in the aforementioned two stories, the contextual aspect of Buraku recognition is immediately apparent: depending on context, people may or may not produce signs of Buraku identity. In light of this general social fact, Goffman proposes dividing stigmatized individuals into two categories: the discredited and the discreditable. The first category comprises those people who have either a swiftly recognizable or recognized stigma. They must deal with the social ramifications of constant stigmatization and are saddled with the task of managing social situations in response. The second category comprises people who have a stigma not yet recognized by other people in a situation. Theirs is the task of deciding when, where, how, and to whom to release information regarding the stigma. Whereas the discredited must manage social situations, the discreditable must manage information. The burdens, anxieties, and potential joys of the discreditable and the discredited are parceled out according to their ability to "pass" or not.

The categories of discredited and discreditable operate too in the Buraku situation, depending on what signs of being Buraku are being produced and others' ability to decode those signs. The people filling one of these two roles actively manage the stakes and appeals of Buraku stigma, happen as it may by management of information or situations. However, there is another type of Buraku person who does no managing, that is, the person who does not know that others may think them Buraku. The language of passing presupposes that the person in question understands themselves to be of a marked identity with the capacity for agency in controlling whether or how to manage the signs of that identity. The unknowing Buraku lacks exactly this knowledge and agentive capacity.

In Goffman's scheme the unknowing Buraku would qualify for membership in a "protective capsule." Not knowing that they in some way diverge from the normal, the unknowing Buraku has neither the responsibility of the discredited nor that of the discreditable. They pass or not without knowing. The management of information and social situations around their stigma may still occur, perhaps by a concerned parent or teacher, but that management happens at a distance from the individual. That capsule, which might last the duration of the person's life, structures the distribution of anxiety regarding and affective engagement with Buraku stigma. The *knowing* person faces the threat of discrimination with management responsibilities, having to manage social situations or personal information in accordance with their sense of ethical and political imperative and personal shame. Anxiety can be allayed, the extent to which management is adept and ethical imperatives are fulfilled. Similarly, the *knowing* person has available affective ties to the category and to others who inhabit it, as well as to potential feelings of nostalgia for its disappearance. On the other hand, the *unknowing* person faces the threat and the pleasures with the luxury of blithe unconcern—

unconcern until the potential moment that they are made to know, whether by discrimination or by the political movement.

It is also possible to interpret the role of the *unknowing* person not simply as a description of a current state of things but as a tendency that is gaining in strength. The number of people who do not find out that they might be considered Buraku, who are not told by their parents, who are not told by their teachers, who are not told by a local political movement, and who never face a discrimination that might make them know—the number of these people is on the rise. The Buraku situation, then, begs the question of what happens to the structure of the *unknowing/knowing* and *discredited/discreditable* and, more to the point here, what happens to a larger political movement when previous indices of a social category no longer index—when the knowledge required to link object to stigma is not present in the stigmatized individuals themselves, and when it is not present in those around them— that is, when the conditions for discrediting someone are on the wane.

FACING THE UNKNOWING:
THE BURAKU POLITICAL RESPONSE TO SILENCE

One might interpret the rise of the long-term *unknowing* as the solution to the Buraku problem. Indeed, the Japanese government made such an argument when, in 2002, it declared Buraku discrimination over and did not renew the 1969 set of laws that had provided government resources to Buraku communities, individuals, and companies. The Communist Party did the same in 2002 when it revamped its Buraku political organization into one focused more broadly on general human rights issues. The BLL, however, publicly disagreed with the government and the Communist Party. It took issue with two points: one, it asserted that discrimination was not in fact over and could be found in still-present-though-dwindling incidents of marriage and employment refusal, Internet harassment, and below-average education rates among Buraku youth; and, two, at a more basic level, it argued that the end of discrimination by itself was an insufficient goal. It argued that the root of the problem lay not in having or not having an object of discrimination but, rather, in there being an inclination to discriminate, independent of an object. "Complete liberation" *(kanzen kaihō)* would only occur when such social inclination was eliminated. How that *kanzen kaihō* might be accomplished, however, was a matter of much strategizing within the Buraku liberation movement.

In December 2005, one month after I had started interning with IMADR, I traveled to Osaka to assist with the interpretation at a conference on "Discrimination Based on Work and Descent" that IMADR had helped organize. For this event, IMADR had teamed with the BLL-associated Buraku Liberation and Human Rights Research Institute (BLHRRI). On the day before the conference, after receiving the international guests from the United Nations, India, and Kenya, we organizers retired to a bar close to the hotel to confirm logistics. The short meeting was led by the director of BLHRRI, Tomonaga Kenzō, a middle-aged man who, though not from a Buraku district, occupation, or family himself, was married to a Buraku woman, had raised his children in a Buraku district, and had been actively engaged in the Buraku liberation struggle since the late 1960s. After running down our preparatory checklist and confirming our activities for the next several days, we were left with some time to chat with each other, and John Davis, a fellow anthropologist from the United States who had done his fieldwork in a Buraku district in Osaka, introduced Tomonaga-san to me as a man "who had all the answers."

I had recently finished reading a book by a younger, freelance Buraku writer named Kadooka Nobuhiko, entitled *Hajimete no Buraku Mondai (Introduction to Buraku Issues)*, in which Kadooka, who was not actively associated with the BLL, suggested that perhaps the end of Buraku discrimination would herald the end of Buraku identity, and that that was potentially not a bad thing. Kadooka's suggestion pointed out a larger debate within the liberation movement—whether there was anything to Buraku identity other than a reaction to discrimination—and I was curious about the movement's stance on "Buraku identity." Seated there at a bar in Osaka across the table from one of the longest-running leaders of the movement, I asked Tomonaga-san whether he thought Buraku identity would and should continue past the end of discrimination. His answer gave me a clue to the end goals of Buraku liberation.

In response to my question, the gist of what Tomonaga-san said was repeated the next day by Kumisaka Shigeyuki, the secretary general of the BLL, who explained the BLL and its goals to the foreign dignitaries. Tomonaga-san told me that it was "not up to the movement to decide whether the identity should continue"; rather, he continued, "it is up to us to create an environment in which individuals themselves can choose to take up the identity or not." Currently, he explained, it was not the decision of those individuals. Instead, discrimination forced certain people, based on perceived relationships with stigmatized industries, to be classified as Buraku, whether they wanted it or not. The movement was trying to create an environment not only in which discrimination did not exist but in which assuming a relationship with the Buraku category of person was a matter of individual volition. Identity, then, in Tomonaga-san's explanation, would be in the hands of individuals.

Tomonaga-san's argument echoes the liberation league's broader argument about "complete liberation." The mission statement of the BLL, revised and adopted in May 1997, is as follows:

> The objective of our league is the realization of complete liberation from Buraku discrimination. We look for the promise of Buraku liberation in a democratic society of autonomy and coexistence, confirmed by human rights—a society in which individuals can set out by themselves on their own lives, with self-actualization, and without having to hide where they came from; a society in which people share and together confirm each other's human rights.

Kanzen kaihō, or complete liberation, then, is a state in which individuals are empowered to make decisions about their own lives, without the coercions of discrimination, and with the support of "coexistence" with other people. This goal, the BLL argues, requires more than merely eliminating discrimination; it requires changing the social structure of Japan through education, legal measures, and direct action against discriminatory acts. In Tomonaga's words, "Discriminatory events are only the tip of the iceberg, beneath which lies a social structure that we must transform to achieve our goals. It is not enough to merely eliminate discrimination, we must transform how people think and act around Buraku issues."[4]

This type of social transformation and empowerment of the individual, however, comes with a catch. The movement aims to create the circumstances in which individuals are granted the license to choose whether, and on which terms, to engage with the Buraku category. At the same time, however, the movement very much has an opinion about which is the ethically and strategically correct choice to make. In the projected, liberated future, they might argue, like Tomonaga-san, that it is "not up to the movement whether the identity should continue"; however, right now, in terms of political strategy of reaching that future of "complete liberation," the rise of the

Buraku people who actively seek to not produce signs of Buraku-ness and the resulting rise of *unknowing* Buraku impede that long-term political objective. A proud Buraku political subject is key to initiating the change that would allow for "complete liberation." This subject should be free to make their own choice but should be disciplined to make a particular choice. Inasmuch as the Buraku liberation movement concerns itself with managing the Buraku population on a numerical and statistical level, tracking education levels, employment, and incidents of discrimination, it is also engaged in a disciplinary project, attempting to discipline into being autonomous political subjects who are simultaneously free to choose whether to associate with the Buraku identity and who actively choose to do so.[5]

Given this set of political goals, the rise of people who choose not to create signs of Buraku identity is troubling to the political movement. As a result, the conceptual armature of the movement for approaching this problem is vast. It has codified modes of characterizing it; these modes both regiment a Buraku subject vis-à-vis attachments to land and kinship and bolster an idea of Japanese citizenship on which that subject sits.

USHIMATSU AS POLITICAL PROBLEM

In August 2006 I headed north from Tokyo into the Tohoku region of Japan in search of what the BLL formally refers to as *mishitei chiku,* or "undesignated districts." This move was in part ironic since there were no designated districts in the greater Tokyo metropolitan area. The "undesignated" here references a system of support for Buraku communities that existed from 1969 until March 2002. For that thirty-three-year period the Special Measures Law provided national funds to local governments to help ameliorate low standards of living and education in Buraku communities. In most areas of the country these funds were distributed to organizations, typically local branches of the BLL, representing geographical and administrative districts. In very few other areas, Tokyo among them, these funds were instead distributed to industrial organizations without geographical reference. Unlike Tohoku, where it was legally possible to register though people elected not to, Tokyo had no designated districts because it was never possible there to register a district. For the areas of the countries that did direct funds to neighborhoods, those neighborhoods had to officially register themselves with the government as, in bureaucratic parlance, *dōwa chiku,* literally "harmony district." While close to 4,600 traditionally Buraku communities decided to register themselves as *dōwa chiku* in order to garner the financial support, an estimated 1,000 Buraku communities remained "undesignated," believing instead that the visibility incurred by designation would draw attention to a community that might otherwise escape from notice and from discrimination.[6] After a year of fieldwork with IMADR, I had become familiar with the Buraku liberation movement's projects. This approach, elaborated in different forms by BLL branches throughout the country, had led many communities to register themselves with the government as *dōwa chiku*. However, the Tohoku region north of Tokyo conspicuously lacked any registered *dōwa chiku*, and the BLL, which cast itself as fighting for Buraku liberation nationwide, lacked a single branch in the six-prefecture region.

Prior to heading north of Tokyo, I first ventured up the stairs from IMADR's basement office to the BLL headquarters in Tokyo. I approached one of the league's staff members and asked him why Tohoku held no *dōwa chiku* and no BLL branches. His response was typical of the movement's assessment of undesignated Buraku districts. He confirmed for me that the absence was not due to a lack of historically Buraku communities; there were plenty of communities, he stated, whose origins could be traced back to the outcastes of Japan's feudal period. The lack of *dōwa chiku* was instead due to a passive political bent prevalent among the inhabitants of these areas, a bent that he summarized with the saying: *neta ko wo okosuna*. This phrase literally means "wake not the sleeping child," equivalent to the English "let sleeping dogs lie." Since the turn of the twentieth century, it has been common liberation movement shorthand for the mind-set that led Buraku communities across the country not to register themselves as *dōwa chiku*, characterized by the "Buraku Issues and Human Rights Encyclopedia" as follows:

> *Neta ko wo okosuna* figuratively expresses the thought that "there is no need to go out of the way to point out the issue's existence to people who otherwise know nothing about it. If we simply leave it alone, it will go away by itself." ... This phrase, whether used by Buraku people or by the general population, should be critiqued on account of its passive approach to solving the issue. ... The *neta ko wo okosuna* mindset ... is a reactive ideology that disrespects all efforts to eliminate discrimination.[7]

In its entry for an undesignated district *(mishitei chiku),* the encyclopedia underscores the BLL staff member's assessment of these areas: "There are a variety of reasons an area might have become an undesignated district. These include such factors as, first, the passive attitude of the government administration to Buraku issues, and second, the fact that the *neta ko wo okosuna* voice is strong among area residents. . . . The Dowa Special Measures went unenforced in undesignated districts, leaving behind miserable living conditions."[8] Both the league staff member and the BLL-supported encyclopedia attribute partial responsibility for the "undesignated" status of some Buraku communities to a strong inclination to avoid or obscure Buraku issues on the part of the districts' residents. This inclination is cast as counter not only to the objectives of the league but to the higher, necessary good of eliminating discrimination. Defining an undesignated district in terms of this inclination couples the inclinations of a set of people with a geographical region: *neta ko wo okosuna* is as much a characteristic of an individual as it is of a geographical and administrative district.

What "undesignated" and *neta ko wo okosuna* do together to link person and place, the use of a third term, common in the movement, *mikaihō* ("unliberated" or "not yet liberated"), they do alone. While this term is not used in formal documents such as the encyclopedia, it is used in daily conversations within the movement, and the staff member working upstairs made mention of it to me, an intern for IMADR. "Unliberated," as much as *neta ko wo okosuna*, picks out a political problem, something to be solved. Here, however, the problem is very clearly operative on two levels simultaneously. "Unliberated" refers to the passive *neta ko wo okosuna* mind-set of individuals, which prevents them from proactively engaging with the liberation movement and which prevented them from designating their district as a *dōwa chiku* under the Special Measures Law. At the same time, it refers to the low standards of living and educational levels of a geographically bound population. The term acts as a metonymic hinge between the movement's biopolitical and disciplinary projects, linking together individuals as possessors of a psychological state—that of complacence, passivity, or obeisance to the status quo—to social and economic conditions of delimited areas. The Tohoku areas that I was to visit, then, were unliberated in a dual sense: unliberated from continued socioeconomic hardship, and comprised of individuals unliberated from a defeatist sense of self.

My month-long Tohoku journey took me through all prefectures in the region. I interviewed city officials, employees of local history museums, butchers, and food industry professionals, and I approached strangers on the street in an attempt to get a sense of the status of the so-called unliberated

Buraku areas. I found several, much more easily than I had anticipated, all of which strangers on the street pointed out for me. Upon my return, I encountered yet another movement term describing these "unliberated districts." A few days after I returned from Tohoku, I had dinner with four IMADR staff members and Matsuoka Toru, a BLL board member and the one Japanese diet member at the time publicly known as being a *Buraku shusshin sha* (i.e., as being from a Buraku district). Over dinner I described to the group the trip I had been on, explaining that I was interested in the desire to not be recognized as Buraku, and the seeming split between the proactive identity-focused approach of the BLL and the approach of the *mikaihō chiku*. Matsuoka-san listened interestedly, and when I was finished with my description, he offered his own much more concise synopsis of my trip: *Ushimatsu gari* (Ushimatsu hunting).

He was referring here to a work of fiction, *Hakai,* or *The Broken Commandment,* written in 1906 by Shimazaki Tōson, in which the main character, a man from a Buraku area, is commanded by his dying father never to reveal his Buraku roots.[9] This man, Ushimatsu, leaves his home district and makes his living as a schoolteacher. While he proves to be a successful teacher, he is constantly plagued with shame over not revealing his background during a time when the Buraku liberation movement is burgeoning, and he is simultaneously filled with an equally plaguing shame over the thought of having people around him know he is from a Buraku district. The book is an exploration of Ushimatsu's attempts at keeping his father's dying commandment, and, despite the hundred years that separated my dinner at an expensive Azabu Juuban restaurant from the publication of the work, my trip to the undesignated districts of Tohoku immediately evoked in Matsuoka-san a comparison to this main character. In searching for the unliberated districts, I had been looking for Ushimatsu.

The rest of the table of activists immediately understood Matsuoka's reference and agreed with his gloss of my trip: they quickly followed his statement with questions about what kinds of Ushimatsu, or his female equivalent, Ushiko, I had found. They also suggested, however, that my journey of hundreds of miles into far-flung northern Buraku districts had perhaps been excessive. The next time I wanted to examine the psychology of undesignated areas, I need not wander so far. Ushimatsu and Ushiko were closer at hand, buried in each Buraku person.

In Matsuoka-san's words, and in the recognition of those at the table, Ushimatsu does not merely refer to the protagonist from a novel written one hundred years earlier. It also picks out a particular type of ideology, codified in BLL parlance as Ushimatsu *shisō* (Ushimatsu ideology) or, alternatively, Ushimatsu-*shugi* (Ushimatsu-ism). And, in Matsuoka-san's rewording of my trip north, it indexes as well an issue distributed along geographic lines, a general characteristic of some types of communities, more prevalent perhaps in the Tohoku region than in the Kansai region. "Ushimatsu" then fulfills the metonymic hinge evident in "unliberated" and *netako wo okosuna:* it ties together a person and a place, rendering either capable of a general psychological state. This process illuminates and creates the scalar scaffolding across which play the tensions of silence of Ushimatsu and of Oguma-san. Approached from this perspective of the BLL, Oguma-san's story is not his alone. It is a story of a general political problematic, recursively active across multiple scales: the individual and the geographically situated Buraku population.[10] According to the movement's Ushimatsu *shisō* read, all of these sites must be engaged in the struggle against *netako wo okosuna*. Here, obfuscating one's identity as a Buraku person leads to a defeatist attitude and a lack of self-esteem. This psychological state becomes outwardly manifest as the inability to struggle against poverty and other forms of entrenched structural discrimination, and that inability takes on individual and geographic boundaries.[11] In the Ushimatsu *shisō* reading, recognition of one's identity as Buraku, both by one's self and by society at large, is cast as a psychological, political, and ethical necessity. Without it, the individual falters, communities remain steeped in "miserable living conditions," the movement stagnates, and gross inequalities continue and thrive.

It is at precisely this point that the Ushimatsu *shisō* approach clashes most apparently with the liberation movement's project of "complete liberation." The individual here pictured is not equipped with the autonomy necessary to make a decision about their relationship with the Buraku category. Furthermore, this lack of individual autonomy is intimately tied to an autonomy of the group.

The scalar link here between the individual and the geographically determined group is what grants the political organization its authority to speak for other people. This link provides a basis for the thought that the struggle of Buraku liberation extends beyond any one individual; instead, it is a matter of the district, and therefore a shared matter of the individuals within that district. The discipline of the individual is linked to the discipline of the population. Through this link, the political organization sees itself as authorized to make claims on the status of other people's Buraku identity and as able to demand that identity of them, for the fight of the political movement cannot happen without the efforts of individuals within a district, however wary. This link forms and confirms the distribution of an ethical imperative to work toward Buraku liberation across districts and across people.

With that distribution comes a categorization of types of Buraku people, and types of Buraku districts. This categorization confers censure and value, and with it ethical and political obligation. On the one end, you have the prototypical Ushimatsu—the kind of person who cannot overcome their inner Ushimatsu, one who has failed to stand up and decry the wrongness of discrimination; on the other end, you have the prototype of the proud activist—one who publicly proclaims their Buraku identity and works for the elimination of discrimination. Likewise, you have on the one end an undesignated, unliberated district whose residents are unable and unwilling to claim a Buraku identity, and on the other you have a district with a thriving Buraku liberation movement, struggling vigilantly against discrimination and any errant Ushimatsus. This is the movement's backlash against a backdrop of silence, an entrenched argument that raises and defines the stakes of Oguma-san's tension, defines the obligations for embracing an identity as a Buraku person, and figures nonproduction not as simple nonexistence but as the deliberate, willful, and shameful obfuscation of Buraku identity, the antithesis of the end goal of the liberated individual.

HISTORICAL PRECURSORS OF USHIMATSU AS POLITICAL PROBLEM

Ushimatsu as political problem has conditions that stretch back arguably a century, if not more. Indeed, the first Buraku political organization, the Suiheisha, established in 1922, issued its first critique of *Hakai* in 1931. Literature scholar René Andersson,[12] among others, argues that this critique, which led to the 1939 publishing of a Suiheisha-censored, revised version of the work, was predicated on a tension between two tendencies prevalent at that time, what historian Kurokawa refers to as the "principle of universalism" (i.e., equality in the distribution of universal rights) and the "politics of difference" (in which a group asserts its sociopolitical situation as different from the majority population).[13] Kurokawa argues that this tension had not been possible prior to the Meiji Restoration and Japan's opening up to internationalization and so-called cultural enlightenment. Prior to the Meiji, there had been no institutionally embedded presupposition that people should be considered universally equal. As such a sensibility became concretized in Japanese jurisprudence and widespread throughout the populace, the difference of the Buraku became that much more prominently marked.

This affective and ethical impulse has a history—particular conditions that have given Ushimatsu life and traction as both a social possibility and a political problem across decades. These conditions hang on configurations of kinship, employment, and location of residence as vectors by which people can be recognized and created as contemporary Buraku subjects.[14] As the evidentiary seat of Buraku subjecthood shifts among these vectors, so too shifts the interplay between obligation—those social factors that obligate subjects to particular forms of life—and choice—those social factors that establish a subject as an autonomous seat of self-authority.

THE MEIJI RESTORATION AND THE END OF THE EDO PERIOD

As I described briefly in the introduction, during the Edo period (1603–1868) there was a formal caste system that divided people in the Japanese archipelago according to four primary work-based categories: warrior, merchant, peasant, and artisan;[15] however, there were three other categories that existed alongside these four: on the one end of the social spectrum, the emperor, who lived a life of forced seclusion under Shogunate rule, and on the other end, the *eta* and the *hinin*, who were allocated tasks seen as improper for the other castes, and too dirty for other people. While there was a great deal of variation regarding the nature of these tasks according to region, the *eta*, which literally means "full of filth," typically dealt with jobs seen as defiled, ranging from the production of meat or leather, to the provision of policing services, to the cremation of dead bodies.[16] On the other hand, *hinin*, which means "nonhuman," included itinerant prostitutes or traveling performers who had lost their positions within the rigidly legislated Tokugawa caste system.[17] As the anthropologist Emiko Ohnuki-Tierney has noted, the types of jobs the *eta* and *hinin*, or, as she calls them, the "special-status people," fulfilled were decidedly nonagrarian, in a world that allotted value according to agrarian productivity.[18] In addition to formal expectations of the types of work appropriate for each of these castes, divisions among these groups were maintained through rigid sumptuary laws, rules governing the use of public space and deferential language, and strict residence zoning. This social system provided a structure in which, in daily interaction, it was difficult to mistake the social caste of other people; while there were similarities in dress between the *eta* and *hinin* castes and the peasants and farmers, subtle sartorial and deferential clues made social identity a visible fact of Edo life.

This situation started to change with the formal end of the caste system. With the promulgation of an edict liberating the "special-status people" from their caste names in 1871, visible signs of social identity were no longer mandatory. While there was much variation in different regions of the reconstructing country, erstwhile *eta* and *hinin* suddenly encountered the newfound promise of mobility across a variety of social arenas. Marriage partners were no longer prohibited or stipulated by law; residence location was no longer mandated; types of labor were no longer legally designated; and the perceptible marking of social status in public space through clothing, movement, or linguistic deference was no longer required. With this restructuring of the legal code came a different set of stakes for choices individuals might make with regard to these social arenas. Erstwhile *eta* and *hinin* could now choose to not cede public space to someone previously of the samurai class and, by the letter of the law, to not have to worry about being legally punished. They also could wear a broader range of clothing without the threat of legal censure. And at the same time, as I note in the introduction, they were also liberated of what occupational security the caste system had provided and became subject to state taxes. With these changes, the ground was laid for a dramatic restructuring of the workings of social recognition.

The Meiji Restoration set into practical effect a politics of equality, rendering the titular choices of individuals the same, agnostic to erstwhile caste status. With this collapse and the institutionalization of formal equality, group affiliation—whether sartorial, verbal, or in other form—moved from the domain of state policy into the domain of individual decision, and individual decision thereby became a location of agency for asserting identity in ways previously not possible. Not choosing to assert an *eta* or a *hinin* identity, then, became an option for those people, families, and districts that had previously not imagined themselves as having such a choice. Within law and social recognition, identity receded from the realms of state-determined caste and instead came to be disciplined as a matter of choice and psychological disposition.

However, while these choices might be made without fear of formal legal reprimand, there was still the matter of general social opprobrium. The Edo social structure, which has frequently been labeled "feudal" among historians of Japan, had long existed as a proper order of things, and its dismantlement was a hugely contested act, rather than simple "development," involving battles throughout the archipelago.[19] The resistance to the reformation took place not only on a legal or political level, but it also existed in the quotidian habits and dispositions of the feudal subjects. The choice of a person of *eta* background not to wear identifying clothing or, worse, not to mark their speech with deference for people previously of other castes was a violation of the sensibilities of propriety that had existed under the previous order of things. And this affront then could serve as a provocation for unmarked Meiji subjects to act on their own to correct what they saw as impropriety, since the state no longer would. It was this type of act, held against the spreading ideology of equality across social castes, that would eventually be interpreted by liberation movements as discrimination.

Erstwhile *eta*'s susceptibility to acts of backlash was intensified by the fact that with the same move that liberated them from their legal status as pariahs, they were also liberated from a monopoly control of an industry that had provided economic support. Throughout the end of the Edo period, the *eta* had controlled the lucrative leather industry, with some such as Dazaimon even amassing tremendous wealth and influence as a result.[20] With the end of the Edo period, and the accompanying end of the policy of national isolation *(sakoku)*, monopoly control of this industry was removed from the *eta*, which, as Japan entered into wars with China and Russia around the turn of the century and into further wars beyond, proved to be a major economic blow to people who already struggled with poverty. The removal of this source of income left the descendants of the *eta* and *hinin* castes without recourse to proprietary economic resources in the face of social censure for violating the expired strictures of the previous social system.

As the realms of marriage, employment, and location of residence were eased from explicit state control, they became consolidated as realms in which certain choices of the erstwhile *eta* and *hinin* might pique public censure. Not all of these transgressions of the previous system carried the same weight: while an erstwhile *eta* and *hinin* might not be reprimanded for not wearing caste-specific clothing, they were more likely to be reprimanded for not using deferential address, and almost assured of encountering extreme resistance in an attempt to marry someone descended from a different caste. Over the next several decades, the first two of these actions would lose their significance as a transgression of propriety, whereas the latter, along with getting a job in a non-*eta* industry, would still maintain a hint of taboo, and then on the obverse become evidence of discrimination. At the same time these arenas of marriage, residence, and employment would become ones in which the nonproduction of signs of a marked identity would trouble the burgeoning *eta*- and *hinin*-derived political movement. As the Meiji Restoration took hold on a daily level, the choice to produce or not produce marked signs of identity was divested from explicit state regulation and instead regimented under the rubric of individual agency that appeared as independent of state control. The production, then, became more subject to institutions of capital bereft of economic protection and the disciplinary weight of social conduct. Such choices came to bear the weight of public censure and political impetus and were channeled and codified under the social arenas of marriage, residence, and employment.[21]

THE FORMATION OF THE BURAKU POLITICAL MOVEMENT

Many historians and activists interested in tracing the history of Buraku issues argue that the social system of the Edo period served to codify, if not create, the category of people who would become the Buraku,[22] formalizing pariah social categories that had, according to some arguments, existed since the Heian period (794–1185) into the governmentally and socially legible categories of *eta* and *hinin*.[23] While the categories of people circumscribed by these Edo caste names underwent drastic change during the Meiji Restoration, this pool of people served as a basis for a political movement that burgeoned in the early years of the twentieth century.[24] The first properly Buraku-led political organization was the Suiheisha, which was founded in 1922 and served as one of many indications of the entrenchment of sensibilities of equality that Kurokawa argues was happening in Japan in this period.[25] The founding document of this organization, the Suiheisha Declaration, interpellates the erstwhile *eta* as Burakumin. At the same time it highlights the coalescing stakes of producing and not producing signs of Buraku identity and shows the regimentation buttressing the rhetoric of individual choice.

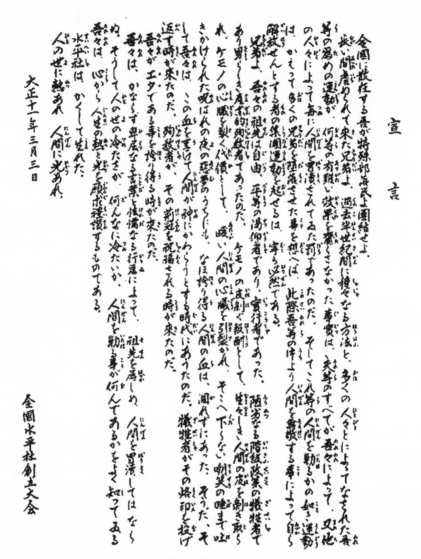

宣 言

大正十一年三月三日

全國水平社創立大會

FIGURE 5. A handwritten version of the Suiheisha Declaration.

Declaration

Tokushu Burakumin throughout the country: Unite!

Long-suffering brothers! Over the past half century, the movements on our behalf by so many people and in such varied ways have yielded no appreciable results. This failure is the punishment we have incurred for permitting ourselves as well as others to debase our own human dignity. Previous movements, though seemingly motivated by compassion, actually corrupted many of our brothers. Thus, it is imperative that we now organize a new collective movement to emancipate ourselves by promoting respect for human dignity.

Brothers! Our ancestors pursued and practiced freedom and equality. They were the victims of base, contemptible class policies and they were the manly martyrs of industry. As a reward for skinning animals, they were stripped of their own living flesh; in return for tearing out the hearts of animals, their own warm human hearts were ripped apart. They were even spat upon with ridicule. Yet, all through these cursed nightmares, their human pride ran deep in their blood. Now, the time has come when we human beings, pulsing with this blood, are soon to regain our divine dignity. The time has come for the victims to throw off their stigma. The time has come for the blessing of the martyrs' crown of thorns.

The time has come when we can be proud of being Eta.

We must never again shame our ancestors and profane humanity through servile words and cowardly deeds. We, who know just how cold human society can be, who know what it is to be pitied, do fervently seek and adore the warmth and light of human life from deep within our hearts.

Thus is the Suiheisha born.

Let there be warmth in human society, let there be light in all human beings.

March 3, 1922
The Suiheisha

The first words of this declaration summon Burakumin to unite in the fight against stigma, shame, and ridicule and for freedom, equality, and pride. This summons hails two interlinked sets of people, and in so doing it identifies two interlinked types of threat. First, the declaration calls out to those who already see themselves as Buraku people, who are actively engaged in the struggle but simply do not have comrades with whom to work. These people are to join together to fight against stigma and overcome a history of having, metaphorically, their skin stripped from their flesh and their hearts ripped from their breasts. Second, the declaration calls out to those who have hesitated to fight for Buraku freedom, those who continue to debase their own human dignity. Here, that which is to be overcome is not an external oppression but an internal weakness. This type of person is presumed to know that they are Buraku, just as is the first, whether they proclaim it or not, and whether society knows it or not. Identity is a given, psychological fact, and the agency to proclaim that identity is presumed and projected to be under individual agency, just as this document itself enacts that proclamation of identity. From this viewpoint, the nonproduction of signs of Buraku identity is problematic in those who, prior to any action or social recognition, *are* Burakumin, or who *are eta*.

The declaration issues a summons to both of these categories of people, linking them together and exhorting them to rise up, unite, and fight for their own human dignity. Not answering this summons works against the ethical fight for freedom and dignity; it also, perhaps more perniciously, denies the attempt to authorize individuals to choose their social identity. Here then is laid plain the basis of the critique that the Suiheisha would lodge against Ushimatsu ten years later. In a time when the Buraku category of person is not a governmentally imposed and regulated category, and when it is possible to *be* Buraku but not be visible as such, Ushimatsu's hiding of his Buraku identity, along with his total flight from the scene, to Texas, is anathema to the ethical and political imperatives of the Suiheisha. In vanishing from view, Ushimatsu, and those who follow him, are once again stripped of "their own living flesh." Ushimatsu's own inner turmoil in the novel is a sign of the persuasive force attained by the stance that Suiheisha represents. For the Suiheisha, the figure of Ushimatsu potentially encourages a tendency among Buraku people, the inheritors of the *eta* and *hinin* stigma, to not claim their identity. The political organization, on the other hand, stresses the ethical virtue and practical necessities of making precisely such a claim of identity.

As scholars such as Neary and Kurokawa have argued, this basic infrastructure of equality and difference was refined over the next several decades, with the intensified introduction of ideas of race around the start of the Russo-Japanese War (1904–5),[26] the rapid spread of socialist ideas throughout Japan following the Russian Revolution,[27] and the reiteration of democratic ideals with U.S. occupation following the Asia-Pacific War. Along with this steady transformation, the Asia-Pacific War heralded a dramatic downturn for domestic political organizations, the Suiheisha included, and prompted a drastic change in the lives of many Buraku people. Increased government surveillance, censorship, and labor demands led to the dismantlement of the Suiheisha in 1942, and carpet and nuclear bombing of Japan's major cities destroyed family records that might have been used to track people as descendants of the *eta* or *hinin* and made the boundaries of traditional Buraku neighborhoods either irrelevant or indistinguishable. As people moved back into these cities following the war, Buraku and non-Buraku people alike came to live in what had been primarily Buraku neighborhoods.[28] In this context, pertinent markers of Buraku identity were lost, making it easier for some of the population to choose not to identify as Buraku, a choice made even easier without a concerted political presence demanding that identification. Furthermore, the war created an increased demand for leather goods, funneling capital into the still-stigmatized industries despite the loss of *eta* monopoly and helping create a Buraku middle class that saw itself as not needing a liberation movement.

POSTWAR POLITICAL SUCCESSES

In the aftermath of the war, the rebirth of the Buraku political movement was slow and complicated by movement-internal political strife, divided along schisms with the Communist Party. By 1969, however, the Buraku political movement had reconsolidated and had found a leading force in the BLL, which had been established by a charismatic and forceful Buraku leader, Matsumoto Jiichiro, during U.S. occupation.[29] In 1969 this, by then, paragon Buraku political organization met with a major success in prompting the Japanese government to pass the Special Measures Law, which would shunt government funds to Buraku people, families, and communities that registered with the government under the name *dōwa* (literally, "harmony"). With the passage of these laws, the ethical and political obligation visible in the Suiheisha Declaration was resuscitated with tangible, guaranteed benefits. If one were to heed the hail of the political movement and register as *dōwa,* one qualified for a variety of financial aid, ranging from academic scholarships, community funds, and industrial support.

As I described earlier, these funds were primarily distributed according to geographic unit throughout the country. Designated *dōwa* districts across the country used these funds to improve the living conditions of their areas and provide educational opportunities for their residents. At the same time that their improvements consolidated the area as Buraku, they also diminished, sometimes completely, drastic visible infrastructural differences between Buraku and non-Buraku districts. These changes to registered *dōwa* districts also permitted the flourishing of local branches of the Buraku political movement, incorporating large numbers of people and rallying those groups against both individual acts and institutionalized forms of discrimination. One primary example of this increased political traction was the closure of family registries *(koseki)* in 1976. Up until that point these family registries had been accessible to anyone who requested them and provided fodder for individuals to distinguish Buraku from non-Buraku families. The BLL rallied against this system, arguing that it provided the basis for discriminatory acts. In 1976 the BLL successfully lobbied the government to reduce access to these documents. While registries are still available to certain lawyers and government bureaucrats, some of whom can be bribed to release this information, by and large this legal change severely limited public access to family genealogies. This change resulted in even more people who might otherwise be thought to be Buraku to go unrecognized as such, unless they chose differently.

In addition to providing the fodder for these types of political action, the Special Measures Law, and the political and community activity it enabled, provided a metric against which the political leanings of families and individuals within a district might be measured. It served as a way to distinguish the proactive from the passive. In all, this law and its enforcement, which continued in various revisions until 2002, cultivated a valorization of Buraku identity within these districts, and at the same time made it more possible for some, particularly those who benefited most from educational and economic support, to leave that Buraku district, and potentially the Buraku identity, behind.[30]

This tendency was particularly pronounced in Tokyo. There, as I mentioned previously, special measure money was not channeled into particular districts; instead, it was funneled into industrial support and into leather research and production. Partially due to this situation, Tokyo, unlike Osaka or Fukuoka, never developed strong Buraku-identified districts, nor did it develop a comparatively strong political movement. Instead, the traditional Buraku areas, which did not take the administrative label *"dōwa,"* appeared merely as relatively impoverished parts of the city. The large number of people who moved to the greater metropolitan area from rural parts of the country during Japan's economic growth spurt in the 1970s and 1980s lacked the knowledge that these less expensive districts needed to interpret these districts as Buraku. Not uncommonly, then, they moved into these areas unaware and unwittingly both made themselves the potential object of Buraku discrimination and diluted the stigma of that neighborhood, making it that much harder to interpret these districts as Buraku. On the other hand, individual Buraku people who moved from more rural areas encountered an urban anonymity unlike what they had experienced in their rural homes. Tokyo, in this massive flow of people, became a petri dish for Ushimatsu-*shugi*.

At the same time the Special Measures Law was slowly reconfiguring the Buraku political movement and the definition of the Buraku category of person, changes in other arenas had similar effects. Japan's economic growth spurt of the 1970s and 1980s overlapped with dramatic changes in traditionally Buraku industries, particularly in the leather industry. Since the occupation, the Japanese government faced an opposing set of pressures with regard to the domestic leather industry: on the one hand, the United States used Japan's status as signatory to the General Agreement on Tariffs and Trade to call for the removal of domestic protections on the leather industry; on the other hand, the leaders of that industry themselves, backed by the political and economic power of the BLL, demanded that this industry remain protected. The primary push for the liberalization of commodities in Japan came in the early 1960s, and though the Japanese leather industry kept some form of legal protection from that time until today, it has suffered greatly from the global liberalization of the leather production trade. The slow dismantlement of protections of the domestic leather industry has allowed for an increased influx of finished leather products into the Japanese market, undercutting the domestic industry's prices and rendering them, slowly and surely, largely obsolete. Take, for instance, trade between the United States and Japan. In 1980, 32 percent of the United States' rawhide exports went to Japan, making it the number-one destination country for the United States' rawhide. This number decreased to 24 percent in 1992, 5.7 percent in 2000, and 3 percent in 2005.[31] The United States was and continues to be the largest international exporter of rawhide. What has changed, however, is the destination of those exports. In 1992, 24 percent of its exports went to Japan, and only 0.7 percent went to China. By 2005, however, Japan had shrunk to 3 percent and China had exploded to 24.8 percent, overtaking all other countries as the number-one destination country for rawhide internationally.

These figures are not limited to imports from the United States. Japan's overall rawhide imports have been on the decrease since their peak in 1975: in 1975, Japan imported 99.9 million skins; in 1998, 3.2 million; and in 2006, 1.1 million.[32] Domestic production of cow rawhide likewise dropped from its 1985 peak of 1.5 million to 1 million in 1998.[33] These changes were palpable in the east Tokyo neighborhood where I did my research: in 1976, this neighborhood housed sixty-two small-scale tanneries. In 2005, when I started my research, this number had decreased to twenty-eight; in 2006, it was twenty-two; and, in 2008, only ten were left.[34] Those factories that do remain face increased pressure regarding environmental issues, on top of steadily increasing economic hardships, as I will discuss in more detail in the next chapter. Many of the remaining factories are quickly trying to develop themselves as niche industries, marketing a particular product or offering a particular process in order to compete with the influx of cheap leather from abroad.

The progressive subjection of the Japanese economy to international competition has led a sea of foreign, cheaper, and frequently undocumented labor into the market. It has also caused many shops simply to succumb and close up shop, allowing less expensive Chinese and Indian leather to instead flood the Japanese markets.[35] These two changes have slowly decreased the importance of tanning in the constitution of Buraku social identity. While the industry remains stigmatized, it does not serve as a primary labor base for people who might be called "Buraku." People who used to work in this industry are turning to unmarked jobs in other sectors, creating another arena in which they need not label themselves "Buraku" if they choose not to do so. While these people might still be identifiable as Buraku by their official family registry or by the location of their ancestral homes, they encounter the possibility of a life untainted both by the danger of arduous labor and the violence of discrimination. For them, however, this possibility is most easily attained by following Ushimatsu's broken commandment and by letting go of signs of their Buraku identity.

THE INCREASING STAKES OF BURAKU VISIBILITY

Even as the foundation for producing signs of being Buraku is crumbling, in another venue there is increased pressure for just such production. As the incitement to multiculturalism has gained in force in the decades surrounding the turn of the twenty-first century, the political stakes for producing signs of Buraku and combating Ushimatsu-*shugi* have in turn heightened. As I noted in the introduction, at the same time that Japan's leather industry has liberalized, the Buraku political movement has met with slow but steady successes on an international level, starting from its engagement with Dalit activists in the 1950s, to its involvement in Japan's ratification of the two international human rights treaties in the 1970s, to its creation of IMADR in

1988. The 2002 expiration date of the Special Measures Law and the attendant national defunding of *dōwa* projects have spurred the Buraku political movement to intensify those international efforts, exemplified in the two momentous successes at the start of the twenty-first century—namely, the consolidation of a new category of discrimination, to be investigated by the United Nations, "Discrimination Based on Work and Descent," and the UN special rapporteur on racism's report on Japan. These successes on an international level have increased the opportunities for solidarity work and for putting pressure *(gaiatsu)* on the Japanese government to push through measures, such as an antidiscrimination bill, that support Buraku and other minorities in Japan. All of that, however, relies on a capacity to combat Ushimatsu-*shugi*.

The end of the Special Measures Law, after thirty-three years of implementation, has had effects in domestic efforts as well. As I stated earlier, the government justified the end of the law by asserting that Buraku discrimination was itself over, and special funds were therefore no longer necessary. The end of this law and the funds that accompanied it left local branches of the BLL with insufficient funding to continue all of its community building, education, and other political activities. This situation prompted in the BLL a sense of crisis, increasing its felt need to produce signs of Buraku discrimination as evidence to counteract the government's claim. At the same time, then, there was a greater sense of urgency to mobilize people to claim a Buraku identity, now that their demise was anticipated publicly by the government, and now that funding was dramatically reduced. In 2006 the situation for political organizations, particularly those in the Kansai area around Osaka, worsened as local governments choked off other sources of funding to community organizations and human rights-oriented organizations. This situation has left the institutions that have cultivated a sense of community within Buraku districts without the support necessary to carry out their work, and the success of the Special Measures Law has left behind districts populated with people not always from Buraku backgrounds, as more affluent Buraku people have slowly migrated out of these communities and as other populations have migrated in. This situation has piqued the movement's sense of urgency; it has been left without funds and with a population either increasingly disinterested in or increasingly unaware of Buraku politics—for them, the possibilities of nostalgia are increasing rapidly, not simply, as we saw in Misato's situation at the beginning of this chapter, for a stigmatized identity now vanishing, but for a past of political and economic clout.

The conjunction of transnational circulations of multicultural politics and neoliberal capital in Japan, decades in the making, lays the conditions for the reproduction of Ushimatsu as political problem. Buraku people are less identified by visible markers of employment, kinship, or even neighborhood association, and, in an environment where the individual rewards for identifying as Buraku are on the wane, the stakes and anxieties of choosing not to produce signs of Buraku identity have shifted. Conversely stated, there are increasing demands on these people to appear as unmarked Japanese citizens. Genealogy, employment, and residence are not merely stripped away from the erstwhile *eta*; rather, these subjects are facing increasing demands to be proper, modern Japanese citizens. In the purchase of these demands does Ushimatsu as a pattern of behavior become more possible, and thus does it become more and more problematic to the political organizations that represent Buraku issues?

Clear here is the fact that Ushimatsu as possibility and Ushimatsu as political problem, along with the optimisms and anxieties they index, do not have even distribution across Japan. The distribution, with its points of high and low intensity, is recursive across different scales of geography and personal biography. From region to region, community to community, family to family, and individual to individual within those communities and families, and even within individuals across different moments of their lives, the Ushimatsu tendency can be more or less enticing, and more or less politically problematic. Each of these scales replicates a gradation of the Ushimatsu tendency and also replicates the perception of that tendency as a problem. Each also entails its own locus of political concern and intervention. For example, regionally, the political activity of the western part of the country, from Kansai to Kyushu, dwarfs that of the east, including Kanto and Tohoku. The BLL can then identify what it calls "problematic" regions—Tohoku versus Kanto—and tailor its political strategy accordingly. Similarly, communities within those regions vary to the degree that they enable and castigate Ushimatsu tendencies. Within Osaka, arguably the heart of the Buraku political movement, districts such as Sumiyoshi and Nishinari are home to strong political movements and offer a strong contrast to neighboring Buraku districts that lack consolidated political organizations. Families also exhibit a similar range—from families that do not ever, among themselves or between each other, speak of their Buraku affiliations to families such as that of the leader of the Osaka Buraku liberation research center, in which every member of the family was raised with being Buraku as a point of pride rather than a point of shame. Finally, individuals themselves exhibit this range of tendencies, across individuals and within them, depending on the context. In the Ushimatsu paradigm, all of these levels are brought into relation with each other, and a political intervention can be made in one as a way to modify another: improvements to districts were a means of improving individuals under the Special Measures Law, and the education of individuals was seen as a way of achieving higher standards of living for a family or for an entire district.

THE NECESSITY OF CHOICE

Emerging from this history and current assemblage of ethical and affective orientations, Buraku political subjects are less and less producing signs of Buraku identity, either willfully so or simply because they lack the knowledge of themselves as such. This "Ushimatsu" tendency provides a scalar scaffolding, from individuals, to families, to neighborhoods, across which the anxieties and aspirations of being Buraku are distributed—the *unknowing* versus the *knowing;* the *discredited* versus the *discreditable.* In turn, the Ushimatsu tendency provokes those unequally distributed anxieties among liberation activists attempting to consolidate a robust and representable minority base to rally governmental and international support. It also foments anxieties because it does not treat what the movement posits as its fundamental problem, of which Buraku discrimination is only symptomatic: a deep prejudice against a very particular difference in Japan.

The anxieties of the movement, however, are not without their tensions. The leaders of the movement are concerned about the choice of their perceived constituency not to embrace a Buraku identity. At the same time, as this chapter has indicated and as the next section of the book discusses in detail, they are struggling to transform a society in which those people are not free to choose a Buraku identity into one in which such a choice could be made. However, in order to create such a transformation, movement leaders argue that people must choose to embrace Buraku identity, affirm it as always having been there even in their election of it. Individuals should be free to choose to embrace their identity, but they should also now be both politically and ethically disciplined, obliged to choose to embrace that identity.

The labor of creating a multicultural Japan entails disciplining populations of individuals, providing them with an interiority capable of enacting that discipline in a way that appears as choice. These Buraku subjects should seek to overcome their inner Ushimatsus and Ushikos and choose to affirm their Buraku identity.

In September 2006, one month after my trip to the northern area of Japan's main island, the Liberty Osaka Museum, in conjunction with the BLL, held a commemorative forum focusing on the significance of *Hakai*, the novel in which Ushimatsu appears, across the century since its publication. The forum was primarily advertised to students and youth involved in the movement. It offered workshops charting *Hakai*'s publication history, its various print and cinematic incarnations, and its reception by the movement, as well as more general panels on the necessity and vicissitudes of valuing one's identity. The event spanned multiple weekends and was planned by Burakumin for Burakumin, to point out the continued salience of Ushimatsu as political problem. The final plenary session culminated in a visceral tribute to this assertion. After the closing words, the final speaker, a young man from south of Osaka, led the assembled group of people in a chant. In unison, the voices of several hundred Buraku people, mostly youth born three-quarters of a century after the original publication of *Hakai*, rang out: *"Ushimatsu shisō, Ushimatsu shugi—kokufuku shiyō! Ushimatsu zō wo koete, Burakumin no aidenteitei!"* ("Let us conquer Ushimatsu ideology, let us conquer Ushimatsu-ism. Overcome Ushimatsu, Burakumin identity!").

PART TWO

Choice and Obligation in Contemporary Buraku Politics

THREE

Locating the Buraku

A POLITICAL ECOLOGY OF POLLUTION

THE FIRST TWO CHAPTERS of this book have examined the tension between producing and not producing signs of Buraku identity. As we have seen, this tension both relies on and effects certain political subjects, ethical obligations, and relationships among people, things, the places they live, the families they inhabit, and the occupations they take up. Just as important in this process, however, is the content of those signs and exactly how they point out Buraku difference. It is not simply that signs of being Buraku have ceased to index. What they index—and how—has also shifted significantly over the past three decades.

As the political movement attempts to create a Buraku subject that both recognizes and claims its Buraku subjectivity, it works to locate the Buraku, both as a physical location and as a character of being. The word *buraku* itself means "neighborhood" or, more rustically, "hamlet"; it refers to a particular physical location and to a generalized, spatial sense of human relation—a "community." Only since the early part of the twentieth century has it become a euphemism for stigmatized areas and even then only from Tokyo down south through Kansai and Shikoku, all the way to Kagoshima. In many parts of Japan, Hokkaido and Okinawa among them, *buraku* still only refers to a "neighborhood," not one necessarily marked by stigma. As we saw in the last chapter, it is that stigma that gives special character to some neighborhoods and affects how they are located with respect to nonstigmatized spaces within urban and rural settings throughout Japan. This stigma itself is located in different ways, both in terms of different practices and in terms of being given different material and symbolic anchors. In the work that locates stigma, the political and social possibilities of what it means to be Buraku shift. Similarly, the very locations that are made to hold a Buraku essence are transformed. Multiculturalism here can be thought of as a particular mode of locating such stigma, and thereby disciplining and shaping what it means to be Buraku.

The question of how Buraku are located involves, on the one hand, how they are physically located on maps. This is a type of knowledge that has preoccupied would-be discriminators, potential employers and marriage partners, and the private detectives they employ. On the other hand, this question involves how an essence of Buraku stigma might be located, and how the political movement locates it as it attempts to develop a Buraku subject that both recognizes and claims, without fear of repercussion, its status as Buraku. These aspects are related. The locating of an "essence" of Buraku stigma, of Buraku-ness, has had profound effects on the geospatial distribution of Buraku neighborhoods. In turn, the geospatial distribution of Buraku areas affects how people can locate them physically as well as conceptually.

In this chapter I couple two attempts to locate Buraku, both physically and essentially, as a way to examine the contemporary Buraku subject and how it sits within a tension between individual freedom and social obligation. Since the turn of the new century, environmental critiques of leather industries have gained unprecedented traction for reasons, I argue, related to how Buraku political organizations situate Buraku difference. Over the same span of time, private detectives, frequently employed by families or employers interested in preventing Buraku stigma from entering, have shifted the standards by which they judge someone Buraku. These two moments demonstrate the stakes of a Buraku difference becoming internalized. Tokyo is a particularly rich place in which to trace out these changing fields of contestation precisely because, as I mentioned in the previous chapter, it has no formally registered Buraku districts. Locating a Buraku in Tokyo relies not on direct state designation and authority, but on myriad other channels of authorization. Tracing these out shows the vast mesh of practices that serve to discipline and position Buraku essence.

TANNERY SLUDGE

Tanning is the transformation of animal skin to leather. Skin stripped from a slaughtered animal and cleaned is submitted to different procedures to eliminate meat, fat, and hair and to bind the proteins, preventing rot and

FIGURE 6. Chemicals draining from a tanning barrel.

increasing strength and durability. These procedures require the application of different chemicals, including sodium hydroxide, sodium hypochlorite, enzymes, lime, in the form of calcium hydroxide, chlorides, sulfuric acid, formic acid, ammonium salts, kerosene, and chlorobenzene agents. The resulting hide is then treated with chromium sulfate, mineral salts, and finally dyes to obtain leather. The effluent generated by this process contains large concentrations of sodium and sodium sulfides, lime, chlorides, caustic soda, and chromium III salts. When released into rivers, this effluent, as a whole, has been shown to have toxic effects on microorganisms: it inhibits the germination of plant life and decreases the fertilization rate of aquatic life. Lime can cause respiratory tract irritation, chemical bronchitis, and internal bleeding, and hexavalent chromium is a known carcinogen.

When not neutralized, this type of industrial effluvium, in rivers and in sewage systems, is exactly what draws the ire of environmental protection groups and city waste disposal engineers. It is also exactly what the outlying Tokyo neighborhood of Higashi Sumida, the only remaining tannery region in the Tokyo metropolitan area, has allowed to run off mostly untreated, day after day for the past ninety years, into a Tokyo sewage system incapable of treating it. Or, worse yet, this water also makes its way out through cracks in pipes and floors into the neighborhood ground and water table. Or, worst of all, it has, at points in the history of this neighborhood, run out through pipes that feed directly into one of Tokyo's largest rivers, the Arakawa.

However, despite the presence of an environmental movement in Japan that was robust during the 1970s and 1980s, despite the potential causticity of these chemicals, despite their urban proximity to 35 million people, and despite decades of their runoff into the dirt and water of east Tokyo, Higashi Sumida and the tanneries it houses have consistently escaped environmental critique and governmental censure—consistently, that is, until the first decade of the twenty-first century. In 2007 the first Tokyo metropolitan ordinance defining acceptable tannery effluent and requiring its filtration and neutralization came into effect, and it came into effect with huge ramifications for the Tokyo leather industry.

Why has it taken so long for the metropolitan government and otherwise eagle-eyed environmental groups to change the effluent standards of Higashi Sumida? Furthermore, if it has been left unproblematic for so long, why might now be the time for this to change? Unpacking how tanneries have become an object of environmental concern hinges on a question of how Buraku are located, and it reveals much about the spatialization of multiculturalism in Japan, tensions within liberalism between individual autonomy and social obligation, and about the status and future of the Buraku category of person. Given the lack of formally designated Buraku districts in Tokyo, asking whether a neighborhood in Tokyo is a Buraku, then, flips the question to: What exactly is a Buraku? What are the techniques different actors use to locate that stigma?

The Buraku people teeter on the knife's edge of environmental and social pollution. While stigmatized work such as tanning pollutes identities and damages bodies, it also, potentially, harms the environment. There has been much literature on environmental problems and the uneven distribution of their hazardous effects.[1] The Buraku situation, however, distinguishes itself in that the marginalized are not seen as the primary sufferers but, rather, as the primary cause of environmental degradation. The question hanging over Buraku pollution is whether it is merely a product of the actions of Buraku people, for example, leather production, or if it somehow inheres in the being of Buraku people and from there transfers to the products of actions, or through social relations to kin or neighbors.

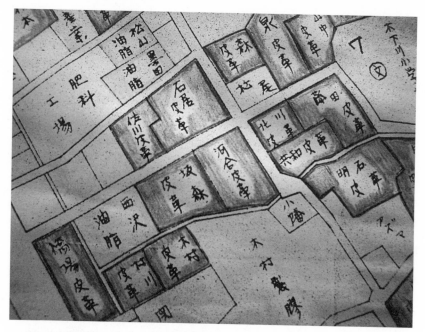

FIGURE 7. Close-up of a hand-drawn map picturing Kinegawa in the 1950s. The brown lots are tanners. The yellow lots are rendering facilities.

PROSCRIBING POLLUTION

As I described in chapter 1, Higashi Sumida, or Kinegawa, as it is affectionately called by some long-time residents, is a small neighborhood in eastern Tokyo filled with a variety of leather processing factories—tanneries, raw skin dealers, rendering facilities, independent leather shavers and dryers, and soap makers. The narrow streets are lined with old, dilapidated buildings made of corrugated tin, rusted and discolored from years of use and exposure to a variety of aerobic chemicals. The neighborhood is fairly cut off from the rest of the city; there is no direct subway or train access, and the buses run significantly less frequently than in the more fashionable western parts of the city. Higashi Sumida now sits as the leather processing heart of the Tokyo metropolis; other neighborhoods that have housed tanneries have steadily lost those industries. That same fate is now hitting Higashi Sumida.

At the time of my fieldwork between 2005 and 2007, there were approximately thirty-one leather-related factories of varying sizes in Higashi Sumida. None of these businesses had more than fifty employees. Most employed no more than ten people and focused on a small handful of tanning steps. The tannery in which I worked was a bit of an exception. It was on the largish side in the neighborhood; it had some twenty-two employees. What distinguished it from the other tanneries, however, was that it handled all parts of the tanning process. It took in raw animal skin and produced sheets of dyed leather, to be sent off to shoe factories to become insoles. It also produced very small quantities of white *"organo"* leather—leather dyed with only natural dyes, and on which the factory printed decorative images. These pieces of leather went mostly to bags and pencil cases. This scale of production was relatively rare in the neighborhood due to financial constraints; the costs of rent, labor, machinery, and maintenance make large-scale production almost impossible for these traditionally family-owned enterprises. The recent change in environmental standards further tipped the balance in the direction of impossibility.

The 2007 ordinance raised the water emission standards for leather-related industries in Tokyo. It imposed a stringent set of water purification demands, which meant that any factory expelling water from the tanning process would need a new filtration system that cost close to 100 million yen (approximately 1 million U.S. dollars). This ordinance had a huge economic impact on the tanneries, placing them under greater economic pressure and pushing an imperative to cut costs at every corner—including, potentially, not providing workers with masks or goggles. It also potentially shoves stigmatized and environmentally unsound industries off to China and India, thereby, though this is a different argument, projecting Japan's erstwhile caste system onto an international arena.

When this ordinance was announced in early 2006, owners of leather factories in this part of Tokyo began to hold weekly strategy meetings. This group of leather leaders foresaw three avenues of action: one, incorporate the majority of the small businesses in the neighborhood into one large corporation, strengthen the leather guild ties, and build a collective drainage and water purification system, dividing expenses among all the area factories and necessitating the coordination of fair billing and maintenance according to relative usage—a bureaucratically daunting task; two, spend the 100 million yen individually—an economically impossible task for most; and, three, after generations of involvement in this industry, give up, close up shop, and turn the children, who are decreasing in number and leaving the industry anyway, on to other professions. Of the thirty-one companies in the area, seventeen discharged some level of unacceptably polluting wastewater. These seventeen companies and the extended families that run them met multiple times over the next year, teasing out the best group and individual courses, deciding which of the three paths to take. It was eventually, only in late December 2006, and after much intense and impassioned debate, decided that each establishment would go it alone.

By the beginning of the 2007 new year, two of the seventeen factories were already making plans to close their doors for good. The rest, which have recently barely turned a profit in an industrial environment enervated by the ascendancy of China's industrial capability, its relatively lax environmental standards, and its summary draw of rawhide, bust out the budgeting pen in hopes of assembling start-up and maintenance costs to meet these new clean-water standards. They did this, however, without much optimism. Most of them flat out could not afford to install the new system and knew that this meant they would eventually have to close their doors or find another place, perhaps outside of the Tokyo metropolitan area, to conduct their business. When I returned to Japan in the summer of 2008, a year and a half after the enactment of the ordinance, seven of the original seventeen tanneries had closed their doors, and of the remainder, only three—including the one I had worked in—had installed water purification systems. The rest were running without permit under the threat of imminent forced closure, hoping to stay operating long enough to fulfill their standing orders. The passage and enforcement of this one ordinance radically transformed the space of Higashi Sumida, moving both industries and workers out of the neighborhood.

The owners and managers of these factories, while facing difficult economic decisions, did not in any serious way have their livelihoods endangered by this ordinance. Most of them had amassed funds for retirement and still owned the land and structures of the tanneries. The workers on the floor, however, faced much more dire straits. Some, such as Tanimoto-san (from chapter 1), have instead been forced back into an increasingly grim job market at the age of fifty, sixty, or older. There, whatever sense of professionalism or enhanced masculinity they may garner from their job is sapped of previous vigor. Professional skill is sacrificed at the start of a new profession, and affirmations of masculinity must be otherwise found, even as these men carry with them from the factory the lingering stigma of having worked in a polluted, and polluting, industry.

While the 2007 environmental ordinance was without recent precedent, that does not mean that it was without precursor at all. The two

FIGURE 8. One of the tannery filtration systems installed in Higashi Sumida.

preceding ordinances that did exist—one promulgated in 1892, the other in 1925—served as touchstones for the factory owners' approach to the ordinance of 2007. In the weekly strategy meetings among the factory owners, hosted by Tokyo's Leather Technology Center, in Higashi Sumida, the first ordinance was frequently talked about as the reason for the neighborhood's existence, and the second ordinance was referred to as the harbinger of decades of political ascendancy on the part of the leather industry. It had been decades and decades since these other ordinances were enacted, and yet they had a certain felt proximity to the discussion of the 2007 ordinance.

The section of Tokyo that holds Higashi Sumida has been devotedly leather focused for a relatively short period of time, only since the first years of the twentieth century. Prior to that, these areas were a mixture of swampy farmland and shogunate hunting grounds at the far eastern reaches of Edo, too far inland along the river to be of much maritime use, but perfectly situated for sportive field trips from the castle and rice cultivation. When the legal shifts following the 1868 Meiji Restoration emancipated the *eta* caste of caste restrictions and of a welfare-providing monopoly on animal-death-related industries, some of these erstwhile *eta* made use of their newfound geographical mobility and moved to locations where their skills could be used. At the turn of the century, with war brewing with China, followed by war with Russia, leather-working skills quickly became prized possessions in strategic urban areas, particularly Tokyo, Osaka, and Wakayama. At the forefront of this migration wave were tanners and leather workers from Shiga-prefecture, who, starting in 1872, moved to an area in Tokyo's Asakusa district, now called Shinya-cho. As wartime demand for boots and bags increased, and as routes and relatives were gradually more secured, the migration trickle turned into a flood. By 1887 the area now known as Shinya-cho was a booming leather center, replete with small-scale slaughterhouses, tanneries, and cobbleries—all parts of the leather production process and all within quick mutual reach. In contrast, what is now called "Higashi Sumida" contained then only three leather-related industries.

The localization of Tokyo leather changed dramatically with an 1892 ordinance, the *Gyojū Kaseijo Torishimari Kisoku,* or the Ordinance for the Regulation of Fish and Wildlife Rendering Industries. As part of an overarching push for a newly rail-enabled modernization and urbanization that did not include noxious leather factories at its heart, this ordinance gave the leather makers of Asakusa ten years to relocate farther out of the city. Their destinations were present-day Arakawa-ku and Higashi Sumida. Though they moved, they left traces in product form: while the tanneries have disappeared from Asakusa's Shinya-cho and Imado, less environmentally damaging and less viscerally animal-associated shoe stores and leather shops still line the streets of these neighborhoods.

As tannery owners found a damp reception in their new locations farther away from the city center, Kinegawa was at that time mostly a swamp, and subject to heavy flooding several times a year. There was a running joke among locals at the time that "if you want to learn to tan leather, you first need to learn to swim."[2] By 1910, the twenty-five tanneries running in Kinegawa joined in a larger push to have the city build a dike along the river. This push was successful, and over the next eighteen years, the city completed this project, eventually resulting in a dike 24 kilometers long, running from the Kita ward of Tokyo down to the mouth of the Arakawa. The dike radically transformed the space of Kinegawa. Flooding was no longer a problem; people could give up their swimming lessons. However, the dike was close to 400 meters wide. Building it decreased the overall space in Kinegawa by one-half. The number of farms in the area dropped, and leather- and animal-related industries came to dominate the burgeoning and cramped urban space. Tanning industries flourished in particular during the First World War, and were called on to produce leather goods for military use. By 1922, there were some sixty tanneries in Kinegawa.

The second ordinance that pushed for the relocation of these industries came just as the industries were solidifying their foothold under these demanding conditions. When the Great Kanto earthquake hit Tokyo in 1923, it destroyed huge portions of the city, resulting in close to 60,000 deaths. Kinegawa, however, was spared severe damages; some roofs fell in, but no one was hurt or killed. However, as Tokyo began to rebuild following the earthquake, the metropolitan government developed a new urban ordinance *(Shigaichi Kenchikubutsu Hō)* that governed land use in the Tokyo area. This new urban plan, passed in 1925, called for the transfer of all "dangerous or unsanitary" industries, such as tanneries or furriers, from the more central portions of the city out to areas such as Komatsugawa or Kasai closer to the mouth of the Arakawa river on the eastern side of the city. The ordinance gave these industries the fifteen-year span until 1940 to relocate. Around the same time, the Tokyo government conducted a survey of sanitation conditions in the city and reported that areas containing tanneries or rendering facilities released noxious smells and allowed polluted water to run off from their facilities into surrounding gullies or rivers, noting that conditions were particularly bad in the summers.[3] The government used this report of the polluting effects of tanneries to justify the urban zoning ordinance. This time, however, the neighborhood united against the ordinance. Leather workers banded together to form the Tokyo Leather Guild *(Tōkyō Seikagyō Kumiai)* and submitted a petition to the government in protest in 1930. After a prolonged fight reaching all the way to Diet and the Ministry of the Interior, the organized leather guild won the fight, securing the withdrawal of the ordinance in 1934. Unlike the 1892 directive, this time there was a thriving Buraku political movement equipped with the language of discrimination and an intimidating mass of angry people that forced this second ordinance into abortiveness.

Both of these ordinances were aimed at relocating leather production farther away from Tokyo's expanding center. The industries were understood to be both an environmental and a social pollutant, even if they provided necessary goods. This push for physical relocation locates Buraku stigma in space. It is the spatial proximity of the industries that threatens the modernizing metropolitan center. An industry must be close for ease of transport, but never too close, for fear of contamination.

The burgeoning political press of the early twentieth century, which grew and changed significantly over the next many decades, both forestalled environmental critique and, simultaneously, laid the base for its current iteration.

Forestalling

As I noted in the last chapter, in 1922, the Buraku people formed their first proper political organization, the Suiheisha (or Leveller's Association). A Tokyo branch was quickly formed later that year. Directed and composed entirely of Buraku people, this organization aimed at mobilizing people who "were stripped of their own living flesh as a reward for skinning animals."[4] With the birth of this movement, Buraku people mobilized against activities that were seen to intensify Buraku stigma—and the second Higashi Sumida ordinance was held as one such activity. The argument at the time was articulated in the movement's records from 1934 as follows: "Buraku people have long faced discrimination because other people erroneously believe contact with us will somehow dirty them. The critique of our labor as itself polluting does little more than replicate that fundamentally incorrect belief."[5] With this argument, the Suiheisha and its postwar successor, the Buraku Liberation League (BLL), coupled action and being. Following similar tendencies with a broader social circulation, this declaration linked types of activity with types of people, and then it proceeded to decry any perceived attack against Buraku people and industries as synonymously reprehensible. In response to such events, as I explore in more detail in the next chapter, they would, in the early days of the movement, gather huge numbers of people to confront offenders and have them apologize for and retract what would come to be called "discriminatory" critiques of Buraku industries.

At the same time the movement pursued these "denunciation sessions," it also used its growing political clout to bolster legislation protecting the domestic leather and meat industries. One example of this tendency is Japan's continued and unique protection of leather commodities. As I discussed in more detail in the previous chapter, in the early 1960s the United States began to use Japan's status as signator to the General Agreement on Tariffs and Trade (GATT) to call for the removal of protections on domestic goods. And, to a large degree, Japan complied: in 1960, some 41 percent of Japan's commodities fit with GATT's definition of "liberalized"; in 1961, that number jumped to

70 percent; and, by 1975, that number had reached 99.9 percent.[6] The only commodities still lacking the "liberalized" designation were lime, leather shoes, and cow, horse, sheep, and goat hide—each a commodity intimately tied to the leather industry. In protest of this protectionism, the United States appealed to GATT throughout the latter half of the 1970s, finally compromising in 1979 and entering into a special U.S.-Japan Leather Accord. In the proceedings for that accord, the Japanese representative gave several reasons for its protective stance toward the leather industry, among them: "Japan's leather companies have a peculiar history as Buraku industries and must therefore be protected."[7]

This nationwide tendency to protect the leather industry was particularly strong in Tokyo. The Special Measures Law delivered money to registered Buraku neighborhoods through the country, with only a handful of exceptions, one of which was Tokyo. In Tokyo, instead of Buraku neighborhoods, Buraku industries were recipients of money, and this legislative difference allowed for the birth and strength of the Tokyo Leather Guild, which provided a space for tannery proprietors to assess and express their common concerns and goals, including that of forestalling environmental critique. It also allowed for the continued existence of leather-working jobs, which were at that time in a position much stronger than they would be at the turn of the twenty-first century.

The capacity to forestall environmental critique, then, comes in two forms, both of which are grounded in a Buraku-led Buraku political movement robust throughout the majority of the twentieth century. First, the movement's struggle against Buraku stigma rendered it taboo, intimidating, or both for any non-Buraku actor to lodge a complaint against a Buraku-related industry. Second, the movement's concerted push for domestic protections around the leather industry resulted in just that—protections, which were particularly strong in Tokyo. However, that forestalling came with a built-in time limit. The set of laws that contributed to Buraku political ascendancy came to an end in 2002, along with a government proclamation that Buraku discrimination was officially over. Suddenly, then, the legislative door to environmental reform was opened, and the dwindling coffers of the BLL softened the threat of Buraku denunciation.

Base-laying

At the same time this burgeoning political movement provided fodder in a fight against spatial and geographical marginalization, it simultaneously paved the way for the current environmental critique of the tanneries of Higashi Sumida. The early political movement protested against the exclusion of Buraku people from full status as Japanese citizens and worked, through its "denunciation sessions," to demand that inclusion. After the war, as the movement started to make use of newly established international human rights mechanisms, this argument changed. The key words of "exclusion" and "harmony" shifted to that of "discrimination," and the key political subject shifted more and more from a national one to a universal human one, one equipped with inalienable rights that could, but should not, be violated. In the 1980s and 1990s, after decades of critique by other movements for their exceptionalism, the Buraku political movement started to develop a sense of commonality with other groups in Japan—the Ainu, the Okinawans, the Koreans—each recognizing the other as a co-minority. As this recognition strengthened, so too did the purchasing power of culture—as both a technique against discrimination and as an inalienable part of a minority identity. Throughout the last quarter of the 1900s, the movement had channeled governmental funds into improving neighborhood infrastructure, widening streets, creating community centers, and providing reasons for Buraku people to gather. In the cultural push, these reasons came to have a consolidated form: more often than not, they included traditional song, storytelling, and culinary celebrations of Buraku foods such as beef tripe stew. The attempt here was aimed at flipping the valence of hitherto denigrated Buraku activities to create a latch point for pride.

To provide an example for this broad gloss and suss out its characteristics, let us look at Yamamoto Shuhei, a man from a Buraku area in Osaka, a social worker and a student of traditional Japanese drumming, Taiko, as well as a subject of photographer Goto Masaru's collection, "Nihon-jin, Buraku-min: Portraits of Japan's Outcaste People."[8] Shuhei's description of his engagement with his drumming provides a prototypical example of this type of culture:

> Taiko has a huge impact on my way of living. When I started taiko at the age of 9, it was just "fun." But I started thinking seriously about it when a friend who plays taiko in a different group asked me, "Why do you play taiko?" Taiko is the traditional craft of the people alienated in Hisabetsu Buraku. It started with a wish of the local adults who wanted to offer an activity that their children could be proud of. Although I did not understand it well in my childhood, taiko was also a symbol of the liberation movement in which my parents and seniors fought against discrimination. Taiko introduced me to

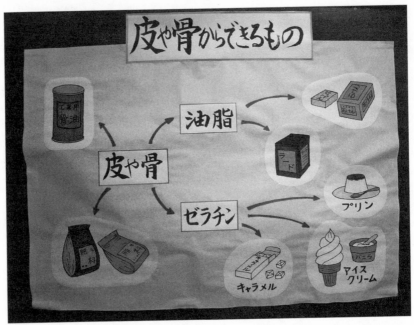

FIGURE 9. A picture of some of the everyday objects made from the hides or bones of animals on display at the Higashi Sumida Elementary School museum. Items shown here include industrial oil, fertilizer, soap, lard, and the gelatin used in caramels, ice cream, and pudding.

the way many such people have lived. I hope to continue living with their thoughts and feelings in my heart, keeping up my head and taking one step at a time, so my life marks a new path.[9]

One essential characteristic of the cultural identity in the type that Shuhei represents is the understanding that identity precedes cultural practices. Playing the taiko does not make Shuhei Buraku; rather, Shuhei *is* Buraku, and the leather-covered taiko drum is a vehicle for him to access a history of discrimination and struggle, and a vehicle through which to buoy himself against his own struggles.

Though a latecomer to this field of culture, the practice of leather making has recently become a similar locus of culture building. To give an example from Higashi Sumida: in 1998, the neighborhood elementary school closed for lack of students. In its stead, in 2000, a group of ex-teachers and members of the tannery guild converted one of the classrooms into a small-scale leather museum, showcasing the history of the leather industry in the neighborhood and teaching the occasional visitor about the tanning process. In

2002 the push for leather production as culture was bolstered with the United Nations' formalization of "Discrimination Based on Work and Descent," a new category of discrimination that provides the United Nations with mechanisms to recognize forms of labor as cultural identity.[10] This formalization provided the elementary school, and the practice of leather making, with a visitor of unexpected promise as the UN special rapporteur on racism, Doudou Diène, included a visit to the elementary school as part of his investigatory mission to Japan. In addition to a visit to the elementary school museum, the local political leaders also organized a tour of the area leather factories, a tour that has now become a standardized portion of the elementary school display. Dubbed *fi-rudo wa-ku* (fieldwork), this tour is now run once or twice a year by the Higashi Sumida Buraku youth group. It follows along the entire process of leather making in Higashi Sumida—from rawhide to finished sheets of leather to the jobs that I described in chapter 1. The tour guides, themselves frequently children of tannery workers and owners, provide tour goers with detailed descriptions of the tanning processes unfolding in front of them, and they do their best to cajole a worker here or there to step aside and talk about his or her work. The questions here typically range from those of technique and process to those of biography and health, inevitably including questions about that person's relationship with the Buraku political movement, a subject that came up not once in my two months of working on the factory floor. The Buraku that emerged from this picture and from that of Shuhei is of a subject, first and foremost Buraku, who can then elect to engage (or not) with these objects labeled "tradition" or "culture." The identity, here in the explanations and administrations of the political movement, precedes the practice. We can see a similar transformation in the discussion of Ushimatsu-shugi that I described in the previous chapter. In the explanations and administrations of the political movement, the Buraku is located in identity rather than practice.

The work of the political organizations, then, in contrast to that of the factory workers, became that of producing an identity, clad in the essentialized authority of an ontological state. If factory laborers, working through the demands of skins of animals, created leather, stigma, and pollution, the political workers, working through the demands of skins of representation, endeavored to produce a pure core identity that could be abstracted from the polluting realm of action. It was a constant source of struggle, however, to locate that core authentic identity and, more importantly for the political movement, to have people cast as Buraku claim that identity within themselves.

The current rally against this tannery sludge, and against the present geo-social distribution of Tokyo tanning industries, begins from a location different from that of its predecessors of a century ago. In between them lies a history of Buraku political mobilization, industrial protectionism, and Buraku cultural cultivation. On the one hand, this movement created a legislative armature that shielded the leather industry for decades. Although that armature is now crumbling under the pressures of neoliberal economic reorderings, another legacy of the movement remains more intact—namely, a widespread taboo in Japan against critiquing Buraku industries. The flip side of this taboo though is a now-hegemonic sense of Buraku identity as an ontological rather than a practical characteristic. And it is this final characteristic that provides an avenue for the 2007 environmental critique of Higashi Sumida sludge, even as it provides the grounds for increasing speculation about who may or may not be Buraku.

RUMOR, SMELL, AND EVIDENCE

If signs of Buraku have turned inward, away from visible markers embedded in odiferous and dangerous tannery work or embedded within state documents and into a state of authentic being, how might that being be tracked? As environmental critique advances, both as symptom and catalyst of a physical and conceptual relocation of Buraku, what are the tools by which those concerned with detecting Buraku go about that task? It is not just the liberation movement that worries about locating potentially hidden or hard-to-ascertain Buraku identity and pulling the inner Ushimatsu out in confession. People invested in whether their children are marrying a Buraku person and people concerned about hiring a Buraku person share similar worries. They talk about who is or is not Buraku and develop a means of identifying people as Buraku and ways of justifying that concern and talk. This type of talk, this type of circulation of information, is one that the Buraku political movement sees as potentially problematic.

The week before I started my apprenticeship at the tannery in Higashi Sumida, I went to my next-door neighbor's house for dinner. He and I lived in a small apartment complex in a neighborhood adjacent to Higashi Sumida. Our neighborhood itself lacked any animal-related industries, but it did house scrap metal processing plants and a waste recycling facility. These facilities, as recyclers of waste, stood in interesting contrast to the tanneries, as producers of waste, situated across the small river that separated our neighborhood from Higashi Sumida.

My neighbor was eighty-two years old and originally from a small town on the Japan Sea side of the main island of Japan. He had moved to Tokyo in his thirties for work after the war and had stayed there through retirement. The apartment complex we lived in was extremely inexpensive by Tokyo standards. We each rented a three-room apartment, with a toilet though no bath or shower, for close to 400 U.S. dollars a month. Within days of my moving in, most of my immediate neighbors, all of whom were older than sixty, had come over to welcome me with gifts of soba noodles and tea, and I had done the same in exchange. They were particularly interested in me as a new neighbor. This was the first time a foreigner had ever lived in this complex, and the first time they knew of a white American living anywhere in the neighborhood. It was at that time that I met Nakajo-san.

He and I both lived alone and quickly began spending time together. Within weeks of my moving in, we found ourselves eating together, doing laundry together, and going to the public baths together. He told me stories of having been in Manchuria during the war, and I told him stories of Texas. I think each of us was very glad for the other's company in a slow and mostly industrial Tokyo neighborhood that otherwise lacked many distractions. By the time I was set to begin my apprenticeship in September, I had already explained my research to Nakajo-san. I had told him that I was interested in the ways in which internationalization was affecting the Buraku political movement and Buraku industries. We had had several conversations about Buraku issues, and I had not noticed anything that might be called prejudice, other than a general sense that Nakajo-san felt it was a shame that Buraku people had to face such hardship. Several times he had referred to them as *kawaisou*, or deserving of pity. And yet that pity did not mean that he was comfortable getting close to Buraku difference.

When I told Nakajo-san that I was going to work at a factory to learn how to tan leather, he reacted with surprise. *"Eeh? Nani? Jo-san ha hontō ni sono yō na kusai tokoro de hataraku ka? Hontō ni kusai yo. Asoko de hataraitara, uchi ni haite ha naranai yo. Kusai kara. Shawa- wo abitara haireru kedo"* ("Huh? What? You're actually going to work in a smelly place like that? It's really smelly, Joe. If you do work there, you're not going to be allowed into my apartment, you'll smell too bad. Maybe if you take a shower first, but . . ."). His professed worry, half in jest, was that the pollution of the industry, in the form of an odor, might cling to me. Nakajo-san's comment might have been meant in jest, but it was a jest he continued. The first day I returned from working at the factory, I went over to Nakajo-san's house in factory clothes to see if he was ready to go to the baths. Nakajo-san saw me approach through his window and called out to me. He would be ready to go momentarily, I should wait just a moment. And, he added with a smile on his face, I should wait outside. Jest or not, Nakajo-san's reaction to my working in a Buraku industry points out several key characteristics of the promiscuities of Buraku pollution, of how Buraku people are located, and of the practical limits to the elasticity of this category of person.

Prior to working in the factory, I had not thought that I might be eligible for Buraku contagion; Buraku-ness could not be located in me. My very apparent non-Japanese-ness, combined with my economic and educational background, my citizenship, and my reasons for being in the factory, would, I thought, preclude anyone from ever asserting that I might be Buraku. However, based on Nakajo-san's reaction, I was subjected to an action that the political movement would, and did, when I mentioned it to them, recognize as Buraku discrimination. Was I more susceptible to Buraku stigma than I had supposed? Perhaps, but only slightly. What Nakajo-san's reaction did was point out the vast range of ways in which Buraku-ness can be located in different people. One person on the other end of the spectrum from me, in terms of susceptibility to contagion, was Tanimoto-san, or "*a-gu*," the newcomer to the factory whom I described in chapter 1. He was an older man, a Japanese citizen with little education, not from a Buraku; however, simply by working at the factory, he was susceptible to being labeled that way. The care he took with his hygiene at the factory and his constant use of gloves and masks even as he buried his head in the tannery barrels to pull out tanning hides bore testament to his desire to remain free both of the polluting substances of tanning but also of the polluting social substance of being Buraku. Another example of this is a Japanese friend of mine who worked as a freelance journalist. She was not Buraku, but she considered working at the Tokyo slaughterhouse, bagging intestines. She was sure that her parents would not mind, but she was worried that her in-laws would object. She thought it possible that she could later be seen as Buraku.

In contrast, take, for example, other people who are not nationally Japanese. The factory in which I worked had twenty-two employees, and the vast majority were Japanese. However, two in addition to me were visibly not. One man, in his late fifties, was from Bangladesh and had worked at the factory for five years. The other man, in his mid-forties, was from Ghana and had worked there for fifteen years. I asked both of them if they were ever looked at as Buraku. They said no—that instead people immediately latched onto their visible racial and ethnic differences. The man from Ghana was married to a Japanese woman. He said that, yes, his fiancée's family had objected to the marriage, but not on the grounds of his job. Rather, they were concerned with the fact that the children would be "*ha-fu*" ("half," meaning racially mixed). In these examples, in contrast to those involving Japanese people, the people involved in Buraku industries proved more resistant, in the contexts of marriage and daily social interaction, to the contagion of Buraku identity. They also appeared somewhat more resistant, arguably because of the different ways whiteness and blackness are marked in Japan, to that contagion than I. Black people were first and foremost black, whereas white people traveled unmarked as simply "foreign." In either of our cases, however, we were rendered exempt from the primary rigors of being Buraku through a national exclusion. Japanese-ness functioned as a presumed backdrop against which the drama of Buraku identity and discrimination might be performed. We were less susceptible to this drama because we were presumed not to be on that stage, in a way that contrasted with the experiences of Tanimoto-san or my freelance friend.

The technique of race *(minzoku)* offers an instructive contrast to highlight the Buraku investment in occupation, residence, and kinship. I refer to race here as a technique in order to locate it in social struggle rather than take it as a given thing in the world.[11] This technique recruits the concept of nature to its cause in order to authorize the ways in which it sorts people and thereby makes demands on them. In some of its original articulations, this technique was developed in concert with colonialism as a means of understanding human differences and justifying the enforced management of people categorized as different from those in colonial centers. Management and civilizing could happen to the extent that certain people were "naturally" amenable to such maneuvers. Recent critical race theory demonstrates race's quality as a social entity and examines the ways in which nature, as a similar social entity, is worked and reworked in being recruited to substantiate racial difference.[12] Within the United States, racial nature, as a human material and symbolic product, arrives in the guise of physical attributes ranging from skin color to bone structure to, more recently, genetic code. Numerous scholars have shown the ways in which race operates within Japan—ways that overlap and diverge with such uses of biological or genetic nature.[13] As race has been articulated in Japan, it has been tied to national belonging, mediated through categories of space and kinship, with the nation being cast as a metonymic extension of the family *(kazoku kokka)*.[14]

The Buraku category of person likewise draws on the category of nature, also linked to notions of kinship and space. Despite these similarities, the Buraku political movement has, until very recently, resisted mobilizing the category of race to describe its own situation, arguing that doing so would locate it outside the putatively racially homogenous Japanese nation-state.[15] It explicitly repudiated such a racial understanding of its situation in a 1965 report from a BLL deliberative council.[16] Over time, however, the movement has become more amenable to using the category of race. This shift is partially due to critiques that the BLL faced in claiming their Japanese-ness as the basis for not being discriminated against. This stance did nothing to critique discrimination against those who were not Japanese; even worse, this stance at times even advanced such discrimination. However, as the purchase of multiculturalism has grown in Japan, seen in solidarity work among such groups as the Buraku and resident Koreans, so too has the BLL's willingness to mobilize the category of race. The visit to Buraku organizations by Diène in 2005 is one example of the increased willingness on the part of the movement to utilize this category. Nonetheless, even as it volleys for an increased capaciousness of the category of race such that it might include the Buraku situation, it also questions the adequacy of this category and pursues other categories, such as "Discrimination Based on Work and Descent," that substantiate Buraku stigma in other terms.

Differences between race and the metrics that mark Buraku difference rise to the surface if we consider how each travels. Race, here ensconced in a particular form of biology, moves through kinship figured as descent. There is also the possibility of contagion by association, but any association not mediated by a relationship figured as biological can be challenged on biological bases. The Buraku category of person is considerably more promiscuous than this, mediated as it has been via the changing vectors of space, occupation, and kinship (figured as both descent and legal status). As we have seen, who can be seen as Buraku has changed dramatically over the past half century, as each of these vectors has transformed. These changes have complicated the political movement's goal to cultivate Buraku political subjects who both recognize and claim their Buraku difference. At the same time, these shifts have also entailed transformations in how the Buraku political movement locates the essence of being Buraku. The vectors that have underpinned Buraku difference have distinct qualities and histories that differently allow for them to index a Buraku identity, and that are remade as they bear the weight of substantiating a Buraku category of person.

To return to Nakajo-san's response to me working at a tannery, the other thing about his reaction that bears commenting on here is the precise thing that he objected to—namely, the smell.[17] As I stated earlier, tanneries use caustic chemicals, some of which are pungent to the nose. However, the firm belief that I would not smell the same, permanently polluted by my labor, was sustained not simply by people's understanding of the chemicals used in the tanning process. During my fieldwork, I interviewed many people who had lived near to but not in Buraku tannery districts. Without fail, every one of them commented on the characteristically bad odor of the area and its residents. In a similar situation, one of the tannery workers with whom I worked recounted a story to me one day of being made fun of at school for smelling bad. He said that he would scrub himself before leaving home in the morning to eliminate whatever odors from his father's tanning job or from his tanning neighborhood that might be lingering on him. However, the other kids would inevitably make fun of how he smelled.

In the first case—people remembering the smell of a Buraku neighborhood—there might be a causal connection between the density of factories and people's offended olfactory senses. However, as the second example indicates, that smell need not actually be present to index Buraku identity. Smell becomes consonant with Buraku identity. In some contexts, such as my conversation with Nakajo-san in which I had actually secretly bathed before I went to his house, the hint of being Buraku itself can be enough to provoke sensory justifications for avoiding Buraku people or places.

This trope—of Buraku people and places smelling bad—is one form of legitimizing Buraku discrimination. Similar to the critique that the environmental movement leveled at tanneries, it is not that Buraku people are not liked; rather, it is that their smell is not liked. In this justification, the relationship between tannery labor and odor becomes convoluted. The labor creates the odor, but as the aforementioned examples show, the odor indicates, and creates, someone who would work in a leather factory. This cultural story is linked closely to that of the environmental movement against polluting tanneries. Both rely on a notion of pollution stemming from action but are linked closely to the type of person. On the one hand, these kinds of association are taken up by the liberation movement as evidence of perduring, deep-seated prejudice. On the other, this kind of rumor is increasingly becoming the basis for institutions such as the private detective industry to determine who and where Buraku are.

As Buraku difference is increasingly channeled inward, non-Buraku people are turning more and more to private detectives with their concerns to root out telltale signs of Buraku people. In that process, the private detective agency, rather than Buraku individuals, communities, or organizations themselves, achieves the authority to determine the boundaries and locations of the Buraku. There are certain patterns to how non-Buraku people express their concerns about Buraku people, and there are particular tools that private detective agencies utilize to locate who is or is not Buraku. These patterns and tools, invested with the power to locate Buraku-ness, have changed over time.

The private detective industry offers background checks (*mimoto chōsa*) of individuals for anyone willing and able to pay the large sums of money required. Though such background checks are now illegal in a handful of prefectures, for example Osaka and Fukuoka, they occur with great frequency in the remaining prefectures and occasionally occur, under different names, even in the prefectures where they are no longer legal. According to a 2003 survey conducted by the BLL, background checks of potential marriage partners were the primary source of business for private detective agencies nationwide.[18] This same survey reveals that the people requesting background checks are typically not the fiancé or fiancée himself or herself but, rather, concerned parents or grandparents who want to know what kind of family is joining with theirs, what kind of person is coming into their family (*miuchi*). These people are worried about Buraku stigma and about the possibility that they or the future progeny of their family might eventually be taken as such. If the background check reveals that the potential partner is from a Buraku family, that information can be sufficient for parents or grandparents, particularly the kind who would pay for background checks in the first place, to oppose the marriage. In requesting an investigation such as this, families assert themselves as standing at a distance from Buraku stigma and coming from a different lineage, with different spatial and occupational affiliations, and they assert themselves as being potentially susceptible to contagion.

The standards by which the private detective industry determines whether someone is Buraku—that is, the way in which a substance or an essence of Buraku being is located—have changed over time, in part due to shifts in the three vectors that have undergirded contemporary Buraku identity for much of the twentieth century: occupation, residence, and kinship.[19] These vectors are deeply interarticulated in Japan: families have their traditional homes (jikka), forms of labor have been assigned particular places, and bloodlines have historical occupations. At the same time, however, each of these vectors has a different material and symbolic capacity to manifest Buraku stigma. As I discussed in the introduction, consider the person who, by blood, is not Buraku but works in a leather factory. Is that person more or less Buraku than the descendant of eta who now works retail at the upscale Ginza Wako department store? How might those people compare to the transplanted couple from Niigata who in search of cheap rent unsuspectingly move into a Tokyo Buraku district? At the root of these questions lies a difference in how these vectors authorize and evidence claims of Buraku stigma. Does identity inhere in the practices of labor and dwelling, or does it inhere in kinship ties of blood or law? Is it seen to unfold in a process, or is it given the weight of inward-oriented being?

The family registry system (koseki) in Japan, which was revamped in 1872 at the end of the Tokugawa period, was established to record addresses, births and deaths, and marriages of individuals in nuclear family units. These records also served as the basis for the administration and collection of taxes.[20] The registry system traces the lineage of eldest sons from the time of the system's inception. It also notes the neighborhoods in which the family has lived since that time. While this revamped system did not explicitly indicate one's previous feudal social status, some bureaucrats would annotate the registries of erstwhile eta and hinin to note that inheritance. Furthermore, with the recording of family addresses, the revamped registry system provided the means for tracking a person's historical relationships with neighborhoods that at one time may have held a meat or leather-related industry. These documents, which were publicly available until 1976 and thus accessible to potential employers or marriage partners, are still a primary focus, as we shall see later, for private detectives hired to research people's backgrounds,[21] and they have proved to be a major focus for the activism of those opposed to Buraku discrimination.

In a 2004 interview between a freelance journalist and a private detective, the journalist quotes the detective as saying, "The easiest way to figure out someone's background is to look at the *tsurigaki* (genealogy)."[22] However, the 1976 legal shift barred public access to official state family registries that provide information about a person's genealogy. Due to the successes of the Buraku liberation movement, these documents were placed outside the legal reach of private detectives and other third parties. With this legislative shift came a shift in the practices of private detectives. In a 1979 statement, Takeuchi, then director of the National Investigators' Network, indicated that, prior to 1976, standard practice in determining whether someone is Buraku had been to check back five generations, which could potentially be done through a family registry. The 1976 legal change made a five-generation search nearly impossible, and as of 1979 standard practice had become three generations, which one typically had access to simply by visiting the person's home address and asking strategic questions about grandparents. According to the private detective interviewed in 2004, the standard practice now is only one generation: "Barring access to [the *tsurigaki*], you can usually find out if you have that person's home address—go there and simply ask people. The neighbors typically know. We define Burakumin as anyone having at least one parent who is a Burakumin."[23]

At the same time the Meiji family registry system was established, the then newly unified Japanese government consolidated, named, and registered Tokugawa neighborhoods throughout the country. This consolidation provided the basis for a clear delineation between Buraku and non-Buraku neighborhoods that would-be employers or spouses could research and that could be tracked with family registries. It provided an additional way for people whose ancestors were not of *eta* or *hinin* designation to come to be seen as Buraku, that is, to become Buraku: if an otherwise non-Buraku person moved into a known Buraku neighborhood, their child would have the name of that neighborhood noted in the family registry and then could be seen as a Buraku. Furthermore, simply living in that area could serve to index one's status as a Buraku. As the tension between a principle of equality and a politics of difference mounted, there was a rise in the attempts on the part of people living in these areas, who lacked the means to move elsewhere, to obfuscate their family's geographical origins and any visible associations within the neighborhood with Buraku-identified occupations, a phenomenon I discussed in greater detail in chapter 2.

The Special Measures Law, enacted in 1969, consolidated even further this coincidence of neighborhood and social identity. In order to be considered for the multiple benefits of the Special Measures Law, a household had to be a resident of a "target area." In order to become a "target area," a neighborhood had to apply for a review and be formally designated a *dōwa chiku* ("harmony district"), which meant that it also had to render its neighborhood and household readily apparent as a Buraku to the government, to large businesses, and to potential marriage partners. In all, 4,603 target areas were eventually designated, and there have been scandals since then in which prominent businesses were found to be circulating lists of these neighborhoods in order to curtail the employment of residents. As a result of the heightened scrutiny involved in formally registering one's neighborhood, many potential "target areas" chose to forego the legal benefits. The BLL estimates that between eight hundred and one thousand Buraku neighborhoods, the *mishiteki-chiku* I discussed in chapter 2, chose to remain undesignated. In this move, the Special Measures Law served to concretize the relationship between space and the Buraku category of identity, providing one of the key objects around which the Buraku dilemma has formed.

The third criterion of Buraku groupness, that of occupation, has undergone significant changes over the past thirty years with the rise of neoliberal flows of industrial capital. This postbellum reconfiguration of transnational capital made it possible to outsource a host of Buraku-identified occupations such as animal slaughter or meat production, and it increased the possibility of imports that obviated the need for local cobbleries, tanneries, or drum workshops. Alongside the high rate of outsourcing of this type of industry, which I detailed in the previous chapter, there has been a similar increase in the number of foreign workers coming to Japan.[24] These workers, frequently from Brazil and Japan's former colonies in the Pacific Rim, desperate for work, and either unaware of or unconcerned about the social stigma that meat-industry occupations carry, have moved into these industries even as the industries themselves dwindle. With this progressive outsourcing of industry and the influx of foreign labor, more and more Buraku youth have moved into other employment sectors, and as a result they frequently find themselves moving from their family's traditional neighborhood as well.

Garbage collection and industry metal work are among the industries to which laborers have moved from leather tanning. With this move, they carry Buraku stigma with them and are changing the types of occupations seen as defiling, with new occupations such as scrap metal reclamation slowly taking on Buraku stigma. However, over the past twenty years particularly, the movement of laborers from Buraku neighborhoods has been so vast that there is less systematicity to the occupations into which they move. In this new situation, the relative weight of the three criteria that could point one out as Buraku is different; in this new configuration, one's occupation is less reliable an index of one's social categorization than familial ties to the Buraku category or place of residence. This difference in criteria is also one of visibility. Family association is a type of information an individual can control more easily than an occupation or a location of residence, especially after family registries became publicly unavailable in 1968. Under these circumstances, the risks of Buraku visibility seem more escapable, and the dilemma that the Buraku political movement faces becomes more pressing.

These shifts in the three canonical criteria of Buraku group membership—familial, spatial, and occupational association—entail a movement of the evidentiary base of the Buraku category of person away from forms of labor, such as meat production and leather production that came to be synonymous with Buraku stigma in the twentieth century, and more to one's relationship with land or kin. With that has come a greater reliance, on the part of detectives, on word of mouth. While the stigma is still linked to the family and the individual, it is here strongly mediated by space and by the narration of that space by its inhabitants and neighbors.

Despite the increasing focus on family neighborhood, family registry information is occasionally leaked. The extant 1976 law prohibits general access to family registries but allows access to lawyers, certain public officials, and tax accountants when deemed necessary. For the right price, these people have sold the family registry information to which they have access. The fact that access to this information is extremely limited grants such a leak the status of scandal, which, when combined with the fact that the individuals being leaked are either employees of the state or high-profile lawyers, makes it fine fodder for media attention. For example, an April 2005 edition of the Asahi Shimbun reported two public notary clerks in Hyogo prefecture illegally releasing the registry information of a woman and her parents in their jurisdiction.[25] Her status as a Buraku became evident in the process. In the three-year period from 2001 to 2004 there were 653 such cases reported in the national media from Osaka and Hyogo prefectures alone, approximately 200 cases a year. These scandals indicate that there still are people deeply invested in finding such information, reliant on the shifting measures by which Buraku are located.

The private detective agencies, which judge Buraku identity for a price, provide signs of two things projected as hidden. The first, for their paying clients, is evidence of a potential Buraku identity; the second, for the Buraku liberation movement, is evidence of a deep-set anti-Buraku prejudice that abides in Japanese society independent of the incidence of discriminatory acts. In recruiting the private detective agencies to this role of evidence, the BLL acknowledges the industry's authority to define who is or is not Buraku. This happens at the same time that it objects to that authority being at a distance from the individuals in question. Granting such authority to private detective agencies is abhorrent, then, for multiple reasons. It weakens the political movement both through the loss of people and in establishing the basis for non-Buraku actors such as the private detective agency to decide, with changing tools, how to locate Buraku.

THE WEIGHTS OF BEING

Political theorist Maruyama Masao tracked the shift from the Tokugawa rule to the Meiji rule as a shift from *de aru koto* (facts of being) to *suru koto* (facts of doing).[26] He argues that modernity is attained to the extent that subjects are granted the freedom to "use" their facts of being strategically, a process that he describes as uneven in the case of Japan. In contrast to life under Tokugawa, which Maruyama characterizes as having facts of being that exist independent of context and that rank types of people, the facts of being under Meiji instead become dependent on contexts. A hierarchy might exist within an organization, but it does not exist as a fact of life across all social institutions. Maruyama's stark dichotomy is a bit misleading, however. The shift he traces, and by which he judges Japan lacking, requires a transformation of "facts of being" as much as it requires a movement toward "facts of doing." In positing individuals who might "use" their social status strategically, Maruyama relies on and projects a notion of a voluntary individual. The understood seat of being shifts from social location to an internal state.

The work of anthropologist Elizabeth Povinelli opens the door to a similar diagonal cut across this stark dichotomy.[27] She allows us to recast this stark periodization with the argument that the attainment of liberalism does not consist in an increased freedom but instead in a remaking of the world in terms of a tension between the "autological subject" with capacities of self-determination and the "genealogical society" posited as restrictive. Following this line of thought, examining how Buraku stigma is located—in being or in doing, an opposition materially rooted in the channels of occupation, residence, or kinship—tells us much about the stakes of liberal multiculturalism in contemporary Japan and shows the effects as people negotiate the dual demands of freedom and constraint emergent in liberal governance.

The current object of the desire to purge the modern urban center of its necessary filth is not the Buraku people themselves but the waste by-products of what they do. Environmentalists and government officials alike can utilize Buraku identity to deflect their critiques of Buraku industry: they are not against a type of person, they are against a type of action. Likewise, as we saw in Nakajo-san's comments, it is possible to be against an odor, born of a type of labor, but not against those who carry that odor. This is a familiar refrain; it is a refrain that drives a wedge into the Suiheisha's assertion of the coevality of action and being. However, possible though this avenue of critique may now be, it is still a precarious one: an odor born of labor clings and pollutes a person; in critiquing the tannery sludge, the environmentalists have charged factory owners and managers with onerous financial tasks, in the end leaving factory laborers without the labor that has for decades supported them. Environmentalists and private detectives alike teeter on the edge of being accused of discrimination, and they teeter on the edge of their own moral imperatives. And here the refrain changes: What if being against a type of action actually destroys both a type of people and a type of place?

The ways in which Buraku are located, physically and conceptually, are shifting. Both the changing grounds of environmental critique and the shifting tools with which the private detective industry pursues Buraku are symptom and catalyst of this transformation. With these shifts in the location of Buraku, different political possibilities and anxieties, as well as different forms of life, are engendered and distributed among Buraku and non-Buraku actors alike. A central tension in this shift is between the confines and freedoms of an authentic, inalienable identity created and bolstered in work. The next chapter examines this tension in the work that the Buraku political movement does to cultivate a public properly attentive to human rights.

FOUR

A Sleeping Public

BURAKU POLITICS AND THE CULTIVATION
OF HUMAN RIGHTS

SOMNOLENT ATTENTION

On a Saturday morning in December 2005, Tomonaga Kenzō leaned into the microphone before him and lightly cleared his throat. The large, windowless auditorium in Osaka grew quiet as attention focused on the director of one of the foremost political organizations of the Buraku people. The director of the Buraku Liberation and Human Rights Research Institute (BLHRRI) offered these introductory words:

> I want to thank you all for making the time in your busy schedules to attend today's symposium. We are gathered to witness an historical moment. The United Nations has recently recognized a new category of discrimination: Discrimination Based on Work and Descent. This category is the culmination of years of work on the part of the Buraku Liberation League and partner Dalit organizations. It will allow us to represent Buraku issues internationally not in terms of race or ethnicity but in terms closer to Buraku experience. This will give us further leverage to fight discrimination here in Japan; likewise, it provides us with the opportunity to gather together with partners from across the world to fight this form of discrimination together. We have the opportunity to advance human rights in this struggle.

Organized by BLHRRI in partnership with the International Movement Against All Forms of Discrimination and Racism (IMADR), this public forum was the culmination of a visit to Japan by three foreign dignitaries, each of whom worked on aspects of this newly recognized form of discrimination. Sukhadeo Thorat, from India, was a scholar of Dalit issues; Abdul Kamala was a graduate student in Kenya working on caste issues among different African tribes; and Chinsung Chun, of Korea, was the newly appointed

FIGURE 10. Leaders of the Buraku liberation movement and foreign dignitaries gathered to discuss "Discrimination Based on Work and Descent."

UN special rapporteur on "Discrimination Based on Work and Descent." Over three days, these foreign guests had toured Buraku neighborhoods, had been treated to traditional Buraku food, had met with political leaders, and had learned the history of Buraku issues across Japan in general and more specifically in the neighborhoods they visited. On their final day, they were the featured speakers of this public forum—all spoke about their impressions and about how the situation in Japan compared to forms of work- and descent-based discrimination in their home countries. The month following this public forum, synopses of the presentations, written by the IMADR staff, were circulated in the IMADR Japanese language newsletter, the *JC Tsūshin* (Japan Committee Missive), to over 1,000 domestic recipients.

Announced at this public meeting were the latest steps in this politics on an international level: the consolidation of the new United Nations' human rights mechanism—"Discrimination Based on Work and Descent"—fought for with the goals of strengthening international ties of solidarity and bolstering domestic support for antidiscrimination legislation. At the same time, the forum was an optimistic enactment of its descriptive content. It presented in its execution the engagement of the United Nations. It offered, in the demographics of its speakers, paths to new solidarity. It also, in being presented to an audience of over two hundred people and farther out across websites and newsletters, was a volley into the future political possibilities of this momentous achievement. This was not simply an event that allowed for new political solidarity among already committed political activists; it was an event intended to rally a public to political and social change.

The public it most immediately addressed, however, was fast asleep. As I sat in the auditorium that December morning, I let my attention slip away from the reports of the foreign guests and comments by the Buraku movement leadership to examine the people in attendance. Two of the 203 people present were IMADR staff (myself included), and ten appeared to be college students: six women and four men, around twenty years old. The remaining 191 people appeared to be Japanese men between the ages of twenty-five and sixty-five, all wearing suits on a Saturday morning. Even more striking than the proportion of ties, however, was the proportion of closed eyes and bobbing or hanging heads. At one point during the two-hour forum, I counted 154 people with eyes closed and heads hanging. Over the course of my internship with IMADR in the following two years, the sight became even more striking: the sleepers were not limited to one particular event; they were present, in large numbers, at every similar public forum. This one slumbering audience was a sample of a larger public assembled around and by some discursive object "Buraku," but a sample they were: the sleepers were endemic to a wider public addressed by this political movement.

A sleeping public—at first blush, such would seem a contradiction in terms. As the cultural and literary theorist Michael Warner argues, publics are constituted by attention, the turning of the sensory apparatus toward something, the focusing of one's consciousness on that thing.[1] But in sleeping, consciousness is lost, and volition is abandoned. At the human rights seminar, the sensory apparatuses are let loose precisely at a moment meant for them to be roused in the struggle for social and political change. Yet, at the same time, each of these people has paid money to attend, and all have made an active decision to step into this room on a Saturday. The political movement might count these people in their annual reports, as a sign of success; similarly, high attendance fills the coffers of the movement. But, at the same time, the political movement is faced with unconscious bodies precisely at a moment when it is attempting to rally public support. These people might be present, but they are asleep.

This chapter examines this disjuncture between presence and sleep to understand the different ways in which attention is assessed, cultivated, and disciplined. The previous chapters have examined the production of Buraku difference and its political stakes; this chapter focuses on how the social movement cultivates attention to those signs of Buraku identity. As much as the Buraku political movement must create a Buraku subject aware of and invested in its Buraku difference, its goals of total liberation *(kanzen kaihō)* also require the cultivation of a public attentive to and working against Buraku discrimination. Philosopher Jurgen Habermas,[2] in line with other thinkers such as John Dewey,[3] argues that publics take energy and effort to cultivate and maintain. They can lie "latent" until properly mobilized— present but sleeping—until the structures that support them "begin to vibrate."[4] Habermas and Dewey do not, however, linger on how exactly that vibration happens. Warner stresses how assembling a public relies on garnering attention, but he, similarly, does not ask how attention is cultivated or sustained, nor does he leave room for contention around what might constitute attention. In the human rights seminar, the Buraku political movement has a public that attends but does not seem to attend to. The gap here between presence and wakefulness illuminates the fact that a public is always a project, one that requires disciplining its members into a particular form of attention. The Buraku political movement attempts to cultivate a public that is not simply behaviorally compliant but that demonstrates an interiority capable of authentic volition. It is in specific projects such as these that human rights, touted as a universal, come to life.

The origin of the sleepers highlights the trajectory of this project. For the most part, these men are non-Buraku employees of companies that have been the subject of another Buraku political tactic, the denunciation session. During a denunciation session, or *kyūdankai,* large groups of Buraku activists gather to publicly decry perceived discrimination, whether by an individual or by institutions such as corporations or government offices. Donning brightly colored headbands and placards, the participants in a *kyūdankai* gather at strategic locations—a perceived discriminator's place of employment or home, a corporate headquarters—and yell coordinated chants, drawing public scrutiny as a means of compelling an alleged discriminator to reconsider their actions. Developed in the 1920s as an alternative to pursuing state aid, the *kyūdankai* quite explicitly demands attention—of the people it addresses and of the wider public from which it hopes to provoke critical scrutiny. Those denounced—individuals and employees of corporations alike—go on to serve as a key constituent of the public addressed by the Buraku movement in their human rights seminars. It is there, even as they are tracked in annual reports and bring in money to the movement, that they are met with expectations of authentic, volitional engagement. When and how these expectations emerge, how the political movement counts the sleepers as insufficiently or sufficiently attentive, says much, I argue, about the staging of volition within publics and about the current form of liberation politics and liberalism in Japan.

The sleeper, straddling the denunciation session and the human rights seminar, invites us to ask, more generally, how do human rights achieve a universal moral authority? As a sleeper moves from someone directly denounced by a second-person pronoun to someone hailed by the wide anonymity of a first-person plural, the pedagogical project shifts, as do the qualities of attention demanded of them. The Buraku political movement finds itself attempting to maintain the sense of urgency that accompanied second-person address, even as it works in the idiom of universality. Its project is to cultivate qualities of attention—assemblages of bodily comportment, cognitive engagement, and ethical orientation—in such a way that attention comes with signs of being volitional and authentic. These two seemingly different modes of attention, linked in the history of the Buraku movement, prompt questions about how boundaries are drawn between coercion and volition. It likewise turns our gaze to the kinds of discipline involved in inclusion.[5] The linkages between these two tactics, joined in the figure of the sleeper, offer insight into how the ideals of human rights—of a free and equal, dignified human subject—are cultivated and formed within Buraku politics. Rather than critique the sleepers as failing to be the proper political subject, I instead follow the traces of the sleeper back from the human rights seminar to the denunciation session to ask what kind of political movement finds itself in an address to a somnolent public.

PUBLIC SLUMBER

Inemuri—to be present but sleeping. The existence of this lexeme in contemporary Japanese suggests that "present sleeping" is a phenomenon so common, and so commonly commented on, as to warrant a ready shorthand. Cultural historian and anthropologist Brigitte Steger makes such an argument as she traces out a culturally based set of rationales for public sleeping in Japan.[6] In making her point, she follows a well-publicized bout of Diet members sleeping in televised Parliament sessions. Steger describes a series of articles published in 1997–98 by the Japanese weekly *Shūkan Hōseki*, in which reporters charted what they labeled some of "the greatest sins of politics and bureaucracy that damage Japan." These articles berate the Diet members for "being lazy" or "insufficiently devoted to their jobs" and include not-uncommon pictures of Diet members sleeping during sessions, as well as responses from the Diet members to written challenges of this behavior issued by the *Shūkan Hōseki*. In their responses, the members of Parliament ignored the charges, dismissed them as false, or explained them as symptomatic not of a lack of attention to the job but, rather, the opposite: "tight schedules and heavy workloads at night," that is, overzealous devotion to work.[7] Their arguments, then, were that sleep itself, not simply paying to attend or being physically present, might actually count as a form of attention—a tribute to the extractive capacities of capitalism as much as it might signal their limit.

Steger provides a sociocultural substantiation of this justification, referencing a boom in books in the 1990s that describe the benefits of work-time sleeping[8] and citing a set of traditional sayings[9] and millennia-old Confucian and Buddhist injunctions in favor of diurnal naps. While the articles from the *Shūkan Hōseki* indicate that sleeping on the job can be the subject of castigation, Steger's analysis makes clear that there are also readily available, circulating arguments justifying such sleep. Indeed, the participants in the 2005 human rights seminar made use of such justifications. While it was difficult to gain access to any of the sleepers—they hurried in and out of events—the few with whom I spoke indicated that they were doing this for their job. They did not indicate whether they slept out of disinterest, exhaustion, or resistance; instead, they indicated that this was yet another task added to already busy schedules. In any case, their sleep still remained a quandary for the political movement, which was pressed to understand this either as a sign of over-attention or under-attention.

Despite the prevalence of arguments justifying sleep as attention, other events in which the Buraku leadership participates render slumber questionable as a form of participation; slumber is notably not present at all events in which BLHRRI and IMADR participate. For example, in early 2006, the IMADR and BLHRRI representatives took part in an open forum to discuss the upcoming restructuring of UN human rights organs. Amnesty International, in cooperation with IMADR and the Tokyo-based United Nations University, spearheaded the organization of the event, which involved over two hundred participants from a wide range of Japanese nongovernmental organizations (NGOs) as well as the United Nations. In this setting, unlike in the December public forum, the audience was awake, actively taking notes and disputing points, and offering questions and opinions during the question-and-answer session. The public audience here was primarily comprised of NGO representatives, whose professional and ethical senses of self hinged on proactive participation. For the Buraku leadership, this grouping of people indicates the promise of the public it addresses. And as aspiration, it also serves as a measure against which sleeping members of that public are problematic. The IMADR leadership left the plenary session invigorated, hoping to, as one member of the IMADR executive team put it, "get the same level of excitement at all our events." Slumber as attention, in moments like these, is found lacking; when weighed against this type of engagement, presence, for whatever money and aggregate numbers it might bring in, is not enough.

The social qualities of slumber are even more problematic, however. Public slumber does not solely disrupt the promise of participation; it also carries with it overtones of a gendered hierarchy that stand in direct opposition to the mission of IMADR. Lack of seniority combines with gender to disqualify some—women and relatively junior men—from public slumber. Indeed, one of the characteristics of being junior or of being a woman, to the extent that these statuses are extricable from each other, is an inability to sleep without censure.[10] Inasmuch as every proscription entails a complementary prescription, women, then, must be alert all the time. Left are the male executives, those more likely to be higher-level managers, the CEOs, and the bosses. These men are the people who face no chastisement if they fall asleep during a meeting and indeed assert authority and masculinity precisely through the exercise of sleep.[11] Sleep, as a cultivated, learned form of attention, possible in the face of anonymous address, brings with it these overtones of a masculinized privilege of seniority.

The slumber of the businessmen in the face of Buraku address, then, even if it is understood as a form of attention, carries other overtones that are inimical to IMADR's mission. Indeed, after the December event, one of the head organizers of the seminar lamented to me that while the event had been well attended, "it seemed like most people were not paying attention," and she worried that "perhaps we should be doing something else." Others, when I asked them, saw slumber as problematic but appeared to be more resigned: "Yes, it is a problem, but what is to be done?" The problem of the sleepers here incriminates the people slumbering, but it also indicts the tactics of the political movement for being insufficiently capable of rallying attention.

The leadership of the liberation movement discusses how to catch and keep the attention of its audience. Working on multiple fronts simultaneously—trying to effect legislative change, build international solidarity networks, and transform domestic consciousness—the movement attempts not only to clamp down on discrimination but, more fundamentally, to root out the mind-set that gives rise to discrimination. Tomonaga Kenzō, whom I first introduced in chapter 2, has played a key role in shaping the projects, conversations, and minds of Buraku leaders for decades. He has served as the director of BLHRRI and has been on the board of directors of IMADR. In his written work, he elaborates the role of education in transforming "discriminatory social consciousness."[12] He argues, and these arguments have shaped the direction of the political movement, that through "social education" people can come to understand the ways in which they, intentionally or inadvertently, reproduce discrimination. Only through such burgeoning recognition can people become both more inclined and able to transform their behavior, a necessary step toward the movement goal of "total liberation" (kanzen kaihō).

Social education, a key component of the liberation movement's set of strategies, requires reshaping one's attention and crafting a different sensory and ethical orientation to one's self and environment. This understanding allows the Buraku leadership to recontextualize the sleepers; rather than being a testament to the failure of the movement, these sleepers can be seen as a "sleeper cell" of sorts, an initial stage in a longer trajectory of social change. They are a problem as they remain asleep, but at least they are present. They are a not-yet-finished aesthetic project, in need of disciplinary intervention, to be guided to the aspirational public of full attention unplagued by gendered hierarchy.

TACTICS OF ATTENTION

This social education, as described by Tomonaga, requires catching, cultivating, and maintaining the volitional attention of a population that currently chooses to be inattentive. Addressees must be disciplined into being the types of people who would, volitionally, choose to be attentive. This social project relies on interpretive regimes through which qualities of attention are judged, weighed, and manipulated.

The canonical literature on publics is less concerned with the qualities of attention than the simple presence or absence of that attention. Reiterating Habermas's assertion[13] that mere presence is sufficient to constitute participation in the public sphere, Warner argues that, in effecting a public, "the cognitive quality of that attention is less important than the mere fact of active uptake."[14] Whether it is a person multitasking at a computer while reading Warner's article, someone watching television while vacuuming the living room, or a person who happens to wander into range, on the way to the bathroom, of a speech being made from a podium, each of these people, through sheer presence, by "coming into range," fulfills "the only entry condition demanded of a public."[15] Even more pertinently here, Warner contends that "it is even possible for us to understand someone sleeping through a ballet performance as a member of that ballet's public, because most contemporary ballet performances are organized as voluntary events, open to anyone willing to attend or, in most cases, to pay to attend. The act of attention involved in showing up is enough to create an addressable public. Some kind of active uptake, however somnolent, is indispensable."[16]

There is, as we have seen, a pragmatic difference between a somnolent and a waking Buraku public. What counts as attention, the qualities through which that attentiveness exhibits itself—whether hierarchized somnolence or active engagement—serve as potential grounds for affirming or disparaging the political goals of the BLL, grounds for qualifying or disqualifying a public. Warner's own example opens this point: while the ballet company, keen on tracking attendance to report to donors and on selling tickets to recoup costs, might count a slumbering audience member as present, attentive, and therefore part of its public, the husband of that sleeper, who has perhaps planned this evening months in advance, might not so readily count his wife's sleeping figure appropriately attentive or as a member of the public. The types of qualities, whether somatic orientations or monetary transactions, that count as attentiveness depend on the interpretive regime brought to bear on the situation and the means by which particular modes and qualities of attention are exacted from those who serve as a public.

The anthropologist Thomas Csordas makes a similar point in his discussion of attention as he argues for taking "a measured step toward filling out embodiment as a methodological field," in complement to a "semiotic" view of the body that he characterizes as working more in terms of textual representation.[17]

While I reserve the term "semiotics" for an understanding of sign phenomena not limited to representation,[18] I am interested, like Csordas, in the social and historical forces that constitute different modes of attention. I stress, however, that such embodiment is always embroiled in a terrain of social contestation, which may or may not be linguistic, and is adjudicated through interpretive regimes, around what counts as attention and who has displayed it when. Through particular pedagogies and debates, people are disciplined into particular forms of attentiveness. Unpacking the social constitution of attention, how precisely people are expected to demonstrate "involvement within [a] situation,"[19] opens analytic inroads not simply to the *exclusions* entailed by a public[20] but to the intricate demands that *inclusion* places on those summoned to attention.

Examining the constitution of attention, which arises from the demands of different interpretive regimes, demonstrates the disciplines of inclusion and also demonstrates the constraints that give rise to volition. Warner argues that "wherever a liberal conception of personality obtains, the moment of uptake that constitutes a public can be seen as an expression of volition on the part of its members. . . . [This] allows us to understand publics as scenes of self-activity, of historical rather than timeless belonging, and of active participation rather than ascriptive belonging."[21] In spelling out how uptake is demanded, disciplined, and debated rather than simply assumed, we gain greater insight into how a liberal conception of personality comes to have force, not simply whether it obtains.

THE CAPACIOUS "WE" OF HUMAN RIGHTS

The December forum was akin to what sociologist Erving Goffman describes as a "podium event."[22] Multiple speakers, including Tomonaga, the three visitors, and the secretary general of the BLL, took turns at the mic, explaining the history, significance, and potential future of "Discrimination Based on Work and Descent," followed by time for questions and discussion. During the forum, the audience was called on to "appreciate remarks but not reply in any direct way"; indeed, the audience gave the floor but, except during the question-and-answer session, rarely got it.[23] The financial, spatial, and auditory setup of the event intensified this unequal structure of presenter and audience. While the presenters were paid for their participation in air travel, hotel accommodations, and meals, every member of the audience had

¥2,000 (approximately 20 U.S. dollars) paid toward their attendance. Similarly, the stage was the locus of the majority of the microphones and audience seats, which were bolted to the ground, that expanded out from the stage in concentric arcs. Those recruited into the role of audience members found their bodies directed toward the stage physically, visually, and auditorally. They also found themselves less authorized to inhabit the role of presenter. They had expressive power as an audience—indeed, sleeping itself is one form of feedback—but less power to individually command an audience.[24] The pedagogical impulse of this setup is evident: the people on the stage are cast as having greater information and authority to distribute that information than the people in the audience.

The event organizers did much to recast this event, not as one based on this fundamental difference in two roles of interaction but, instead, as one of conversation among equals, seeking to capacitate choice and authenticity as the driving factors of participation. Wireless mics were available for all participants during the event and prior to the event, the organizing staff had tested the acoustic speakers to make sure that the sound blanketed the space evenly, working to diminish the auditory effect of unidirectionality emanating from the stage. In the spatial and auditory setup, the staff members strove to affirm the opportunity for any participant in the event to assume the role of presenter. They sought to project uniformity across the actors, and to deemphasize the differences between audience and presenter. These two orientations sit alongside each other, at times uncomfortably and at times indicative of a trajectory of "social education." In the eyes of the organizers, the promise of the event was to educate people sufficiently so that they might eventually join in the "we" as authentic, volitional equals.

Rhetorically, Tomonaga's call for attention while opening the forum came in the form of an equalizing universal. His use of the first-person plural "we" expanded out in concentric arcs, including the leaders on the stage and those assembled in the audience, extending to the nation, but then beyond—to nations united and the boundaries of the human. The content of his message presented a reasoned appeal to ethical commitments projected as universal. This universality is a performative achievement, or at least an attempt at one. In the background of its potential success is the ability of the message to be "excerptible,"[25] that is, for the message to be presumable as direct discourse with consistent referential content across divergent arenas of action.[26] Human rights were a presupposed good, the end of discrimination posited as a common goal—this knowledge and the ethical commitment required to decipher the meaning of his words were performatively projected as universal.[27] Proper attention here involves choosing to fulfill these universal ethical obligations.

The organizers use the term *ooyake* to describe the public attentive in this way. In the newsletters, e-mails, and websites advertising these events, the movement leaders use the phrase *"Kōkai Shimpojiumu"* or "Public Symposium." The two Chinese characters that make up the term *kōkai* are, first, *kō*, also read *ooyake* (which, by itself, means "public"), and, the second, *kai* or *hiraku* (which means "open"). Drawing on the work of historians Mizoguchi and Yoshida, sociologist Eiko Ikegami traces the usage of the term *ooyake* in Japanese back to the seventh century and argues that for the duration of its use, this word has indicated a sense of "horizontal commonality," even when used to describe different planes of hierarchical social arrangements.[28] IMADR and the BLL use this term to refer to all of their activities that include potential strangers. It implies a sense of openness, being inclusive not just of any particular person reading the message but of an indefinite set of others, a projection beyond physical readership. The language ideology and the material ideology in effect here are consonant: horizontal commonality is presupposed as prior to mediation.

In the preparation for this event, one of the key organizers and administrators at BLHRRI distributed an internal memo to those helping plan the event. This memo included a time line of the different events across the visit of the international guests, both in Japanese and English. In the description of the *Kōkai Shimpojiumu*, the administrator had estimated the potential attendance of the event (*"ippan sanka yotei 200nin"* or "general attendance est. 200 people"). The attendance estimate, *"ippan sanka yotei,"* comprises six characters, the first two of which constitute a commonly used lexeme: *ippan*. This word can be translated as general, but it is also frequently translated as meaning "public" itself, as in *"ippan kara no akusesu"* or "public access," or *"ippan kara iken wo tsunoru"* or "to gather public opinion." This alternate term to describe the group of people who might attend the event also implies a sense of openness, along with one of generalizability—a sense of equality across constituent parts, and a sense of a mass noun rather than a count noun to describe a gestalt whole.

The internal memo, as well as the more widely circulated newsletters and billets, described the presentations of the different international guests as *"kōhyō"* or "public announcements." The word choice to describe the presentations or "public announcements" relied on the character *ooyake* (also read *kō*), though this time in combination with *hyō* or *arawasu* ("to describe"). The use of this term, in contrast to the comments made by the visitors during their tours of different minority neighborhoods, perhaps described as *"hatsugen"* or "statements," also implies a sense of officiality. The presentations, then, are open, relatively official descriptions, proceeding outward from one person into an indivisible mass of perhaps unknown people who have chosen to be there. In reality, these statements very much proceeded from a place of individual sincerity: Thorat and Kamala in particular were invited to "share their thoughts and opinions on what they had seen over the prior days," which stood in contrast to the request to Chun to report on the status of UN policy on this new form of discrimination. In the description of the event, and in the actual event itself, authority was simultaneously constituted through the invocation of a large anonymous public[29] and through the invocation of individual experience.[30] It is important to note here too the relationship of the present public to the one projected in the circulation of the newsletters. The first public, the one present at the event, is taken to be a stand-in for this larger public. There is a sampling effect happening here, in which those in attendance who potentially take their learned lessons home with them index countless others who are potentially susceptible or amenable to the forum's message. The possibilities and challenges of the entire group are indexed and held by this smaller group.

The public of the human rights forum, then, is one ascribed to a collective of unidentified strangers, vested with the potential qualities of both impersonal officialness and personal authenticity, and laden with the optimism of political change. The group of people delimited by the public, including those who are doing the majority of the organizing and publication, is envisioned to be equally engaged in voluntarist efforts to combat discrimination and "to change things." There is a temporality here marked out by the circulation of the newsletters and the occurrence of public forums and other trainings governed by an overarching expectation of education based on sharing and working together. The foreign guests were not the only people to speak at this event. The mixture of personal and impersonal speech opened up the possibility for other actors to speak as well. Organizers from the research institute and from IMADR also spoke, as did representatives from the different companies whose employees were so visibly in attendance. Beyond these people stood the further possibility of anyone else potentially speaking, just as anyone could theoretically contribute to the newsletters of the movement. This was a collective of people advancing together in the steady stream of education with the shared goal of effecting social change through the discourses and the practices of human rights.

It is this pedagogical project that opens the door for the sleeper, and for slumber as a form of attention. Abstract and universal, public address here leaves open space for someone to be attentive at some moments and not at others—to be present but sleeping, even as the movement attempts to instill in its addressees an ethical orientation that would obligate them to tune in. The sleeper, then, indicates trajectory and trouble. It calls into question the current ethical commitment of those present: "It seemed like most people were not paying attention." But he (for that is what *he* is) does more than that: the sleeper also provokes questions about the effectiveness of movement strategies and, particularly when considered in light of their origin, worries that the sleeper, present though he may be, might never awake.

THE INESCAPABLE "YOU" OF DENUNCIATION

While the Buraku liberation movement has utilized public forums since the 1960s, it has used the *kyūdankai*, or denunciation session, since the early parts of the twentieth century as part of its strategy to eliminate discrimination. Developed with inspiration from Confucian forms of self-critique and consciousness-raising, these denunciations harnessed anger and umbrage to publicly castigate—with screams and brightly colored placards—offending others. Replete with a flair for public drama, these denunciation sessions were to foment the shame of public scrutiny and compel an offender's self-critique. This tactic gained the movement's attention, but as a political presence both forceful and fearsome. It was explicitly based on consciousness-raising techniques, and it carries those overtones into the human rights forum, contrasting with the ideology of this second public. As I outline later, the denunciation tactic expanded and developed over the decades following its inception to form the basis for the current addressed public of the BLL and IMADR, but with a public shaped around demands very different from that of the human rights seminar.

The denunciation sessions were born in an era of political uprising in the region. The Russian Revolution had occurred in 1917; China had seen the Xinhai Revolution in 1911 and the May Fourth Movement in 1917. Within Japan, a similar left-wing and proletarian movement was burgeoning. The Suiheisha formed in 1922, the same year as the formation of the Japanese

Communist Party. It was in this broad regional milieu that the Suiheisha developed its first proper political tactic, the denunciation session, explicitly modeled as a technique of self-critique. These sessions were also developed concomitant with a distrust of and a lack of support from the state. In the 1920s, just as now, Japan lacked legislation that prohibited or punished discrimination. With the redrafting of its constitution under the U.S. occupation thirty years later, the government would incorporate an injunction against discrimination: "All of the people are equal under the law and there shall be no discrimination in political, economic, or social relations because of race, creed, sex, social status, or family origin."[31] However, this article was never coupled with actionable legislation, leaving it merely a guideline and not a protective measure, and leaving Japanese citizens in the same place they were at the 1922 birth of the Suiheisha. In explicit reaction against previous state-led movements for Buraku assimilation, with the Suiheisha, the Buraku chose to rely on themselves alone.[32]

At its first national meeting in 1922, the Suiheisha adopted a resolution to "carry out a thorough denunciation whenever the words Eta or Tokushu Burakumin are used with the will to insult."[33] The denunciation sessions that would follow this decision—1,432 sessions in the next year alone[34]— were marked by two sets of characteristics. On the one hand, they were marked by independence on the part of Buraku people. Denunciation sessions were to be an antidiscrimination measure conducted by Buraku people themselves. On the other, they were marked by a focus on individual action and intent. This combination of characteristics intensified the sense of rupture between the discriminator and the discriminated and typically involved the outpouring of anger on both sides.[35]

Take, for example, the "Suikoku Soto Incident" of 1923.[36] The incident began on March 17 of that year with a man transporting a dowry from one neighborhood in Nara to another. On his way, he was stopped on the street and asked where the goods he was carrying were from. Raising four fingers to pejoratively denote Buraku people by associating them with four-legged animals, he answered "from those people in Shitanaga."[37] A witness reported this incident to the local branch of the Suiheisha, and a representative gathered a police officer and went to the home of the man who had disparagingly referred to Buraku people with four fingers. Instead of that man, however, a member of the right-wing patriots' assembly came out and said, threateningly, that he would apologize in the other man's stead, and that the Suiheisha should just drop the issue. When the Suiheisha representative refused to accept this apology and asked for the original man, the right-wing man grew belligerent, insulting the Suiheisha representative and refusing to produce the original man. In response the next day, the Suiheisha branch gathered some two hundred people and went back to the house, demanding that the original man apologize. They instead found members of the patriots' assembly armed and ready to fight. And fight they did, with people on both sides sustaining injuries. The situation further escalated from there. The next day the Suiheisha branch gathered over a thousand people and decided together that it could not allow the actions of the patriots' assembly, so it gathered weapons of its own and brought the fight back to the assembly. This time people on both sides were shot and injured, drawing the attention of the local police who eventually had to call for aid from Osaka and Kyoto cities, which dispatched army units to stop the fight. In the end, seventeen members of the Suiheisha were imprisoned for ten months to a year, and eight members of the patriots' assembly were given shorter terms. While this account is taken from a BLL adherent and reflects that perspective, it still shows the basic characteristics of *kyūdan* sessions from this era. While bloodier and larger scale than other *kyūdankai* of the early period, this denunciation session involved Burakumin working autonomously, and angrily, against what they saw as the intentionally insulting actions of others.

This approach changed slightly over the next several decades, partially due to coalition work between the Buraku movement and labor movements. In this coalition, the Suiheisha was exposed to a different theorization of the origins of discrimination, that is, that discrimination issued forth not simply from the intentions of other people but from an underlying social material basis.[38] For example, a denunciation session against a member of the Tokugawa family in the mid-1920s reflected a presumption of social structure underlying individual intent. In their letter to the descendant of the man for whom the feudal period of Japan was named, the central committee of the Suiheisha assigned responsibility for over three hundred years of suffering, sweat, and blood on the part of the Buraku people to the Tokugawa line, and present responsibility to the inheritor of that line, Tokugawa Ichimon, whom they called on to recognize this legacy of subjection.[39] This incident was not directed solely at Tokugawa Ichimon, the individual; it was directed at a social system that valued certain types of people over others; Tokugawa, as the stipulated progenitor of this system, was made accountable.

However, as the historian Yagi and others argue, such broadly focused denunciation sessions were rare at the outset of the movement. For the most part, the first two decades of the practice's history (1920s–1940s) were characterized by an oftentimes extremely angry focus on individual acts of discrimination, though rarely violent to the degree of the Suikoku Soto incident. In response to these individual acts, the Suiheisha would gather large groups of Burakumin, help coordinate placards and headbands, and take its resistance directly to the offending individual. It would gather in a public place and prevent the individual or group from moving, screaming at them until they elicited an apology and a promise not to repeat the act. While this tactic had the beneficial effects of providing agency to Burakumin who otherwise felt powerless and providing concrete opportunities for Burakumin to gather and support each other, it did little, as the movement would argue later, to change the underlying discriminatory social structure. Offenders typically tended to capitulate simply for pragmatic reasons of not being able to access their workplace or of not being able to conduct their daily business without being accompanied by a screaming group of angry Buraku people. What is more, given the pervasive nature of anti-Buraku prejudice at the time, what media coverage that these events garnered typically worked against the Suiheisha. Newspapers reported the acts as violent or threatening, creating for the Suiheisha a reputation for being "frightening."[40] Combined with general Buraku prejudice, this image would follow the movement for the next half-century, despite changes in the *kyūdankai* practice.

The major shift in the theory and goals of the denunciation session as political tactic came postwar. During the war, the Suiheisha movement, like all other social movements, had been dismantled by the government and had to remake itself in the aftermath of the occupation. With this remaking came a rethinking of the denunciation session and its potential role in the movement for liberation. A particularly well-known denunciation session from 1951 illustrates this point. That year a part-time employee of the Kyoto sanitation department published the short story "Tokushu Buraku" in the October issue of the journal *All Romance*. This story was about a love affair between a man of Korean descent and a Japanese woman and was set in an actually existing Buraku district in Kyoto. The story described the Buraku neighborhood as festering with disease and crime, which was the point that incited a denunciation session. The denunciation session was conducted on the basis of an argument that the story circulated an exaggeratedly negative image of a Buraku neighborhood, and that it provided fodder for future discrimination. However, rather than only denouncing the author of the story and the editors of the journal, the liberation movement at the time decided to denounce the city of Kyoto for leaving Buraku districts in such bad conditions that they would inspire discriminatory thoughts on the part of people like the short story's author. This was the first time that the movement did not simply reproach an individual or a group that committed a discriminatory act but instead prioritized tackling the systemic reasons that prompted discrimination. The leaders of the movement extended the *kyūdankai* through all sectors of the municipal government, from sanitation, to housing, to economics, to water provision, to education, pointing out to government bureaucrats in each of these areas the ways in which they were, consciously or not, perpetrating Buraku discrimination.

For example, in one moment in the *kyūdankai* process, as recorded in the notes from the session,[41] representatives from the Kyoto fire department denied the implication that they did not provide Buraku districts with the same level of service as did other districts. A member of the *kyūdan* party asked one of the representatives to produce a map of all fire hydrants and fire alarms in the city and then produced a corresponding map of Buraku districts. None of the fire facilities was located in any of the city's Buraku areas, the combined population of which totaled some 3,000 people. This fact was even more striking, the *kyūdankai* members pointed out, given that houses in Buraku districts were tightly packed and made of flammable materials. The notes from the session report the fire department official's surprise at this fact and his realization that, without directly knowing it and without directly intending it, the distribution of the fire department's services was indeed discriminatory. The members of the *kyūdankai* group conducted similar sessions across all branches of the municipal government, and it became clear that the most underserved areas were invariably Buraku districts.

This incident started a spate of similar *kyūdan* sessions, targeting the social and structural underpinnings of Buraku discrimination. The "*All Romance* Incident," as it came to be known, heralded a change in the uses and goals of the *kyūdankai*. One statement by one of the organizers of the session became widely known, and widely used, to stress the importance of this shift in tactics: "Discriminatory incidents reflect a wider discriminatory mindset. Therefore, in order to fight discrimination, we must fight that which gives rise to this mindset."[42] Following this incident, the *kyūdankai* still served the purpose of eliciting apologies from individuals or groups who discriminated against Buraku people, but the primary goal shifted to the transformation of society. Offenders were no longer to be simply encouraged to apologize; rather, care should be taken to have them understand that what they did was wrong. The focus became not the denunciation of the offender but an education of that and like offenders. Instead of only changing one person's behavior, a successful *kyūdankai* would sow the seeds for a broader, more systemic change. It was, in the words of a previous secretary general of the Suiheisha who was interviewed after the war, "a method of guiding both the discriminator and the public more broadly to a more enlightened understanding of discrimination."[43] Here, then, a trajectory of consciousness-raising was initiated, with the *kyūdankai* and the cultivation of a public as the beginning of that trajectory. The movement reports this era as the theoretical coming of age of the tactic, which they would argue is the "artery that fostered the life of the movement."[44]

These goals were slowly codified and systematized under the leadership of the BLL in its role as postwar successor to the Suiheisha. In this new process, individual intent was no longer necessary for the conduct of a denunciation session, as the BLL headquarters' current online description of the *kyūdan* process makes clear. On the premise that a discriminatory event is symptomatic of deeper social issues, the website gives two occasions in which a *kyūdankai* is appropriate: the first, when someone intends to insult a Buraku person with their action, and the second, when Buraku discrimination might occur as a result of a person's actions, independent of that person's intent.[45] It was this second reason that moved the BLL to press the *"All Romance" kyūdan* not only to the author of the article or the publisher of the journal but to the Kyoto municipal government.

This change in theoretical focus, and the creation of a trajectory, can be seen in the *kyūdan* process that the BLL developed along with the theoretical shift. The BLL headquarters' current website provides the following recommendation for the order and process of a *kyūdan* session, from the occurrence of a discriminatory event to creating structures subsequent to the completion of the *kyūdan*:

Encounter with discrimination (either witnessing or experiencing directly)

If possible, confirm on the spot with the offender that the act was discriminatory.
Inform the liberation league.
Have the league conduct an investigation of the event.

Confirmation session (to be conducted in a public space)

Secure the participation of a third party, either a government representative or someone from a human rights organization. Confirm the alleged circumstances from the alleged offender.

Denunciation session

Write, as a group, an outline describing the events of the incident, what action should be taken, and what the end goals of that action are, based on extended group discussion of the confirmation session.
Confirm a consensus opinion among the leaders of the kyudan session.
Decide a step-by-step plan for how to proceed.
Hold a session with the offender, make sure to hear their account of the event and their motives. Keep your temper and seek to guide them to a realization that what they did was wrong. Video record the session.
Take breaks as scheduled and as necessary. Leaders of the session should discuss strategy and how the session is proceeding.
Work together with potential partner organizations. E.g., labor unions, human rights groups.

Ongoing process after the session

Draft and make public a general overview of the denunciation session.
Involve the government in the continued social enlightenment of the offender. This should be their responsibility.
Develop, if applicable, a critique of how the state may have created the basis for the incident.
Work for furthering the enlightenment of the coworkers or neighbors of the offender, including organizing voluntary study groups.
Encourage the individual's company or other organization to make further efforts to prevent the spread of discrimination.
Strengthen that organization's relationship with the BLL.

This *kyūdan* process, which the BLL website describes as "organized and systematic," was consolidated in order to achieve the "transformation of humankind" by the means of "focusing not just on the phenomena of discrimination but upon its essence," as explained in the BLL headquarters' literature on how to conduct a *kyūdankai*, a document circulated to all branches as a suggestion. First, the confirmation session is included in order to make sure that the two involved parties, the offender and the offended, agree on the actual events of the incident. A third party is incorporated in order to ensure the fairness of this agreement and to broaden the effective scope of the session, potentially transforming the ideology of that third party as well. This confirmation session is to take place in a public space, both to ensure the fairness and to remind the alleged offender that they were being watched by a wider public. The *kyūdan* session itself consists of a face-to-face meeting between the group organizing the session and the offender's party, with the participation of the third party. This meeting, however, should not be held until the group leading the *kyūdankai* has drawn up a denunciation outline. The outline should be written collectively through group discussion, not by one person, and should very clearly state "what, in light of the end goal of full Buraku liberation, the goals of the *kyūdan* session are to be."[46] Here, then, there is an idea that actual acts of discrimination are only symptoms of a larger problem: the state of civil society in Japan. The true final goal of the *kyūdankai*, in focusing on the essence of discrimination, is to transform that public.

This method works very differently from that of the public forum. Here, instead of an emphasis on horizontality, there is a performance of difference. Rather than speaking in terms of a general, inclusive "we," the denunciation session performs a separation between the person or entity being denounced and a broader public. Attention is cultivated—demanded, rather—by articulating a startling rupture between the transgressor, "you," and a public that the movement refers to as the *seken-sama*. Frequently translated into English as "public," *seken-sama*, in contrast to the *ooyake* of the "public forum," refers to a bounded group. The power of the *kyūdankai* lies in forcing someone outside of that group:

> Instead of simply getting angry at the offender, work to create an environment in which such actions are inexcusable. It is important here to make the offender seem isolated from that environment. If a person refuses to attend a kyūdan session, publicize the events of the incident, making as plain as possible the problems involved, gain the participation of a representative from the government, and use the public disapproval you generate to demand reflection on the part of the offender. Other options of generating this public opprobrium include involving other organizations, such as local human rights organizations or the neighborhood association to which the offender belongs. Show them the truth of the matter and with their help create the circumstances under which the discriminator will understand the problems with their action. If the person continues to refuse, publicize the inevitable anger that those trying to convince the person will feel, isolate the person in the process, and further create the circumstances to demand that person's reflection.[47]

In invoking this *mawari* type public, in focusing its attention on one individual, the kyudankai creates a public that disapproves of discrimination, personified in government or NGO officials, neighbors, or coworkers.

Through the use of this tactic, the movement seeks to create a split between that "isolated" individual and a *mawari* or *seken-sama* that that person might otherwise feel a part of. In so doing, it performatively creates that public, and it creates the grounds for an individual to desire to reform his or her ways in order to belong to that public.

The demands on the actor addressed by the *kyūdankai* are significantly different from those on the addressee of the public forum. Whereas the addressee of the public forum is considered one of the group, part of a whole of people working toward the end of discrimination, the addressee of the *kyūdankai* is constructed as distant from that public, and, furthermore, scrutinized by it. A successful *kyūdankai* creates the transformed individual as part of that concerned public, and available for future summons as part of that public. The differences between the public of the public forum and that of the *kyūdankai* were reiterated to me by Mushakoji Kinhide, the founder, first secretary general, and current board member of IMADR.

Over dinner, during a trip to the World Social Forum in Nairobi in 2007, I had the chance to ask Mushakoji how it is that the *kyūdankai* effects change: Why is it not possible for the alleged offender to simply ignore the requests of the BLL? Mushakoji explained to me that the secret of the *kyūdankai* lies in the concept of the *"seken-sama,"* a term with, as Mushakoji was to explain, very different connotations than the "public" or *"ooyake"* of the "public forum." The *seken-sama* is based on a sense of exclusion, in contrast to the general openness conveyed by *ooyake*. The *seken-sama* refers to a bounded group, among whom there exists the potential for *wa,* or "harmony." While the *ooyake* might be open, the *seken-sama* is laced with the threat of exclusion if harmony is disrupted, something to be avoided at all costs. Mushakoji's explanation here resonates with an oft-repeated proverb in Japan, *deru kugi wa utareru* ("the nail that sticks out gets hammered down"), or, as the literary and cultural critic Norma Field echoes, "To create an awkward moment is a sin in Japan; to cause disruption puts one beyond the pale."[48]

Mushakoji, who has made this argument about the *seken-sama* in books and in the classes he teaches as a university professor, went on to point out too that "discrimination" *(sabetsu)* was a post-World War II notion—that public censor prior to that, in the era in which the *kyūdankai* was developed, functioned not because of a notion of universal human rights or a notion of underlying human equality but because of a notion of the necessity of harmony within a specified group. He substantiated this argument that "the *kyūdan* session is the exact opposite of the idea of human rights" by tracing the history of the *kyūdankai* to Confucian, with later influence by Maoist, consciousness-raising sessions. Given this analysis, the tactical question for the Suiheisha, then, was how to have anti-Buraku activities count as a disruption to the *wa*, so as to invoke the scrutinizing force of the *seken-sama*. The answer was to disrupt the *wa* in response and pin the responsibility on the alleged aggressor.

The potency of the *kyūdankai*, its ability to force individuals or city administrations alike into reflexive reconsideration, lies precisely in directing attention, of a broader public and of a transgressor alike, to a rift between them. This capacity to create a sense of disjuncture is the standard by which the *kyūdankai* is assessed in the interpretive regimes of the movement. The Buraku liberation's guide to denunciation asks whether the offender has been sufficiently made to feel as if their behavior sets them apart from others. It asks organizers of the sessions to ensure, through public displays and media reports, that the "eye of the surroundings" be brought to bear on the situation and the offender. Visually and audibly enacting such a break, the *kyūdankai* draws an ireful scrutiny that motivates a transgressor to be attentive to their culpability. In the eyes of the movement, denunciation is successful to the extent that it summons from an offender an attention of public scrutiny and potential ostracization and summons from the surrounding *seken-sama* disapproval and chastisement. Attention here is laced with shame and scrutiny, on the one hand, and disapproval and distance, on the other.

TRACES, FROM YOU TO WE

These two styles of political address, their backing interpretive regimes and the forms and qualities of attention they entail, are easily counterposed. A human rights symposium reaches out in the language of universality, attempting to effect the felicity conditions for the broadest circulation of message possible. According to this regulatory ideal, space is to be broad and horizontal, across which a message might circulate without impediment; time is unfolding, and likewise smooth. The projected public is composed of strangers all equal, all hailed equally by these statements, and all of whom can choose to give their attention. The denunciation session, in contrast, is intentionally lodged in a discrete moment of interaction. Space is punctuated by dense locations of intervention, and time is singular and urgent. Political actors are not all equal under the hail of human; rather, they are split between those who discriminate and those who do not; the discriminators must be forced into a situation in which they are attentive to and remediate the deleterious effects of their actions. On the one hand, we have the projected public of modern nation-states; on the other, we have a *seken-sama,* or "surrounding eye," rooted in the specifics of context.

This neat cleavage, however, falters if we turn our gaze away from the stage of the human rights seminar and instead out to the sleepers. Whereas Mushakoji argues that human rights and the *kyūdankai* are fundamentally opposed, others in the movement, such as Tomonaga, have argued that both sit easily under a broader pedagogical trajectory of education, with the denunciation session sitting at a moment prior to human rights seminars. Whether understood as opposed or as different moments in a pedagogical strategy, these two tactics are hinged together historically and conceptually by the figure of the sleeper.

In 1975 it came to light that a private detective had assembled a list of all Buraku districts throughout the country and sold that list to companies across Japan. The detective had noticed that close to 99 percent of clients who asked for a background check on a potential marriage partner did so to see whether that person was from a Buraku family.[49] Similarly, companies who asked for background checks on potential employees were looking for the same information. He surmised, correctly, that he could make a large amount of money if he "put together a full list of Buraku districts."[50] This he did, tailoring different versions specific to different regions of the country. When the BLL learned of this situation, it quickly organized a *kyūdankai,* found the man who had created the lists, and discovered that over two hundred companies had purchased them, including some of the top business names in Japan. In the proceedings of the *"Chimei Sōkan* Incident," the BLL organized local and national newspapers to evoke public censure and raise awareness of Buraku issues across the country. During the *kyūdan* session, it used media attention, large and sustained protests, and repeated argumentation to have company representatives admit that what they had done was wrong and relinquish the lists, and also vow to work proactively against discrimination from that point forward.

The BLL website gives this incident as an example of the potential successes of a *kyūdankai.* In describing this incident, it says: "Responsibility does not end only with the person who bought the lists, thinking it was their duty as an employee. That is only where the work begins. From there, move on to explain the discriminatory environment of the company, and work to change that. Gain the support of the workers, even if they had no part in the incident. Ask the company to conduct Buraku study sessions. And, what you must be most persistent in, have the company join with the BLL and work together."[51] This was exactly what many of the companies that had purchased the lists did: varying somewhat from company to company, they organized human rights and discrimination training for employees, incentivized that training with bonuses and credited work time, and paid for annual subscriptions to BLL publications. Reformed companies came together to organize as a *Dōwa Mondai Kigyō Renraku Kai* (abbreviated as *Dōkiren*), or an Industrial Federation for Dowa Issues. This organization still exists and has grown larger over the years, pulling membership from further denunciation sessions and from companies that were never denounced. The *Dōkiren* coordinates human rights training for member companies, and, while membership no longer indicates some initial act of discrimination, the organization incorporates BLL programs into that training program.

An incident in 1979 provoked the organization of a similar group for religious organizations. During the third World Conference of Religions for Peace, the director of the Japan Buddhist Federation and head of the largest sect of Zen Buddhism in Japan was asked what the Japanese federation of religions was doing to combat Buraku discrimination in Japan. The director's response provoked critique from those in attendance, and, when news of the response reached Japan, provoked a *kyūdankai* from the BLL that stretched across the nation. At this international venue, in front of hundreds of representatives from all over the world, the director of the Japan Buddhist Federation said:

Presently, there is no Buraku issue in Japan. I, as a Japanese person, should know. However, there are apparently those who, for the supposed cause of "Buraku Issues" or "Buraku Liberation," are still making a large fuss. At the present time, there is absolutely no discrimination in the country of Japan. This is why we need not include the issue of Buraku discrimination in our report. This is a matter of the honor of Japan.[52]

The BLL used this quote as an opportunity to investigate religious organizations across Japan, and to examine how they might be perpetuating Buraku discrimination. This inquiry spanned several months, and by its end the BLL had successfully fostered self-critique in many religious organizations, which, as part of their reform, came together to form the Religious Federation for Dowa Issues *(Dōwa Mondai Shūkyou Renraku Kai* or *Dōshūren)* in 1981. Like their *Dōkiren* counterpart, this organization has grown beyond just those denounced, removing any immediate connection between membership and an original discriminatory event. However, the organization continues to manage the obligations that were consolidated with the outcome of the denunciation session—namely, the coordination of human rights education across its member organizations and its support of BLL activities.

These two organizations—the *Dōkiren* and the *Dōshūren*—have been constituent members of IMADR since the BLL founded the organization in 1988. IMADR is primarily supported by membership fees ranging from ¥3,000 to ¥30,000 (roughly 30 to 300 U.S. dollars) for the IMADR newsletter and other publications. The members of the *Dōkiren* and the *Dōshūren* pay these fees and also pay for their members to attend Buraku public forums. This financial support provides IMADR with a budget to maintain its activities independent of state aid. The fact that these reformed organizations support IMADR, that their representatives attend events, and that they have implemented human rights educational requirements provides the BLL with fodder for heralding the *kyūdankai* as "a space for someone who has discriminated to realize their full human potential . . . a space for the public to reform its own consciousness"[53] and equips organizations with evidence of their commitment to the struggle against discrimination.

At the December forum, the head of the Osaka *Dōkiren* spoke in language generalized beyond denunciation sessions. He framed his organization's mission in terms of a commitment to facilitate the "construction of a society in which human rights are realized." Educational programs were key: "In addition to training aimed at sharpening the knowledge, skills, and general capacities of company leaders, we also provide training and education directly to all employees. We train people to be company leaders in areas of human rights protection." As a result, he argued, "industry representatives make up a large proportion of people attending human rights awareness trainings across the country" and "leave a strong impression of industries addressing human rights." The fact of attendance, that is, "mere presence," here serves as a sign of participation in a public, and as a sign of the success of both the educational programs of these organizations and, more deeply, of the *kyūdankai* as a political strategy. What goes unmentioned, here, however, is that it is precisely this audience that is, for the most part, asleep.

In some cases, mere attendance is coupled with other signs of sincerity. Take, for example, Murase-san, the director of a human rights program for a prominent corporation. Murase-san's company had been the object of a *kyūdankai* before he was hired in the early nineties and established a human rights program as a result. Murase-san was hired to manage that program, which he did with great enthusiasm. In addition to incentivizing participation in discrimination study sessions for the employees, he himself sought out multiple opportunities to further his own understanding of issues of discrimination. His efforts included participating in a study tour of India conducted by the Tokyo branch of the BLL and participating in the English class that I taught in preparation for that tour. Although he was one of the few non-Buraku people in the group, Murase-san displayed a high level of interest in issues of discrimination and was always well prepared for class. He was an avid attendee of the larger Buraku public forums.

However, such qualities of attention beyond mere presence are not required for the educational programs. The system at Murase-san's corporation, for example, requires employees to attend two human rights-oriented trainings a year. The company provides a list of events that qualify, and it covers all entry fees. To secure credit, the employee must attend and bring back the billet from the event. Even the most stringent programs only require that employees supply a paragraph response to the event, something easily drafted from information handed out to the attendees.

The existence of the sleepers demonstrates the cultivation and grooming of attention as a social project. Standing between the denunciation sessions and the human rights seminars, the sleepers highlight the discrepancies and variations in what counts as attention from one political tactic to another. The interpretive regime of social education, standing above denunciation sessions and public forums alike, hinges together two sets of desires: on the one hand, the desires of employees to get paid on a regular basis and not cause trouble at work (i.e., "disturb the *wa*"), and, on the other, the desires of the BLL to have companies actively engage the elimination of discrimination and to have a stable budget. However, in moving from one tactic to another, employees are not required to bring any quality of attention to human rights issues other than presence. When they were addressed by the second-person "you," slumber is unimaginable; in the human rights seminar, they can hide within the anonymity of the first-person plural. They choose to attend, but their obliged attention ends there. They can attend, but they cannot attend to.

The public addressed by the Buraku political movement is not one that, in a totally straightforward manner, chooses to lend its attention. Only through specific disciplines, among them the denunciation session and the human rights seminar, have the people who compose that public learned the modes of attention that qualify them for inclusion. They have learned where and how to be attentive; they have learned when to ask questions, when to respond with shame and apology, and when it is they might sleep. This situation prompts questions that can be asked of all publics: How are they mobilized? How are the institutions that undergird them made to "vibrate" and thus awaken a "latent" public? How is attention cultivated, groomed, and sustained? The techniques that go into capacitating volition here do not preclude the Buraku public from being a public; rather, I argue, any public relies on similar techniques for mobilization. The work of this discipline, I contend, is foundational to the labor of multiculturalism.

Canonical examinations of publics and the public sphere have moved quickly over a consideration of qualities of attention. As I discussed earlier, in Warner's description of the ideology associated with the bourgeois public sphere, membership is constituted by mere attention, and that attention, its type or degree unquestioned, is performed as volitional. As a result, publics in this description can "be understood within the conceptual framework of civil society, that is, as having a free, voluntary, and active membership."[54] However, as the Buraku situation makes patent, the basis for membership in any given public is not mere volitional attention; rather, it is a matter of the cultivation of modes of attention proper to that public, a social process the legitimacy and forms of which are open to debate. This fact, as embodied in the sleepers, causes trouble for the Buraku movement: it expresses frustration, heavy with resignation, over facing a somnolent public; or, it makes recourse to an ideology of social education that locates these sleepers at an initial stage of intervention, as of yet insufficiently disciplined to perform the aspirational duties of the burgeoning public.

Examining the public as a project that disciplines forms and qualities of attention places strain on canonical distinctions between coercion and volition. In his discussion of deliberative democracy, which is what the Buraku movement is attempting eventually to facilitate, Habermas locates public and political legitimacy in a procedure of communication at the base of which lies the operation of reason. Deliberative democracy, founded on rational critical debate, in this read is the antithesis of coercive. Coercion would place "constraints or limitations on the range of topics open to public discourse."[55] Rational critical debate only effects procedural, rather than topical, constraints: "to talk about something is not necessarily the same as meddling in another's affairs."[56]

However, as the Buraku situation points out, the deliberation at the base of a public requires of its participants particular somatic and ethical qualities of attention. The reflexive capacity for critical debate, part of what the BLL aspires to achieve inclusion in, requires the adoption of a perspective of an anonymous "we" that consists in very particular ethical, temporal, spatial, and somatic orientations. Directing attention is a form of meddling. Some people are more able to be recruited to attention than others; some might need more disciplinary intervention to be included than others. This disciplined inclusion is partial, differential, context dependent, and never a given. Unpacking the cultivation of attention and the processes through which a public is mobilized opens up an analysis as to what kinds of people might be included, the differential disciplinary effects of that inclusion, and the complementary forms of exclusion.

Standing between two different disciplinary projects, between the context-specific hail of "hey you" and the universal aspirations of the "we shall," the sleepers are not simply an initial stage in a trajectory of social education, nor are they an indictment of the public altogether. Instead, they are an indication of the constant work to shore up the attention of any public. As Habermas and Dewey argue, a public is a project. The anonymity of the "we" includes in it an impersonal space in which people can hide outside the possible range of address, without the correctly cultivated forms of attention necessary for a deliberative public. If we understand attention as a range of qualities manifest in assemblages of bodily comportment, cognitive engagement, and ethical orientation, we can see the ways in which any public, in its conduct, must constantly meddle to sustain itself. Tracing the denunciation session into the human rights seminar invites us to understand the freedoms of publics in terms of the constraints from which they are born, to examine how particular modes of attention are cultivated, how that inclusion might be disciplinary, partial, or differential, and to critically pursue the coercions that give rise to the possibility of volition.

PART THREE

International Standards and the Possibilities of Solidarity

FIVE

Demanding a Standard

BURAKU POLITICS ON A GLOBAL STAGE

"WE ARE GATHERED HERE TODAY . . .":
ASSERTING SIMILARITY ACROSS DIFFERENCE

On a spring day in 2006, Professor Yozo Yokota called to order a meeting of some forty representatives of nongovernmental organizations (NGOs) from across the world. Representing over eleven different countries, from South and East Asia, Africa, and the Middle East, these representatives had gathered in Geneva to spend two days discussing the new United Nations (UN) category "Discrimination Based on Work and Descent." Across those early March days, they would outline their strategies to combat this discrimination and, in some cases, share their own experiences of discrimination. Based on this information, and information gathered in a questionnaire circulated the previous year, the UN special rapporteurs Yokota and Chin-Sung Chun would prepare an official document to be distributed to the UN Human Rights Sub-Commission, concerned NGOs, and governments of the countries represented in this room. The document, "Proposals and Guidelines for the Elimination of 'Discrimination Based on Work and Descent,'" would be a compendium of the divergent experiences of groups across the globe as they fought this form of discrimination—both a guide to NGOs searching for new strategies, and a reminder to people that they were not alone in this struggle.

As the eyes and ears of the assembled representatives came to rest on him, Professor Yokota spoke out in English. He welcomed everyone to this "Informal Consultation" and thanked them all for their time and efforts in making this meeting possible. He extended particular thanks to a Denmark-based NGO, the International Dalit Solidarity Network (IDSN), for hosting

FIGURE 11. Special rapporteurs Chun and Yokota, along with the leader of the International Dalit Solidarity Network, at a meeting about "Discrimination Based on Work and Descent" in Geneva 2006.

and coordinating the event. Yokota then provided a brief history of this category of discrimination at the UN level. First recognized by the United Nations in August 2000, "Discrimination Based on Work and Descent" was from the outset, he explained, a nebulous form of discrimination. The two special rapporteurs initially appointed to investigate this form of discrimination did not start their inquiry with any preset definitions; rather, they conducted what he called "wide-ranging explorations."

They found that a tremendous number of people, as many as 250 million worldwide, faced something that could be called discrimination based on work and descent. The number of potentially included people and groups was so large, and the people were so diverse and diffuse, that the special rapporteurs feared that they would not be able to isolate any common, baseline characteristics that extended across the entire population. They found the task of their UN mandate daunting and decided to change tactics. In 2005 they drafted an open-worded questionnaire and distributed it internationally, making it available to as many NGOs, human rights bodies, and governments as possible. Though they were disappointed with what they saw to be a paucity of responses (nineteen NGOs, nine governments, and one national human rights organization), the special rapporteurs were able to cull some common characteristics from questionnaire responses.

This "Informal Consultation" was the second stage of their project. The goal here was to specify with greater refinement "the common features and differences among all the different examples of this discrimination" and to "determine how this form of discrimination sits alongside other forms of discrimination such as that based on race or ethnicity." Each responding group would be given time to present its case to the entire group, and then everyone would refine the list of common characteristics and effective strategies, with an eye toward producing the "Proposals and Guidelines" document.

Professor Yokota stressed the importance of thinking in terms of similarities in order to provide a framework for understanding differences among the various groups. He offered an example of two groups prominently engaged in this issue: the Dalit of India and the Buraku people of Japan. Drawing from questionnaire responses, he asserted:

> In Japan the most important connection among those facing this type of discrimination is actually their place of origin, what neighborhood they are from. Therefore in Japan, we need to stop the practice of finding out the place of origin of individual people. But in the case of India, only sometimes does the location have something to do with the kind of discrimination. But more importantly, the names play a key role in identifying who is and who is not a certain kind of person. However, the difference between Japan and India is not so important. In both cases, the people are connected to a type of people who have been involved in a certain kind of work.[1]

In Professor Yokota's description here, we have a move worthy of the sociologist Georg Simmel: at the same time the prospect of solidarity among these groups proffers similarity, it also presumes a divide among the groups present.[2] The cases of India and Japan are marked out as significantly different in order to show that they are similar. Yokota acknowledges that the mode by which people are tracked as certain kinds of people is different in each country: people are tracked by name in India and by place of origin in Japan. The strategies necessary to combat discrimination against these people vary accordingly. However, he also stresses to the assembled NGOs that these differences are secondary to an overarching similarity: types of people connected to types of work. Buraku and Dalit can be seen to be equivalent because they both have the same determining relationship with types of work.

Professor Yokota concluded his introductory remarks with an injunction, phrased as a reminder. In order to come to a true understanding of the real bases of discrimination, there was a need to learn directly from representatives of discriminated communities. Therefore, the focus, for the duration of the "Informal Consultation," would be on lived experience facing and fighting discrimination. With this statement, Professor Yokota drew a line between two kinds of people in the audience: those that actually face this form of discrimination,[3] and those there in solidarity (such as myself or the governing board of the IDSN, all of whom are white Europeans with no direct connection with types of labor that might stigmatize them). Precedence and authority were to be granted to the former. It was from their experiences that differences would be ascertained, and rendered commensurable, under the rubric of "work and descent."

"Discrimination Based on Work and Descent," as an official category of discrimination recognized by the United Nations, provides a capacious conceptual umbrella for grouping vastly divergent experiences of people across the globe. It establishes a standard of comparison that posits as commensurate different people and different experiences of discrimination, and it allows them to be compared and contrasted in new ways. This category relies on and asserts a proportionality of experience, relating types of people, types of occupation, and types of discrimination. This proportionality serves as a metric that allows actors such as the special rapporteurs or the representatives of NGOs to decide whether particular groups of people count as "people discriminated against on the basis of work and descent," all grouped together in a bond of solidarity.

However, the exact qualifications for inclusion in *certain* people or *certain* experiences—that is, what pain or difficulty might evidence this form of discrimination, and what types and numbers of people might experience it worldwide—are still very much a matter of question and contestation. As this new category circulates and gains traction in such text artifacts as the questionnaire and in such meetings as the "Informal Consultation," it offers Dalit and Buraku groups, as well as groups from Yemen, Kenya, Senegal, and beyond, new potential allies and new political and rhetorical resources for domestic and international struggles to transform their conditions of life.[4] The work underlying this commensuration relies on and confirms the authority of such organizations as the United Nations or the IDSN to arbitrate such decisions of inclusion.

In this chapter and in the next I investigate political solidarity as a project of commensuration hinging on a cultivated sympathetic engagement established via the pain of discrimination. When people and social movements produce evidence of the pain of discrimination, what work does that do, what bridges does it allow, and what commitments does it demand? Taking up the work of philosophers David Hume and Adam Smith,[5] I treat sympathy foremost as an operation of "fellow feeling," not a feeling in itself but an affective conduit, a sympathy *with* rather than a sympathy *for*. This is an operation not merely of reason but of the senses and of the body, where reason and moral orientation arise through entering into another's sentiment. Sentiment here moves from object to agent through the function of the imagination: my sentiment is fired by what I imagine I would feel in your situation. I gain an idea of your situation off your body and your circumstances, a habituated ability cultivated through experience. Nurtured well, that idea swells, gaining in "force and vivacity," into a passion mimetic of yours. On these grounds—bodily, material, aesthetic, and habituated—I can feel *with* you. Extending sympathy takes the work of disposing the imagination, an endeavor, Hume and Smith insist, fueled by cultivating a sense of proximity, whether that proximity is one of shared qualities, that is, resemblance, or of contiguity. As the anthropologist Danilyn Rutherford phrases it, characterizing Hume, "[t]he vividness of one's commitments depends on whether the people and outcomes involved are experienced as close or remote, relatively accessible or not."[6] Key here is the disposition of that imagination, and the assertion of standards is one such technique.

Building on previous chapters' examination of Buraku politics in domestic realms, this chapter and the next examine the work of sympathetic commensuration underlying transnational solidarity projects as a key moment in the transnational circulation of multiculturalism. I examine the work that goes into projecting similarity across presupposed difference, the standards that are called on to authorize such work, and moments of blockage in these sympathetic transfers. This chapter looks specifically at the legal standards that back a Buraku politics of international solidarity. With an eye to how "Discrimination Based on Work and Descent" is created as "new" among other legal strategies, I examine how this standard serves as a conduit through which Buraku actors can address an international audience, making themselves sympathetically available across national borders, and the revised self they achieve in the process of linking their international forays to domestic efforts.

In December 2005 three international visitors came to Osaka to attend a public forum on "Discrimination Based on Work and Descent." Sukhadeo Thorat, from India, was a scholar of Dalit issues; Abdul Kamala was a graduate student in Kenya working on caste issues among different African tribes; and Chinsung Chun, from Korea, was the newly appointed UN special rapporteuse on "Discrimination Based on Work and Descent." Their three-day visit to Osaka included tours of Buraku neighborhoods, meetings with political leaders, and explanations of the history of the Buraku liberation movement, and it concluded with the public forum I discussed in chapter 4. In one session on the conduct of the movement, Thorat asked about the apparent lack of affirmative action legislation in Japan and why the Buraku movement was not pushing for such legislation. He explained that affirmative action legislation had played a large part in much of the Dalit movement within India, and he wondered why Buraku organizations were not engaged in a similar struggle. Tomonaga Kenzō, the director of the Buraku Liberation and Human Rights Research Institute (BLHRRI), whom I had met for the first time the evening the visitors arrived, had been the primary organizer of the conference and answered Thorat's question. He explained that the consensus decision within the Buraku Liberation League (BLL) was that affirmative action legislation ran the risk of fostering the dependency of Buraku people on the state rather than fostering empowerment and self-sufficiency. The Special Measures Law, which had directed funds to registered Buraku communities and businesses,[7] had just come to an end in 2002, and one of the league's tasks over the past several years was that of weaning Buraku neighborhoods, families, and organizations from an overreliance on that type of support. Affirmative action legislation ran the risk of intensifying such a reliance.

While the type of affirmative action legislation that Thorat asked about is a very specific type of minority group legal support, this vignette serves to characterize the ambivalent status that legislation has occupied in the strategies of the Buraku liberation movement. The movement, and the variety of organizations that work in its name, has had a long and complicated relationship with the law and with state intervention. From the "Emancipation Edict" of 1871, through the antistate phase of the early movement, to the call for special Buraku measures in the postwar period, to a call for a basic law on Buraku discrimination in the 1980s and 1990s, and, finally, to a wider call for more general antidiscrimination legislation, the liberation movement has shown both a hesitancy to rely on the state for any provision of aid and an increasing tendency to view the law as one strategy of many to be used on the road to its goal of "complete liberation." This ambivalence has also been fueled by acrimonious debate within the movement regarding what categories of difference—race, ethnicity, or something else—might be applicable to the Buraku situation.

DOMESTIC LEGISLATION

As I have discussed in other chapters, the 1871 "Emancipation Edict" that liberated the "abject classes" from their class distinction also liberated them from the monopolies that they had held on industries such as tanning, depriving some of them of whatever economic stability they may have enjoyed up until that point and at the same time granting them a formal equality.[8] The popular backlash against the inclusion of these "abject classes" provided the momentum for a Buraku political movement that started to burgeon in the 1890s. The first meetings consisted primarily of discussion groups centered on such topics as how to resist the recently reinstated emperor system and how to combat discrimination. These groups became popular across western Japan and served as a means of fostering a realization that experiences of discrimination were shared by similar groups in other locations.[9] However, this initial movement was characterized by the idea that discrimination was somehow warranted, that is, that there was something wrong with these "new commoners" that needed to be corrected before they could join the rest of society. In 1905 new political initiatives by the Meiji government made it difficult for political activity to be organized independent of the state; and the *Yūwa* (or "conciliation") groups were required to include "a trusted member of the community such as a school-teacher."[10] These outsiders were tasked with reporting back to government officials, acting as state monitors of the groups.

These types of groups flourished over the next two decades, simultaneously functioning as a way for the state to monitor and control the *Yūwa* movement and creating a national network of *Yūwa* groups that served as the basis for the next transformation in the political movement. In the late teens and early twenties of the twentieth century, there was a burgeoning sentiment opposing state involvement in the political movement. When the

Suiheisha (or "Levellers' Association") was established in 1922, it made use of the *Yūwa* network and its cache of participants. However, it positioned its mission in direct contrast to that of the *Yūwa* movement: "Previous movements, though seemingly motivated by compassion, actually corrupted many of our brothers. In the light of this, it is necessary for us to organize a new collective movement through which we shall emancipate ourselves by our own effort and self-respect."[11] This focus on emancipation via "our own effort" came to characterize the Suiheisha movement in its initial years as it swept across *Yūwa* groups, throughout its heyday in the late twenties and thirties, and on through to its decline and demise from 1938 to 1942. With this focus, the Suiheisha limited participation in its movement to people they christened *Tokushu Burakumin* ("residents of special neighborhoods"), ejected the government liaisons that had been a constant part of the *Yūwa* groups, and, more broadly, spurned the idea that the state could be a potential source of assistance. The Suiheisha, working in solidarity with workers' and tenants' movements, saw the state not as an agent of assistance but rather as a culpable agent in the perpetuation of structural Buraku discrimination.

The Suiheisha movement lost momentum in the face of the government crackdown on political organizations during the Asia-Pacific War, finally succumbing to pressure to end its activities in 1942. While the Suiheisha lost organizational ground during the war, one of its prominent leaders, Matsumoto Jiichiro, rose to and remained in a position of political influence throughout the war.[12] Elected to the Diet in 1936, he remained part of the Diet throughout the war and was key in re-creating the Buraku political movement following Japan's defeat. Almost immediately after Japan's surrender, former leaders of the Suiheisha met to strategize the rebirth of the movement. Within the year they formed the National Committee for Buraku Liberation, with broad support from most of the more left-leaning political parties, including both the Japanese Communist Party (JCP) and the Japanese Socialist Party (JSP), both of which explicitly reference their support for the Buraku liberation movement in their postwar manifestos.[13] In the first election after the establishment of the new constitution, nine Buraku people were elected to the Diet, seven of whom were members of the JSP, including Matsumoto. With this level of involvement in the government proper, the new Buraku movement argued for greater possibilities for the role of government in ameliorating Buraku discrimination. However, there was little popular enthusiasm for this newly revivified movement during the occupation, a situation that the political theorist Ian Neary argues resulted from a hope, held by people otherwise busy merely subsisting, that the changes being enforced by the Supreme Command for Allied Powers would eliminate Buraku discrimination.

Spurred by the efforts of Matsumoto, the movement's foothold in the government's left of center parties remained strong through U.S. occupation. This foothold was then complemented by a dramatic rise in popular support in 1951, stoked by a widely publicized discriminatory event. This *"All Romance* Incident," discussed in the previous chapter, provided the National Committee for Buraku Liberation with an opportunity to publicize continuing disparities in governmental service provision between Buraku and non-Buraku districts. This incident served as a rallying point for the movement's rebirth, and as a rallying point for demanding government responsibility in improving the conditions of Buraku districts. Subsequent critiques of local governments led to visible improvements to Buraku districts, which in turn flamed the fires of the movement. In 1955 the National Committee renamed itself the Buraku Liberation League, which leaders argued would have an expanded appeal beyond the "vanguardist overtones" of a "national committee."[14]

The BLL was able to combine this upswing in popular support with its continued foothold in the JSP and the Diet to parlay its accomplishments into broader support from the government and some of the political parties. The JSP, for instance, issued a report in 1957 arguing that "although complete Buraku liberation was only possible through the creation of a socialist society, even within the capitalist structure it was possible and necessary to improve the Burakumin living environment and their life chances," and it urged the government to create a special commission with the goal of drafting a comprehensive national policy for improving the conditions of Buraku people.[15] On the other hand, the JCP issued a statement in response, arguing that there was nothing "special about the problems faced by Burakumin workers. Their poverty was just one product of the contradictions within capitalist society and therefore the main target of the Buraku struggle should be the overthrow of the class system rather than making special demands on that system which would weaken their solidarity with the rest of the working-class movement."[16] This counterargument was a continuation of a communist line of thought that had existed since the turn of the century, namely, that Buraku discrimination was an artifact of an incomplete bourgeois revolution—as capitalism set in, Buraku discrimination would inevitably disappear on its own. Thus no special attention was required, and in fact special attention would only hinder the approach of the Communist revolution.[17] The difference between this line of thought and the BLL's would increase in severity and vehemence over the next decade, and the contrast provides insight into the BLL's resulting strategy vis-à-vis the state.

The BLL, along with the JSP and its associated labor unions, asserted that special measures were required to improve the living situations in Buraku areas. As the BLL's primary political tactic, the denunciation session, grew in usage and became more theorized, there came a greater awareness that the problems that Buraku people faced were systemic, across the nation, and a greater insistence that national measures were required to relieve these problems. During the 1957–58 period, riding on rising popular support, the BLL pushed this line of approach with the leading Liberal Democratic Party (LDP), with the support of the JSP and labor unions. The LDP prime minister at the time conceded that policies were necessary to address the problem,[18] and later that year the LDP, which was besieged with protests from left-wing groups against the renewal of a Security Treaty with the United States, made a pledge to form a committee to consider the issue. This pledge came to fruition in frustrated form in 1961, when the LDP, which appointed a former leader of the *Yūwa* movement to head the *Nihon Dōwakai* (Japanese Harmony Association), declared that it would cease to work with the BLL.

The *Dōwakai* was tasked with producing a report on Buraku issues, which it did in 1965. Despite the declared break with the BLL, the report closely resembled the stance of the BLL. The report asserted: (1) that the Buraku people are in no way ethnically or racially different from other Japanese people; (2) that the Buraku issue was not a remnant of the feudal period that would simply disappear with the advancement of capitalism; and (3) that the Buraku issue was not best solved by being ignored. Instead, it was argued in the report that the problem should be engaged proactively.[19] These points on the part of the government report opened the door for the BLL's willingness to work closely with the government to solve the problem and also were directly contrary to the prevalent JCP point of view, which cast Buraku discrimination as a fading anachronism. This report and the government footholds it opened for the BLL contributed to an eventual break between the JCP and the BLL, with the JCP going on to form a separate organization, the Zenkairen, in 1979 and criticizing the BLL's too-close involvement with the government.

For the BLL, however, the *Dōwakai* report signified a major outpouring of governmental support, and it worked closely with the government to ameliorate discrepancies in Buraku living conditions. In 1969 the *Dōwakai*, with aid from the BLL, used the report as the basis for drafting the "Law on Special Measures for Dowa Projects" (SML). Initially slated to be in effect for ten years, this law in its original form was extended and ran until 1993. This set of laws allowed for the direction of government funds, both national and municipal, to projects that improved the physical environment, including housing and public spaces, in Buraku districts; fostered education achievements; bolstered public health; promoted Buraku industries; and provided employment protection. Over these twenty-four years, the original SML distributed some 13,880 billion yen (approximately 139 million U.S. dollars) for the improvement of streets and schools, as stipends paid directly to Buraku families, and for school- and nonschool-based educational programs.[20] In fostering these successes, the law also exacerbated the rift between the JCP and the BLL, with the JCP arguing that funds should be directed not only to Buraku people but to other impoverished people as well. Overall, the BLL argued for the need for special attention to Buraku plight, and subsequently it was critiqued by the JCP and other marginalized groups, such as resident Koreans, of monopolizing the governmental administrative window.

As the 1993 expiration date for the SML became closer, the push grew stronger within the BLL not for the extension of special measures but instead for the implementation of a fundamental basic law that would (1) institutionalize national commitment to the goals of the 1965 report and establish a legal framework for a comprehensive approach to the Buraku problem; (2) obligate the government to take action in a broad range of areas beyond urban renewal; and (3) prohibit a wide range of discriminatory acts and provide the statutory basis for direct legal attacks on discrimination by individuals and groups.[21] This push, however, was not without its critics, from both outside and within the movement. With the end of the SML, the JCP argued that there was no longer any barrier preventing the end of Buraku discrimination, and the LDP also agreed that a basic permanent law was unnecessary. From within the BLL, there was a critique that a permanent law would supplant the BLL's signature tactic of the denunciation session and thus cede to the state the authority to judge what counts as discrimination, essentially devolving the movement back to the position of the *Yūwa* movement at the turn of the century. Though this internal debate, in combination with the hesitancy of the ruling party, led to the defeat of the push for a basic law, this push was the first time the BLL had sought to institutionalize antidiscrimination measures as a state function rather than as a role of the movement.

The legal scholar Frank Upham argues that the push for a basic law, which had started in the mid-1980s, signified that "the BLL was ready to acknowledge the potential role for law in combating discrimination."[22] This push marked a shift from seeing the law and state intervention as a way to change the structure of Buraku districts and to distribute services to seeing it as a way of meting out punishment for events labeled discriminatory. Instead of a basic law, however, the BLL succeeded in pushing through a revised and narrowed form of the SML, with an extended expiration date, first in 1997 and then extended to 2002. The government rejection of the basic law in 1993, and then a subsequent rejection of a general antidiscrimination law in 2002, prompted much argument and conversation within the movement as to the end goals of Buraku liberation, a conversation that continued beyond the final end of the SML. The end of the SML heralded a major shift for the Buraku movement, what scholars commonly refer to as the "third phase" of the Buraku movement, the first being that up until World War II and the second being the run of the SML. Now Buraku political organizations are faced with limited domestic funds and limited domestic support in their attempts to implement an antidiscrimination bill or even simply to fund their activities. This waning domestic support has contributed to their increased use of international venues for accruing support and the adoption of a new vocabulary for addressing Buraku issues.

INTERNATIONAL LEGAL MECHANISMS

Three years after Thorat's question about affirmative action legislation, BLHRRI welcomed a different set of international visitors to Osaka. In August 2008 it hosted a conference entitled "Present Day Buraku Issues—From an International Perspective," to which it invited young international scholars working on Buraku issues as well as a handful of young Japanese scholars, whom they called "the next generation of movement leadership." This event consisted of one day of Buraku tours, three days of paper presentations and discussion, and a final public forum attended by approximately two hundred BLHRRI associates. Tomonaga Kenzō, again a key organizer of this event, opened the presentations with a description of the Buraku liberation movement, as he had done with Thorat and company three years prior, but this time he focused on the history of what he called "Buraku internationalism." Ian Neary argues that while internationalism was a strong component of Matsumoto Jiichiro's approach to the liberation movement immediately following the war, the primary push for the use of international legal mechanisms started to develop in the 1980s, alongside an increased emphasis "on the 'human rights' dimension of the Buraku issues."[23] The formation of the International Movement Against All Forms of Discrimination and Racism (IMADR) in 1988 is one sign of this shift. In a similar move, during Tomonaga's tenure as director, the Buraku Liberation Research Institute (BLRI) changed its name in 1998 to the Buraku Liberation and *Human Rights* Research Institute (BLHRRI). The internationalization of the Buraku movement in the 1970s and 1980s coincided with an increased appeal to a broad notion of human rights, a shift likewise evident in the presentation that Tomonaga gave at the 2008 academic conference.[24]

Tomonaga's presentation, entitled "The Role of the Buraku Liberation League in Building a World without Discrimination," offered a vision of the Buraku movement characterized, from its beginning until the present day, by an international orientation. Tomonaga located the roots of Buraku internationalism in the founding moment of the movement: the declaration of the Suiheisha. He argued that the declaration reflects "thinking based on an advanced, international humanism," and that the declaration, in its emphasis on respect rather than pity, contained the seeds of the modern notion of human rights. Tomonaga cited as evidence of this internationalist trend the Suiheisha's solidarity work with the Korean organization *Hyonpyonsa* in the 1920s and its protest against the Nazis' oppression of the Jews in the 1930s. This orientation, Tomonaga continued, was equally evident in the activities of Matsumoto Jiichiro following the war. Tomonaga argued that, under Matsumoto's guidance, the movement strengthened its focus on the possibilities of international solidarity, and he cited as examples Matsumoto's development of relations with China, his visitation of "outcaste" communities in India, and his attendance in 1956 of the meeting of the International League against Racism and the Ostracization of Jews.

This orientation took a more legal direction in the later portion of the twentieth century. In 1976 the United Nations adopted its two covenants on rights, the International Covenant on Civil and Political Rights and the International Covenant on Economic, Social, and Cultural Rights. As Tomonaga presented it, this UN change provided scaffolding for the BLL and the BLRI, with which Tomonaga was already involved, to forge their burgeoning emphasis on the international, this time, however, in the guise of law rather than simply solidarity work. The BLL and the BLRI used this adoption as an opportunity to hold public symposia in Japan, both to heighten awareness around Buraku issues and to foment awareness that there was increasing international recognition of these issues. They worked alongside other groups to have the Japanese government ratify these covenants domestically and to obligate themselves to respond to this international legal armature. Japan did so soon after, in 1979.

Having successfully used these UN mechanisms as a means of rallying public and governmental support, the BLL and the BLRI then increased their push to have the Japanese government ratify the United Nations' 1969 International Convention on the Elimination of All Forms of Racial Discrimination (ICERD). The struggle for this ratification was protracted; Japan finally became a signatory to the ICERD in 1996. During those two decades, the BLL and the BLRI worked together to form IMADR, the name of which is a direct reference to the ICERD, in part as a liaison to the United Nations and more generally in the hopes of creating, as Tomonaga phrased it, "an international Suiheisha." While IMADR's mission and day-to-day activities include more than working through UN human rights mechanisms (a potential source of tension within the movement, which I discuss further in the next chapter), the mission was intended to serve as a space for different Japanese advocacy groups to become aware of and respond to UN conventions and the domestic government's response to those conventions. In 1993 IMADR received consultative status with the Economic and Social Council of the United Nations and established a permanent office in Geneva to facilitate its work within the international human rights arena. After obtaining this status, IMADR, along with the BLL and the BLRI, successfully led the campaign to have the Japanese government ratify the United Nations' Committee on the Elimination of All Forms of Racial Discrimination (CERD).

The ICERD served as one of the two avenues that would allow the Buraku liberation movement to lobby for international recognition of the Buraku as a minority group deserving intervention and aid. In ratifying the ICERD, the Japanese government obligated itself to submit periodic reports on the domestic status of relevant issues to the United Nations and to respond to the recommendations issued by the United Nations based on these reports.

In March 2001, the CERD, upon consideration of the first and second reports from the Japanese government, stated that Japanese Buraku discrimination falls under the purview of the ICERD as "discrimination based on descent" and recommended measures for protection from discrimination as well as the complete preservation of "all civil, political, economic, social, and cultural rights of the Buraku people." The Japanese government responded with its long-held stance that Buraku discrimination is not, unlike racial or ethnic discrimination, based on "descent" (here translated as *monchi,* a translation decision I discuss in greater detail later), a category of discrimination prohibited by the Japanese constitution. After careful consideration, the CERD disagreed with this assessment and adopted "General Recommendation 29," which asserted that "discrimination based on 'descent' includes discrimination against members of communities based on forms of social stratification such as caste and analogous systems of inherited status which nullify or impair their equal enjoyment of human rights." In such political maneuvers, the ICERD opened for the Buraku political movement one avenue of international recognition. It placed the Buraku minority, primarily constituted under the conceptual category "descent," alongside other minority groups constituted by race, ethnicity, and religious difference.

The other avenue of international legal recognition available to the Buraku political movement was the UN Sub-Commission on the Promotion and Protection of Human Rights. Since its formation in 1947 until its dissolution in the summer of 2006, the sub-commission was tasked with investigating discrimination of any kind related to human rights. It was under this organ that the United Nations conducted research into "Discrimination Based on Work and Descent." In his presentation, Tomonaga related how representatives from the BLL and the research institute had been actively participating in the meetings of the human rights sub-commission since the early 1980s. After multiple reports from the Buraku liberation movement insisting that Buraku discrimination was a form of discrimination distinct from racial or ethnic discrimination, the sub-commission finally adopted a "Resolution Based on Work and Descent" in mid-2000 and resolved to appoint special rapporteurs to investigate this form of discrimination and to draft proposals on it. This category recognizes Buraku issues under a rubric of "work" as much as "descent." It allows for the examination of the Buraku minority group not alongside other groups constituted by race or ethnicity but, instead, alongside groups such as the "outcastes" of South Asia. In so doing, it places a very different set of demands and expectations on how the political movement comports and articulates itself internationally.

The Buraku liberation movement, as enacted under the auspices of the Suiheisha, the BLL, the JSP, the JCP, and even the LDP, has had a complex relationship with domestic and international legal mechanisms. While some of these organizations deny the validity of such an approach altogether (e.g., the JCP), others, such as the LDP, the JSP, and the BLL, have used legislation as a way of ameliorating the perceived problem. However, even within these organizations there is dispute. For a long time the predominant position within the BLL was that law could be used to make positive changes to the education, housing, and social welfare of Buraku districts but was not an appropriate means for combating direct discrimination. However, as the movement started to increase its emphasis on internationalization and to make greater use of the language of human rights, this tendency shifted, and it has become a more accepted and even predominant approach of the movement to volley for the creation of antidiscrimination legislation. The consolidation of "Discrimination Based on Work and Descent" is one such example of this tendency.

A QUESTIONNAIRE CIRCULATES

Prior to the "Informal Consultation," the special rapporteurs circulated a questionnaire on "Discrimination Based on Work and Descent" internationally to UN member states and networked organizations. The movement of the questionnaire in the process of consolidating "Discrimination Based on Work and Descent" offers an inroad to this new standard and the creation of people, things, and words as similar or different across arenas of action. As I noted in the introduction, it has become commonplace to argue that the contemporary moment is characterized by increased movement and an increasing rate of movement—of certain privileged words, objects, and people—across a variety of boundaries.[25] This movement is frequently framed as "circulation." Linguistic anthropology has cautioned against the temptation to view the circulation of a text as a simple matter of production, transmission, and reception, arguing that such an approach tends to presume both text and context.[26] Instead, it pursues an alternative line of inquiry attentive to the work involved in framing one instance of a text as related to another. This "interdiscursive" understanding allows us to rework notions of "friction," for example, not simply as the movement of "universals" but, rather, the creation and re-creation of something the status of which as universal is, if anything, an achievement.[27] These insights are equally applicable to realms beyond discursive signification. People and objects too are equally formed in such work—down to their intimate passionate orientations to pain. The cultural theorists Dilip Gaonkar and Elizabeth Povinelli push in this direction, arguing for attention to how things "entail, demand, seduce, intoxicate, and materialize rather than simply mean."[28]

Take, for example, the first time a Buraku activist visited the UN offices to argue for the inclusion of Buraku issues alongside issues of racial and ethnic discrimination. During this first visit, in the late 1960s, Matsumoto Jiichiro was hard-pressed to create a context in which who he was and what he represented might be understood, much less actively engaged. Compare that experience to how Kumisaka Shigeyuki, current secretary general of the BLL, or Tomonaga Kenzō might now, after decades of interaction with different UN offices, be recognized, greeted, and handled, under the guise of an informational session on "Discrimination Based on Work and Descent." Where Matsumoto had to work hard to be understood, Kumisaka and Tomonaga enjoy an easy reference to precedent; there is a context for their reception, and precedents for how to respond. The differences between these two situations show that there is nothing semiotically flat about the circulation of people bodily from place to place. What that body signifies and what responses it provokes are not the same in these two contexts. Indeed, these two contexts themselves are given shape in the transvaluation of this body.[29] What the United Nations can and cannot do changes across this semiotic transvaluation. In the forty-year gulf that stands between these two sets of activists, work has been done to create contexts in which Buraku identity can signify, and can, further, be seen as related to that of a Dalit activist from, say, Chennai.

The jump from discursive activity to other things such as people or objects is made less jolting if we also consider the fact that any discursive activity only travels as a concrete text artifact, that is, as an object. Whether as books, magazines, or other pieces of paper,[30] as audiotapes,[31] or as blog postings or Internet chats,[32] examples abound of how the material form of a text artifact is consequential to its circulation and the manner in which it is contextualized.[33] The movement of any of these things—people, words, and objects—is the product of the semiotic work of framing. In a similar line of analysis, the anthropologists Benjamin Lee and Edward LiPuma argue that "if circulation is to serve as a useful analytic construct for cultural analysis, it must be conceived as more than simply the movement of people, ideas, and commodities from one culture to another. Instead, recent work indicates that circulation is a cultural process with its own forms of abstraction, evaluation and constraint, which are created by the interactions between specific types of circulating forms and the interpretive communities built around them."[34] They focus on three such interpretive communities, which they argue are constitutive of Western modernity, namely, the nation-state, the public sphere, and the market. I want to push their analysis further. In distinguishing these interpretive communities, Lee and LiPuma leave aside questions of the cultural variability within any one of them. Each of these genres of commensuration is amenable to an internal semiotic analysis of how the effects of similarity or difference are achieved, with attendant consideration for the immanence of social forms in the interaction and maneuvers of authority and warrant.[35] The question remains as to exactly how we might examine these negotiations of similarity and difference and the standards that enable them.

Tracking the movement of the questionnaire in the process of consolidating "Discrimination Based on Work and Descent" offers an inroad to these negotiations, and the creation of people, things, and words as similar or different across arenas of action. The BLL office becomes a different thing when recognized by the UN special rapporteurs through the medium of this text. Likewise, the United Nations, here in the form of two special rapporteurs, asserts itself, in circulating the questionnaire, as a potential purveyor of help on these issues. Other groups, such as the Dalit groups from South Asia, create themselves as potential partners in this struggle. As the linguistic anthropologist Susan Gal pithily puts it: "When texts move, both text and context are transformed."[36] The work involved in circulating these texts, and in turn creating both text and context, is a process of creation and transformation.

This approach has two implications that I would like to highlight here. Framed this way, as process rather than product, these questions of movement immediately implicate questions of authority and political economy. Adjudicating similarity across arenas of action is intricately tied to structures of power and value that constitute the political economy of this category of discrimination, thus begging the questions of access, legitimacy, competence, and values.[37] For example, Professor Yokota, whose presentation opens this chapter, spoke in English to a group of people not all of whom are native English speakers. There were no officially provided interpreters here to translate among English, Japanese, Tamil, Arabic, or Kiswahili. The question then arises, which groups, present or not, have the basic resources necessary to enter into this conversation, that is, either the capacity to understand English or the resources to employee an interpreter? The very room in which Professor Yokota spoke underscored this question of authority. Frequently used for large international meetings, the room was equipped with simultaneous interpretation booths and a display board listing interpreted languages with respective headphone channels. However, during the consultation, the booths were empty, the display board blank, and the headphones silent. This silence spoke—these groups were to provide interpretation for themselves if they were to be provided for at all.

A woman representing a group from Yemen explicitly addressed this question of political economy and resources, extending it beyond the proceedings in the room alone. A graduate student of anthropology from New York University, not a Yemeni herself, and not, despite Professor Yokota's emphasis on minority experience, a member of the group for whom she spoke, pointed out: "The very fact that I am representing this group says something. I am not from this minority. They have no access to government or to transportation." This non-Yemeni graduate student provides this group with its only means of even recognizing the questionnaire as something to which it might be able to respond. Her situation and the group's situation prompt the question, which groups lack such means altogether?

My analytical approach to movement, and its systematization as circulation, as a process of commensuration, has implications for the exercise of comparison more generally. "Discrimination Based on Work and Descent" functions as a standard of comparison, bringing together divergent people and experiences. Given the attention to how contexts and actors themselves are made and remade in interaction, Japan, India, and the United Nations, or Buraku, Dalit, and the human rights worker, cannot be taken as self-evident containers among which texts, people, and things circulate. Rather, these locales and subject positions are co-constitutive; they emerge in a processual, dialogical fashion. Comparison in this case must start with an analysis of how the very objects of comparison emerge within the transnational circulation and commensuration of texts, people, and contexts.[38] How do "work" and "descent" achieve persuasive force? What does the work underlying this achievement do to those who perform such work, and which disciplinary force lies behind "human rights"? And, which types of political action here are rendered possible, obsolete, or even unthinkable?

A NEW SPACE FOR WORK AND DESCENT:
LABOR, CONSTITUTIONAL LAW, AND GRASSROOTS
ORGANIZING

The special rapporteurs on "Discrimination Based on Work and Descent" released their questionnaire in early 2005 with the aim of specifying the forms of this type of discrimination and the types of people affected by it. They did this to fulfill their mandate of establishing a new international instrument that would draw on relevant existing human rights obligations and apply them to situations of work- and descent-based discrimination around the world. The questionnaire, circulated to governments, national human rights institutions, and any nongovernmental organization that saw itself working on this type of discrimination, asked for responding institutions to, among other things, provide a list of affected communities, offer a number of people facing this type of discrimination, and describe in detail the forms of this discrimination.

In Japan the questionnaire was received by the government and a variety of human rights-related NGOs, and it was completed and returned as a joint project among three primary Buraku-related organizations: The BLL, IMADR, and BLHRRI. These organizations produced a collaborative forty-four-page response that was translated into English and provided detailed answers to these and further questions. They defined and identified the kind of person in Japan facing this type of discrimination (the "Buraku people"); they provided numbers of these people in Japan (an estimated 3 million); and they offered a concise description of the ways in which the Buraku people suffer from discrimination based on work and descent.

As staff members from the BLL, IMADR, and BLHRRI worked on this questionnaire, first translating it from English to Japanese and then responding to it, they situated it with respect to other forms of law and political movements. At times these linkages were intentional and strategic, and at times they were unintentional. Likewise, their practices of work were at times matters of word, phrase, or stylistic choice and at other times matters of framing or association. These lexical and pragmatic linkages collectively establish "Discrimination Based on Work and Descent" as new or unprece-

172 · CHAPTER FIVE

FIGURE 12. Chinsung Chun, UN special rapporteuse, leading a discussion about "Discrimination Based on Work and Descent" in Osaka, 2005.

dented, as different from other movements, or as a continuation of them. At the same time, this labor creates and sustains them as particular political subjects. I provide two examples of these achievements, showing the types of political subjects and possibilities they delimit.

There was much debate among the staff of the BLL, IMADR, and BLHRRI about how "Discrimination Based on Work and Descent" might be appropriately and advantageously translated into Japanese. This debate unfolded over hours of face-to-face meetings, e-mails, and phone calls that volleyed between Osaka and Tokyo. "Discrimination" was an easy word. It circulated widely among organizations in Japan that worked on issues of human rights, within and outside of a UN context. The translation into Japanese is standardized: "discrimination" is *"sabetsu."* This term is composed of two characters. The first is used to imply a difference between two things, and the second is used to indicate a separation between those different things. Combined, these characters form a lexeme that invokes a range of political and ethical sensibilities very similar to the word "discrimination" in English. To label the actions of someone else *sabetsu* is an accusation of moral infraction. This word has been used in legal terminology and among political movements since the immediate postwar period. It presently contains the resonances of infraction and opposition. IMADR's name in Japanese is *Han Sabetsu Kokusai Undō,* or "The International Movement Against Discrimination." This word is likewise the standard translation for discrimination as used in other already existing UN regulations, such as the CERD. Thus in choosing to move between "discrimination" and *"sabetsu,"* the staffs of the Buraku political organizations were following and affirming a heavily regimented convention. In so doing, they asserted this new form of potential law as of a piece with similar UN regulations, with the current push for antidiscrimination *(han sabetsu)* legislation in Japan, and with IMADR's ongoing activities. This relationship was already implied in the English original, and IMADR and partner organizations had no desire, nor any authority, to question it in the Japanese rendering.

"Work" was only slightly more problematic. The word unanimously agreed on by the staff members was *"shokugyō."* The term was suggested by a head member of the Buraku research institute and allowed to sit unquestioned by all other participants. I later asked that person about the taken-for-granted aspect of that choice, and he explained that *shokugyō* was a word that implied neutrality in its description of one's employment. The term also is frequently rendered into English as "occupation." This is a word used by government bureaucrats more than labor movements. They preferred terms such as "labor" *(rōdō),* and they similarly spoke of "exploitation" *(sakushu)* instead of "discrimination" *(sabetsu).* The choice of *shokugyō,* which was justified as simply being unmarked, actually served to create a sense of continuity with bureaucratic efforts and a sense of rupture or, rather, nonrelation with a labor movement.

As I alluded to earlier, the most difficult word for the group was "descent." The discussion here pivoted around whether it should be translated as *seikei* or *monchi,*[39] neither of which is a term particularly familiar to a general audience and neither of which is used in everyday conversation by Buraku people to refer to themselves. Though both unknown, these two options, *monchi* and *seikei,* both refer to a hereditary family system, equivalent also to "lineage" in English. However, despite this referential similarity, the indexical overtones of each lexeme are vastly different. They each hook up in vastly different ways with already existing means of managing human rights in Japan. Discrimination on the basis of *monchi* is formally forbidden by Article 14 of the Constitution of Japan. Furthermore, over the past sixty years, the Japanese government has steadily refused to recognize Buraku as a group constituted by *monchi*. The people from the IMADR office, an organization with greater focus on grassroots movements and on human rights beyond just the Buraku case, argued that the translation of the "descent" from this UN document as *monchi* could be a way to pressure the Japanese government into mobilizing its already existing constitutional law to deal with Buraku discrimination. However, representatives from BLHRRI argued that *seikei*, which had no legal life, would allow this new form of discrimination to stand unencumbered by these old, stagnating political efforts. Adopting *seikei* as the translation, which is what eventually happened, would therefore more likely have an effect on the Japanese government and on the legislation it might enact.[40]

The final translation of "Discrimination Based on Work and Descent," to be used in the dissemination of the questionnaire and to describe this new category in the literature and websites of these organizations, was *"Shokugyō to Seikei ni Motodzuku Sabetsu."* In something as seemingly simple as a set of lexical choices, requiring a sometimes contentious set of conversations among the respective leaderships of the BLL, IMADR, and BLHRRI, a range of relationships was framed between this form of discrimination and previous political efforts. This effort was affirmed as a continuation and extension of human rights-focused political movements in Japan; it was divorced from any relation to labor movements in Japan; and it was framed as a new beginning, different from previous legal struggles around constitutional law. In addition to structuring the set of issues with which they would engage, the coalition of the BLL, IMADR, and BLHRRI, in choosing this translation as opposed to, say, *"Rōdō to Monchi ni Motodzuku Sakushu"* or "Exploitation Based on Labor and Descent," also asserted the types of groups it might have as its interlocutors: groups focused on human rights and discrimination, whether lawyers groups, NGOs, grassroots organizations, or even corporations. Equally, this choice of lexical framing asserted the BLL, IMADR, and BLHRRI as organizations that dealt with these issues, engaged with each other, and were available for engagement with the aforementioned types of groups. Internally, the conversations that led to this translation also cast BLHRRI as more interested in engaging with bureaucratic (as opposed to "grassroots," a distinction I discuss more in the next chapter) pathways and confirmed its greater authority alongside the BLL to make decisions that also directed the actions of IMADR.

A second example of the structuring of continuity and difference in the creation of this new category of discrimination lies in the way in which the

BLL, IMADR, and BLHRRI evidenced discrimination and is less a matter of lexical choice than a matter of form and style. The fourth question on the questionnaire was, simply, "What are the types of discrimination?" In response, the BLL, IMADR, and BLHRRI provided a detailed description of discrimination against Buraku people, which they broadly categorized into two types. The first type was *"sabetsu no jiken,"* rendered into English as "Discriminatory Events." These events primarily comprised volitional actions of individuals against other individuals. The second type was *"sabetsu no genjitsu,"* or "The Reality of Discrimination," which was a description of the more structural forms of discrimination faced by Buraku people.

The first type, "Discriminatory Events," was broken into several different categories. First was marriage discrimination, that is, refusal of marriage because of a potential partner's purported Buraku origin. This was followed by employment discrimination (refusal of employment on those same grounds), discrimination within workplaces (slowed upward mobility, verbal harassment), and discrimination in local communities (resistance to administratively merging with a Buraku district within the city-town-village merger project presently taking place across the country). These listed forms of discrimination fall along the commonplace characteristics of what makes one Buraku—prohibition of kinship, employment, and spatial relationships.[41] These are the characteristics that the websites of each of the preparing organizations give in their introductory descriptions of Buraku issues, and they are the characteristics given by academics such as John Lie and Ian Neary, who work on minority and Buraku issues in Japan.[42] They also correspond closely to the primary categories of discrimination described in the *Annual Compendium of Nation-Wide Discrimination*, an annual publication now in its fifteenth year and an initiative of the BLL. A comparison of the questionnaire and compendium is telling.

The major difference between the compendium and the questionnaire response is in the form that the evidence of discrimination takes. The compendium, which has assumed a generic and standardized form in the past five years, culls real-life examples of discrimination that prototypically indicate each different category—marriage discrimination, employment discrimination, and so on.[43] It then describes those typical incidents with great specificity, providing examples of actual discriminatory letters and using photographic reproductions of those letters to prove its case. It speaks to an audience, an "out-group,"[44] that perhaps doubts its message, and the authors of the work state that the abundance of detail is necessary to eliminate that doubt. In its act of describing these forms of discrimination in detail, the BLL projects an ignorance and a doubt to its audience, as well as a knowledge, an authority, and a determination to ending discrimination itself.

The questionnaire response, in contrast, lacks the abundance of detail, though it provides the same general typology of "discriminatory events." It speaks in sound bites and glosses; it references details, but it does not provide them. The audience that is envisioned and projected in this description is one already won over to the fight against discrimination and, projected as that "in-group,"[45] it is already inclined to believe what the authoring organizations say in their questionnaire responses. The UN special rapporteurs and the answering organizations are framed as being on the same general side of what is cast as political struggle; the shorthand of the BLL, IMADR, and BLHRRI's response presumes a shared set of knowledge and a shared set of political and ethical commitments. These are organizations that can work together to end discrimination. The political efforts around "Discrimination Based on Work and Descent" are then available as a continuation of the compendium efforts of the BLL, but with a different set of interlocutors and a different set of political horizons.

The second type of discrimination provided in the questionnaire response was of a similar form, reinforcing the presumptions and assertions of the form of the first type. The section entitled "Reality of Discrimination" entails a description of structural discrimination manifest in the gap in living standards between Buraku and non-Buraku people, particularly with respect to housing, the range of occupation options, and educational standards. Here, too, like the "Discriminatory Events" subsection, there was a scarcity of detailed specificity—not because details are not available but because this genre and the way in which it has already authorized the questionnaire respondent do not require it.

The form of argument underlying both types of Buraku discrimination described on the questionnaire—"Discriminatory Events" and "Reality of Discrimination"—characterizes the Buraku movement in two other ways. Both sections evidence discrimination by indicating a variation from some norm. Buraku people do not have normal access to normal marriage; they do not have normal access to normal education; and they do not have access to the kind of housing deemed (necessary and) normal. Each of these instances of discrimination has in common the general generic form—we are not that, and therefore we are discriminated against; that which is deemed normal is being withheld from us, or from other subpopulations. In creating this form of argument, the movement also establishes a metric by which to gauge normality. For instance, on a different level Buraku people who seek marriage are deemed normal, whereas those who do not but, rather, seek to abolish the marriage system and the family household system altogether sit in opposition to that normal as abnormal.[46] Interesting to note here is the fact that whether this political strategy challenges norms or not is a matter of perspective. For those seeking inclusion in the norm, the norm is not challenged, but frequently for those who already occupy the norm, the mere inclusion of Buraku people, whether in marriage or in one's neighborhood, is a challenge to the institutions of marriage or to sensibilities of propriety.

These arguments of those struggling against anti-Buraku discrimination also establish a relationship with the state. The BLL push for United Nations' help to establish legislation to address the Buraku gap from the social norm fixes the state in a role as a purveyor of assistance. The scope of possible critique of the state then shifts; the BLL's call for legislation condemns the state for incorrect or insufficient implementation of its stated goals rather than for its involvement at all, something, as we saw earlier, which was deemed unnecessary and unwanted in the early part of the movement. This focus on the norm, as well as the reliance on the state, also positions this UN-level endeavor as a continuation of previous Buraku political strategies. The shift in the domestic movement, particularly since the 1970s, from a stance of self-reliance and critique of the state to a stance in which the state is cast as purveyor of assistance is then repeated here on the UN level, casting this current endeavor as an extension of and consonant with other contemporary approaches that rely on the state.

"OUR GRANDPARENTS' TIME": CONNECTING BURAKU PAST TO DALIT PRESENT

In his opening remarks Professor Yokota commented on the large differences among the various groups assembled at the "Informal Consultation." Indeed, these differences bore out in the presentations over the next two days. One of the first group presentations was from a Nepalese Dalit organization. The presenter, a self-identified Dalit man in his mid-forties, framed his discussion with an assertion of the ineffectiveness of law, particularly in areas in which the Maoist movement was contesting state military control.

He detailed the different types of discrimination suffered by the Dalit people in Nepal, ranging from physical violence to unequal access to education and social welfare, and, in his PowerPoint presentation, he provided a graphic photographic testimony of the range of discrimination. He showed pictures as he enumerated atrocities that went unpunished by the state: kidnapping, torture, murder, and rape. He also showed pictures of malnourished children and untreated wounds. Discrimination in his presentation was a matter of bodily harm, including both sudden and extreme violation of the body and steady, long-term degenerescence.

His presentation was followed by a presentation from Kumisaka Shigeyuki, secretary general of the BLL. Kumisaka's presentation lacked a graphic accompaniment; it lacked both a PowerPoint presentation and detailed descriptions of the gruesome effects of discrimination on the bodies and lives of people who face discrimination based on work and descent. Instead of graphic visceral details, Kumisaka's presentation consisted of his reading a preprinted script in English, a script that had been distributed to everyone in attendance prior to his presentation, to ensure that they would be able to decode an English strained through thick Japanese phonology. Kumisaka provided detail, but his was of the emotional strain of being denied marriage or employment based on one's origin; it was also of passed legislation, political strategy, and obtained social benefits. Several frames intersect here to create the sense of a difference in mediation: the *im*mediacy of physical pain is presented in visceral pictures; emotional struggle is conveyed through the medium of words.

If such work went into staging these experiences as different, comparable work went into staging them as both evidence of the same type of discrimination. In her opening remarks Special Rapporteuse Chun had commented on some of the "best practices" exhibited in the responses to the questionnaire, highlighting legislative advances in India and Japan as two primary examples. These were practices to which other groups should aspire, and perhaps one day to attain. Similarly, she noted that Japan had first succeeded in passing special Buraku-focused laws in 1969, well before its Indian counterpart. That temporal gap was evident in the other aspects of discrimination as well. While discrimination in India still frequently took the form of physical violence, such attacks "had become" exceedingly rare in Japan. A presenter from a Dalit group in India made similar comments on the second day. In his presentation, he lauded the advances achieved in Japan and stated that he hoped one day India "would reach" such a point. He thanked the representatives of the BLL for their presentation, which offered everyone at the table a productive model toward which to strive.

Over this two-day conversation, remarks such as these provided a framing of the different modes of discrimination experienced by the various groups. This framing rendered commensurate emotional strain and physical torture as evidence of discrimination, made sensible in respect to each other with the insertion of a model of linear temporal progress. Emotional strain and physical torture here are of the same kind; the difference is only one of degree: over time, physical pain gives way to emotional pain. During the consultation, in Dalit, Buraku, and UN mouths alike, the Dalit were made to be *now* what the Buraku people were *sixty or seventy years ago*. The special rapporteurs relied heavily on the past described by the BLL-generated report to project a future for the Dalit in Nepal and India. The first draft of their guidelines for the elimination of discrimination based on work and descent took the Buraku liberation movement's history as a schematic means for ending this kind of discrimination in South Asia and speculated on its utility in African countries. This framing transformed the past successes of the Buraku movement into future goals for the other groups and their respective governments. There were adjustments to this linear narrative, where the Buraku organization thought it "could have done" better, or where other organizations had pursued tactics divergent from what the BLL had done. For instance, in line with Thorat's questions to Tomonaga regarding affirmative action, several representatives for India argued vocally for legislation in support of affirmative action, contrary to Buraku strategy. However, these adjustments were cast as accessories to the central, normative narrative of linear progression.

Just as the framing of linear progression made past successes of the BLL into potential goals for the other groups, it also made Dalit presents available as examples of Buraku pasts, even if Buraku communities themselves never actually faced the kinds of physical threat that Dalit people currently face. In order to compare experiences with present-day Dalit movements, representatives from the BLL regularly made the move via their own past. This framing was captured particularly well by a Tokyo sanitation worker in a related situation I explore in the next chapter. Speaking to a group of his Buraku fellows prior to their departure on a solidarity trip to South India, he offered a word of cushioning advice to those who had never been to Dalit communities before: "They're like our grandparents' time. It's a Buraku of seventy years ago—dirty and dangerous."

An even more striking example of this tendency to approach Dalit experience through a narrative of linear progress comes in an encyclopedia of Buraku issues published in 1995 by the Buraku Liberation Press. Though the book only contains a discussion of present-day Buraku discrimination, the first few pages of the work, which are all pictures, begin with brutal images of slain Dalit—kneecaps ripped off, legs twisted and torn—and from there the work progresses into the corrugated tin homes and narrow streets of prewar Buraku neighborhoods, and then further on to pictures of wider, tree-lined streets of the successful Buraku neighborhoods of the 1980s.

The discursive device of linear progress provides a framework for the amelioration of differences among the various groups that gathered for the UN "Informal Consultation." It provides a means by which people create apparent unity by putting others into their own stories, either as "our past" or "our future." This framing rendered commensurate emotional strain and physical torture as evidence of discrimination, made sensible in respect to each other by their insertion into a model of linear temporal progress. Emotional strain and physical torture become of a kind; the difference is only one of degree: over time, physical pain gives way to emotional pain. At the same time, it links the current UN-level endeavor to previous and simultaneous Buraku political initiatives. A narrative of linear progress is apparent in all three of the aforementioned examples: in the "Informal Consultation," in the grassroots activist trip to India, and in the BLL publication. This stylistic similarity makes available a sense of continuity across all three of these examples, giving each the grounds for recognizing the others as engaged in the same endeavor.

This narrative also characterizes that endeavor in which these two groups are engaged, both those gathered at the UN consultation and those working in Japan in the Buraku political movement. The device of linear narrative takes discrimination, manifest in one instance as emotional or physical pain, as the entry point into political action. Discrimination is the tacit, taken-for-granted object of political concern. Discrimination and concern are then available for distribution across the minority/nonminority divide that Professor Yokota noted at the end of his introductory remarks. Minorities face discrimination, and they become the proper location for the working of sympathy on the part of nonminority allies.

This shift has a quality that we might call particularly liberal and modern. The primary sympathetic relation here, between, say, Buraku and Dalit people or the Kenyan blacksmiths and Senegalese caste people, is mediated by a third party, a set of people who do not directly face discrimination based on work and descent but who are concerned by it. Their concern, also a form of sympathetic engagement and fellow feeling, stems not from an underlying similarity based on a form of discrimination but on an abstracted notion of the universal human. Whereas what the Buraku actor might feel with her Dalit comrade is based on imagining a similar pain—either recalling an experience or imagining its possibility in the future—the Danish representative from the IDSN is fueled in his concern through an imaginary of an abstract human vulnerable to the abuse of its inalienable rights, a set of concerns and presumptions on which the United Nations is based. It is this abstract human that gives rise to the possibility of a sympathy *with*, but also, faced with the impossibility that the Dane might suffer a similar abuse, gives way to a sympathy *for* that then enables and demands, even, a fellow feeling between Dalit and Buraku people based on their shared woundedness, even as it allows the IDSN representative to indulge sympathetic pleasures of what the anthropologist Michel Rolph Trouillot has called "the convenience of the unmarked."[47]

As the political theorist Wendy Brown argues in *States of Injury*, liberalism brings with it an incitement to *ressentiment*—manifest in a pressure on those marginalized to present themselves as pained rather than to "conjure an imagined future of power to remake itself."[48] In its quest for progress, liberalism keeps an eye on where it can be improved, where it has been insufficiently tolerant, where it has inflicted the "grievous wound" of misrecognition.[49] Its logic demands a wounded other to fuel its drive for improvement.[50] The "Informal Consultation," "based on direct experiences of discrimination," was to a large degree about sharing pain, partaking in what Brown points out as the fixing "of the injured and the injuring as social positions."[51] At the same time, however, the "Informal Consultation," like the trip of Buraku activists to Tamil Nadu, which I discuss in the next chapter, was a moment in which shared pain served as the basis for conjuring an alternate future. The Buraku situation indicates, contra Brown, that a past-bound woundedness need not be contrasted with a future-oriented horizon of possibility. Rather, this situation crosscuts this dichotomization, indicating the future possibilities of a solidarity based on past wounds—one that is not merely therapeutic or reactionary. These possibilities, however, rest in practices geared at projecting a symmetry across Buraku and Dalit experiences, a set of practices that sometimes falters.

Approaching the construction of "Discrimination Based on Work and Descent" as a project of commensuration opens inroads to the various materially and symbolically grounded practices that create the bases for intuitions of continuity, innovation, and rupture among different political groups. It demonstrates how the categories of "discrimination," "work," and "descent" gain purchase and form the basis for international solidarity, and in so doing give form to the political subjectivities and horizons at work in this endeavor. This project of commensuration is key to the labor of multiculturalism and gives a glimpse of how it might be that now, just as the forms of labor that have historically given rise to the Buraku category of person are fading, a multicultural mode of managing social difference might gain traction. The Buraku endeavor of building "Discrimination Based on Work and Descent" resonates with other human rights and minority groups in Japan and internationally, it builds a sense of newness in its divergence from older arguments around constitutional law, and it breaks from a long history of labor movements despite a formal similarity in lexical choice. Groups such as the BLL and the IDSN work to identify, expose, and eliminate discrimination and the pains that accompany it. They call on the state to provide aid in this endeavor at the same time they assist each other.

These moves allow for work to be reworked, returning denuded of any class-based politics and clad instead in the robe of multicultural minority identity. The stripping down of class analysis, of relation to a Marxist labor movement, is, here, precisely what makes this category amenable to use in the context of multicultural politics. We are outside of the factory, here concerned with breaches of a supposed formal equality among citizens. Using the terms of labor is a precarious venture here, particularly pit against the BLL's beleaguered relationship with the JCP. There is always the possibility of the argument being co-opted or undermined by Communist rivals. However, stripping labor of these associations, and starting "new," provides this Japanese organization with an avenue to use a labor-based argument in a drastically different setting.

I have focused on one particular path by which Japan is achieving multicultural status on an international level. This one path relies on the constitution of labor as the basis for an identity that in turn allows for Japan to appear multicultural on an international stage. However, this multiculturalism, narrated here in the language of labor and enabled and led by a Buraku political movement antagonistic with a Communist movement, occurs only under a condition in which a socialist class politics is subsumed. The success of Japan as multicultural in this context hinges on the dissolution of traditional class politics, instead shifting the political gaze to those wounded through discrimination. In this traffic of sympathy, this is the new standard erected and bolstered.

SIX

Wounded Futures

PROSPECTS OF TRANSNATIONAL SOLIDARITY

SYMPATHETIC SELVES

When I was in junior high school, I first learned that I was Burakumin when kids made fun of me. When I was in high school, some of my classmates refused to hang out with me or date me. Now I work with the Tokyo Liberation League.

I am originally from Tsuruoka city, in Japan. I live in Adachi, Tokyo. I first learned that I was Buraku when I was twenty. When I was in high school, my parents wouldn't talk about it. My friends explained it to me. I work with the Buraku Liberation League.

I was born in a Japanese Buraku. I knew I was Buraku from a young age. But I didn't participate in the Buraku Liberation League. When I was twenty-three years old, I participated in the BLL for the first time. I became interested when I heard of the false arrest of a Buraku man for a crime he did not commit. I want to fight against discrimination.

These stories are not mine. They are stories, drafted in English, of a small group of Japanese sanitation workers and Buraku activists who, in 2006, participated in a solidarity trip to Tamil Nadu, India, to meet with "outcaste" Dalit people there, to tour their neighborhoods, homes, and workplaces, to learn about their circumstances, and to share experiences—challenges and successes—in facing a form of discrimination based on descent and occupation.

This week-long trip was the second such trip in three years and if all went according to plan would be just one of many such trips taking Buraku people west to India. Preparation for this trip began months in advance. The Buraku contingent organized a monthly study group; people who had participated in the first trip presented impressions from that first venture to broader audiences in the hope of encouraging participation. On that first trip, they had gone with no language preparation, a fact they lamented over while there; they had exchanged pictures and experiences with the Dalit through an interpreter, but they wanted the felt proximity of direct communication. As I mentioned in chapter 2, eight months prior to their second trip they organized an English-language class and—having heard of this native English speaker working with the head offices of the Buraku Liberation League (BLL)—hired me to teach them.

The twelve students in this English class, all between forty and eighty years old, were absolute beginners in the language. At the first meeting, we discussed their goals—which types of English they might want to learn for their upcoming trip. We drilled English reproductions of several Japanese sentences they had identified as key in describing their situation as minorities in Japan: "Buraku discrimination is a form of caste-based discrimination," and "Buraku people face discrimination in marriage, employment, and education." Beyond these statements and a smattering of travel phrases, we devoted most of our time to developing what we came to call "my story"— succinct statements, some of which begin this chapter, that could be used to explain to Dalit comrades how the Buraku activists came to know they were marked as Buraku, how they became involved in the Buraku liberation movement, and what type of work they currently performed.

After we had finally covered enough key phrases and grammar to move on to "my story," I asked each member of the class to bring three sentences of their "my story" to share with the rest of the students. We went around the class, with each person standing and sharing their three sentences. I made corrections and extracted words and phrases that I thought might be of common use. About fifteen minutes into this exercise, the onus of presentation fell on one person, who had come extraordinarily prepared. She stepped up with her three sentences in grammatically perfect form and she included grammar points I had taught in the previous lesson. She explained to us that she had not learned that she was a Burakumin until junior high school. She described the way in which some of her later high school classmates had refused to associate with her at all, and how some boys refused to date her once they learned her background. This last sentence she managed only with a struggle, emotion welling up in her voice, flushing, and turning red. It had been almost forty years since she had been in high school, but still there she was, stammering and almost crying with the pain of those memories. I immediately felt guilty for asking her to share these memories with the rest of the class. I apologized later, but she told me not to worry about it; this was something she wanted to share with Dalit women in India, and she needed to practice it with people here to be sure she would be able to say it and be understood when she got there. It was something she needed to say.

These stories are self-narrations, framed as the expression of personal and private, painful and possibly triumphant experiences of being Buraku. They are produced, however, set within a vivid topography of others. They are written and performed with an eye on a particular audience—the Dalit—and composed to fire the imagination of those Dalit people, transforming them from distant strangers to closer comrades who might understand, even if only slightly, the situation of the Buraku in Japan and in understanding start to feel with the Buraku. In anticipation of this audience, these Buraku people create texts about themselves, and in internalizing this projected topography, in the practice of addressing it, in firing their own imaginations of that audience, they retexture themselves. In attempting to persuade the Dalit to feel with the Buraku, they also learn a particular way of beating in time with themselves, a particular mode of feeling themselves and being Buraku. Their self-narrations, as a practice, create grounds for the presence and the power of personal and private, painful and possibly triumphant experiences of being Buraku.

At the crux of these genres of self is the figure of pain, centered on wounds, material and emotional, and produced through discrimination. The struggle here, sometimes triumphant, sometimes still embattled, was to overcome this pain, to ameliorate the unequal distribution of resources that might allow life to thrive, and to right any misrecognition that placed individuals and groups under erasure or inflicted on those people a debilitating self-hatred. It was the tenacity of this pain that served as the potential basis for solidarity between the Buraku and the Dalit. It is pain that fires the imagination and allows for a sympathetic transfer between the Buraku and the Dalit—as I said in the last chapter, not a feeling *for* but, rather, a feeling *with*. These social practices of the stories, embedded in the large project of transnational solidarity, were to serve as a means of unearthing and dismantling this pain, of expressing the self correctly, and of being heard across a gulf of national, economic, and racial difference. They were a form of self-care, enabled through a connection with others, as well as a form of self-fashioning. This care of the self, achieved in building a relation with a Dalit other, required a particular disposition of the Buraku imagination that might bring the Dalit within sympathetic range. In this chapter I investigate the mechanisms and aesthetics by which this disposition is achieved, the standards called upon, and the inter-ruptions that, at times, stymie that sympathetic flow.

TYPES OF INTERNATIONAL POLITICAL ACTION: FROM GRASS ROOTS TO THE GOVERNMENT

When the BLL founded the International Movement Against All Forms of Discrimination and Racism (IMADR) in 1988, it did so with the aspiration of internationalizing its original liberatory impulses, of creating an "interna-tional Suiheisha."[1] This internationalization focused on working at the UN and governmental levels with international human rights mechanisms such as "Discrimination Based on Work and Descent." It also included fos-tering "grassroots" work such as the study tour I just described. These types of activity are parsed out under the three fields of engagement with which IMADR was tasked at its inception: *empowerment, solidarity*, and *advocacy*, each of which carries a different ethical and political charge, and each of which allows for the enactment of transnational solidarity in slightly differ-ent manners.

IMADR describes itself as "an international non-profit, non-governmental human rights organization devoted to eliminating discrimination and rac-ism, forging international solidarity among discriminated minorities and ad-vancing the international human rights system."[2] These three core values form the basis of IMADR's concrete activities, from educational seminars and study groups, to media releases, to maintaining an informational website and newsletter in English and Japanese, to organizing the visit of UN digni-taries, to facilitating exchange among their international partners, and they form the basis by which IMADR evaluates itself annually in preparation for the board of directors meetings. The first core value, *empowerment*, consists in the effort "to promote the capacity of discriminated groups to raise their voices and represent themselves in activities to combat discrimination." The second, *solidarity*, is the effort "to promote cooperation and solidarity among discriminated peoples in ways that rise above regional, national, and gender differences." The final value, *advocacy*, is manifest in the activities "to promote implementation of human rights instruments through the voice and power of discriminated groups, and strengthen legal standards, institutions, and organs for the elimination of discrimination and racism; to promote their effective use by the discriminated."

IMADR's website and other literature give equal weight to these three core values and demonstrate how they might be reciprocally nested, each providing the building blocks for the next at the same time that they intensify and promote the prior. For example, empowering people might help them approach a point where they could work in solidarity with others and be able to mobilize human rights instruments to better their situation, but at the same time developing human rights instruments might serve as the grounds for a solidarity that could facilitate empowerment. This asserted reciprocity, however, does not mean that these values receive the same amount of weight in daily practice. Nor does each of these core values index the same type of political engagement, the same type of politically engaged subject, or the same type of political motivations. The differences among the indexical overtones of the core values both reflect and create ideological characterizations of each of these types. These differences are then available as an interpretive and evaluative framework for use across multiple different scales.

During my fieldwork, the leadership of the BLL headquarters and the Buraku Liberation and Human Rights Research Institute (BLHRRI) repeatedly demonstrated a preference for and emphasis on advocacy work at the UN level. During board meetings, they held IMADR accountable for such projects that very much overlapped with their own. On the other hand, IMADR staff members occasionally expressed doubts with regard to the effectiveness of UN human rights mechanisms as a sole or even primary route of political intervention. Take, for example, a meeting between leaders of IMADR and the Feminist Dalit Organization (FEDO) in which a "grassroots" approach comes to fill a space oppositional to that of a "UN" approach.

The leadership of the FEDO came to IMADR's offices in November 2006 in the hope of discovering "a potential partner in solidarity." This brief excerpt from their meeting gives a sense of the weighted relations between "grassroots" and "UN" or fund-raising work.

> IMADR: This is the fist time we have met here, and thank you so much for coming and for your presentation yesterday. I look forward to future collaboration and am glad we have this time to exchange views. I definitely would like to hear your experiences collaborating with the BLL, both in Nepal and on the Japanese side. You mentioned yesterday that you feel empowered, but what has happened to your Japanese counterparts—probably the same? IMADR is a catalyst, sometimes invisible. We have focused on UN-level work but over the past 5 years, we have focused more and more on establishing exchanges and networks

among minority populations, with the cooperation of the majority populations as well. I would also like to hear what your expectations of us might be, that is, what we can do for each other. From what I have understood, there are many issues on which we overlap—trafficking issues, UN level, minority women. Hopefully this time will allow us to develop strategies for future collaboration. What are your impressions so far?

FEDO: I have been here before but have had a lot more opportunities to talk to people, the Buraku, and others this time. When I was in Kagoshima I had learned about Okinawa, but this time we had a home stay with the Buraku community and see how people live. It was interesting to see how people feel about their family members and how they lead their lives.

IMADR: Effective measures must be installed with the support of grass roots. We don't say that we don't need the international pressure from international NGOs, but we focus on grass roots. Without this level of initiative, these programs often fail—for example, the Roma in Slovakia. The government has built beautiful houses, but . . .

FEDO: We asked Dalit women—if we built a five-story house for them, how would you feel. Just building a house is not enough. Must have grassroots support and activity.

IMADR: . . . Huge money-collectors frequently spend their money without the actual people knowing about the money or having access to it. European agencies have started to finance programs that deal with Dalit issues, but they still overly focus on themselves. There needs to be more centralization on the groups, and work coming from those groups. IMADR needs to be something different, not deciding how the money might be spent, but empowering people themselves. . . . The work is talking to people and empowering them. We NGOs in the north are asked about transparency and reports but this kind of measurement is sometimes not applicable to what is happening on the ground. We are trying to be an agent to have money given to the people themselves. In the future, I would very much like to continue our relationship. I think there is a strong fit between our goals.

FEDO: We always like the idea of creating the network and giving solidarity to each other's actions. Thank you very much for your commitment to us. I am excited about the possibility of potential future solidarity.

There is a contrast here between two types of political action. The "UN-level" work is characterized as overlapping with the "distribution of money" and the "regulation of its expenditure." These types of "larger" agencies tend to "focus on themselves" more than they focus on the "empowerment of discriminated against people." Their politics are conducted with a combination of little knowledge of what is happening "on the ground" and a large amount of bureaucratic paperwork to simulate lines of accountability. "Grassroots activism," in contrast, centers on the possibilities of "collaboration," "empowerment," "mobilization," and "mutual benefit." Instead of "merely knowing" "politics and history," this type of engagement also considers "culture." In the description of the FEDO's activities, this mode of political engagement includes "homestays, talking to people, seeing how they lead their lives, and how they relate to their families." In pursing this type of politics, IMADR seeks to "build connections" and "establish exchanges and networks among minority populations." In this conversation, grassroots work is given greater ethical and political weight; it is projected as less mediated, more direct, and riper with future political potential. Grassroots work will not simply "build houses," it will allow people to claim those houses as their homes.

This interpretive framework, which contrasts "UN work" with "grassroots work," travels. It establishes two different authoritative standards to undergird international political work. This contrast is available for use in characterizing individual political actions as well as types of individuals or institutions across different scales of interaction, coming to effect insofar as it is recontextualized alongside and bundled with other frames that sort and categorize actors and actions. As I gave a glimpse of in the first chapter, one particular place that this framework has traction is in the relationship between the BLL and IMADR, where distinctions of physical location, age, gender, and decorative style all combine to carve out different types of political orientations. The more "grassroots" IMADR was located in the basement of the BLL building, in a space that was converted from a garage when IMADR was founded, both literally and figuratively, under the management of the BLL.[3] Whereas IMADR staff members, five of the six of whom were female, were between the ages of twenty-three and forty, the all-male BLL leadership was age fifty or older. Indeed, there was only one woman working on any of the BLL floors of the building. The mostly female staff members of IMADR, unless they had to attend a formal meeting, a press conference, teach class, or talk to a Diet member, were typically dressed in very casual business wear. The BLL men, however, were always in suits. The BLL office space was dominated by working cubicles, each piled high with mounds of paperwork. The walls were covered with pictures of founding (male) members of the BLL, posters for political parties and leaders receptive to the BLL cause, and iconic memorabilia from the movement's history, among them the crown of thorns emblem of the movement and a copy of the Suiheisha Declaration. IMADR's office lacked the cubicle walls and was decorated with posters showcasing the UN human rights declaration, with a variety of items that conveyed a stronger sense of internationalism: a poster of a young white boy giving a young black girl a flower, a calendar featuring different African tribes, gilded, South Asian cloth runners across cabinets, and an assortment of eclectica, such as a stuffed tiger in a pink shirt with the word "lucky" across it, a Nepalese version of a cabbage-patch doll, and a rabbit dressed in an American flag. Most of these items were either gifts from IMADR's partner organizations throughout Asia, Africa, and South America or souvenirs brought back from staff trips to those locations. While they did not clutter the space, they definitely lent it a palpably different feel from the upstairs offices.

These bundled dimensions of distinction—political persuasion, physical location, age, gender, and sartorial and interior style—exist alongside and parallel to the differences among IMADR's different core values of empowerment, solidarity, and advocacy. Thus we have, on the one side, empowerment and solidarity aligned with IMADR's younger, more female staff, indexing an interest in something called "grassroots social change" that is imagined to be "closer" to the movements on the ground and closer to a real form of democracy. Advocacy, on the other hand, maintains a twinge of older, stodgier masculine professionalism. While these different dimensions need not always work together, and while no one dimension entirely determines any of the others, the link among these bundled characteristics makes possible cross-dimensional (or interpragmatic) associations. This set of constrasts provides grist for the labor of characterizing, judging, and making types of people, types of political projects, and types of ethical sensibilities and, in the act of firing that imagination and extending sympathetic engagement, characterizing the self.

The relationship between IMADR and the BLL is just one venue in which a contrast between the grassroots- and UN-level is salient. For example, IMADR and the BLL collaborated to attend the 2007 World Social Forum. At this event, "grassroots activists" gathered in a stadium outside of Nairobi, surrounded by a fence, barbed wire, and security, for three days of meetings. As a result of this "protection," the participants in the World Social Forum faced criticism by local political organizers as being insufficiently oriented to grassroots concerns—of siding with bureaucracy and governments.[4] Likewise, similar contrasts exist within the BLL itself, and the actions of the BLL headquarters, which target domestic and international legal and political change, can sit counterposed with the actions of local branches, the Tokyo

FIGURE 13. A meeting at the 2007 World Social Forum among activists, including Buraku and Dalit organizers, to discuss caste and descent-based discrimination.

branch of the liberation league, as one example, that focus more on local communities or on the smaller-scale connections between a handful of Tokyo activists and Dalit organizers based in Tamil Nadu, India.

IMADR and the BLL, as well as the scholars Arjun Appadurai[5] and Francoise Lionnet and Shu-mei Shih,[6] laud "grassroots" political engagement as a novel and potentially powerful form of politics and contrast it with "UN- or government-based politics." Lionnet and Shih in particular tend to emphasize the possibilities of this type of politics, but at the same time they forgo an analysis of the work entailed in achieving this category or the authority presupposed and created in conferring it. The constraints and potentially unmeetable demands, along with new possibilities, come with the work required to constitute and confer the statuses of "solidarity" and "empowerment." IMADR and the BLL, including its Tokyo branch, must strategize around these constraints, even as they enliven new possibilities. The optimistic descriptions of Appadurai and Lionnet and Shih, which dwell more on possibilities than on the full complement of work, possibility,

FIGURE 14. Buraku activists meeting with their Dalit counterparts in Chennai, India.

and constraint, then prompt the question, for whom are these engagements hopeful? Certainly they inspire hope for the organizations involved, but this optimism is tempered by the distress, confusion, and restrategization that accompany this work of creating a hopeful grassroots solidarity.

CREATING "MY STORY," CREATING MYSELF: TRAVELING TO INDIA

It was in the context of IMADR's "grassroots" activism that I was introduced to the Tokyo branch of the BLL (or, Toren, for short). In early 2006 two men from their office, their director and one of their office staff, Mizuno, came to IMADR to discuss potential opportunities for collaboration. Prior to the meeting, the entire office, myself included, took these visitors to a nearby Korean restaurant that we frequented. The lunch conversation centered on Tokyo Buraku districts, with the two Toren officers good-naturedly lecturing the rest of us on this history. In addition, however, the lunch also served to introduce the Toren leaders to two native English speakers also familiar with Buraku issues: Malaya and me. Months later, when the Toren was looking for an English teacher to help it prepare for its study tour to India, their director asked IMADR if either of us would be interested in this paid position. I was interested, and Malaya was otherwise busy; the task became mine.

The study tour, which was conducted with the aim of promoting an exchange between the Dalit and Buraku people, was a collaborative effort between the members of the Tokyo Toren and its related Tokyo Buraku Liberation Research Center and members of a Chennai-based Dalit organization headed by Dalit lawyer and activist Caroline Ezhil. The trip had grown, in part, out of a decades-long friendship between Mizuno and Caroline's family. IMADR supported this connection as an example of its core values of "empowerment" and "solidarity" and referred to this connection as a "grassroots" one. The BLL Toren members likewise classified it as an example of the internationalization of the Suiheisha. The study tour, which did not rely on international human rights mechanisms nor aimed to use international pressure to influence a domestic government to enact legislation, likewise would qualify for Appadurai's designation of "deep democracy."[7]

This solidarity project hung on the interplay of similarity and difference between Buraku and Dalit experiences of discrimination, discrimination that was tied to forms of labor. The trip exists in a longer history of solidarity projects between Buraku and Dalit organizations, reliant on a burgeoning sensibility that Buraku and Dalit people face similar situations, in this case made relevant in contingent factors of friendship between Caroline and Mizuno. Particular work was required to assert similarities across a presupposed chasm of difference and claim the possibilities of "empowerment" and "solidarity." This work, much of which relied on a hinge of shared pain, was at the same time risky, plagued with possibilities of failure but also productive of ethical implications that threatened the entire project.

BURAKU AND DALIT GRASSROOTS SOLIDARITY

Since the 1950s members of the Buraku liberation movement have conducted trips to India to investigate possible similarities with the Dalit and to assess the potential for collaborative political work. As I mentioned in the last chapter, the leader of the immediate postwar liberation movement, Matsumoto Jiichiro, himself visited India multiple times to forge connections and build a base for collaboration. During the 1960s and early 1970s, with the passage of the Special Measures Law, there was a larger focus on domestic issues than on international ones. However, the then-named Buraku Liberation Research Institute (BLRI), which was established during that time period, took as one of its primary goals the investigation of something it called "caste-based discrimination" throughout Asia. It focused in particular on South Asia and India. While there were related projects throughout the first decade of the institute's existence, they remained, until the mid-1980s, secondary priorities compared to domestic research. At that point, the BLL was starting to engage more fully with UN human rights mechanisms and was expanding its political vision across a global horizon.[8]

In the late 1980s and early 1990s, just as IMADR was starting its activities, the research institute intensified its research regarding trans-Asian caste-based discrimination. As part of this project, it and the BLL encouraged Japanese scholars to visit countries in South Asia and sponsored and supported visits to Japan by Dalit activists and organizers. It published information regarding these activities in the BLL, IMADR, and BLRI newsletters, which were distributed to all BLL branches throughout the country. Eventually, the research institute, renamed the Buraku Liberation and Human Rights Research Institute in 1998, created a permanent study group devoted to exploring this form of discrimination. This group, which consists of members of BLHRRI, IMADR, and a variety of university professors and graduate students primarily in the Osaka area, holds monthly meetings, organizes conferences, and publishes its proceedings. Its efforts resulted in the 2004 publication of a work entitled *Ajia no Mibunsei to Sabetsu (Asia's Caste System and Discrimination)*, which describes the roots and rigors of caste-based discrimination in China, Korea, India, Nepal, and Japan, and which uses the category of labor as the basis for a transnational form of discrimination and identity.[9]

This burgeoning line of engagement provided fodder for action and strategic planning for the Buraku political organizations. It also, as news of these research projects, visitations, and trips circulated in movement periodicals, served to widen the imaginary horizon of Buraku people associated with the movement and beyond. For example, over tea one day in late 2005, I was asked to explain my research by a friend, Uchizawa Junko, a freelance journalist who researches meat and leather production globally. She wanted to incorporate a description of me and my hometown, Lubbock, Texas, into a book that she was working on detailing meat production around the world.

The previous summer she had come to my hometown to tour the ranches, feedlots, and slaughterhouses that help support my hometown's economy. She was then in the final stages of finishing her book and wanted more details about my project to flesh out her description of her trip to Texas.[10] I explained my research as an examination of the effects of internationalization on the Buraku political movement. At the word "international," or *kokusai,* she launched into a description of political movements and workers' conditions in India, a country she had visited multiple times while working on her book. Uchizawa's immediate association of "international BLL" work with conditions in India is in no way isolated; it indicates a larger trend within those familiar with the Buraku liberation movement. The movement's well-advertised push to recognize similarities with Dalit organizations in South Asia has become a touchstone across the movement, and the association of Buraku internationalism and the Dalit that my friend Uchizawa here exhibits is commonplace.

The Toren India study tour is another moment that both reflected this association and intensified its visibility and political solvency, serving to dispose the Buraku imagination to recognize Dalit as proximate. The friendship between Mizuno and Caroline, the foundational prompt for the study tour, was itself born of and creative of this association. During college in Kyoto, Mizuno had interned at a newly established and very small Buraku liberation center that had been set up by the United Church of Christ in Japan (UCCJ). Mizuno worked closely with the center's director, Imai, growing closer over the several years he interned there.

Three years into Mizuno's internship, Imai grew sick. Weeks before he passed away, he urged Mizuno to visit India. Imai had been to India shortly before Mizuno started his internship and there had become friends with Caroline's father. Mizuno agreed to his friend and mentor's suggestion, but it took him several years to amass the money to make the trip. After college he worked a host of part-time jobs, including waiting tables, and at the same time continued volunteering with the UCCJ liberation center. At one point he helped host a delegation from India, touring Buraku areas throughout the country. Caroline's father was part of that delegation. Becoming closer to this Dalit leader, Mizuno redoubled his efforts to travel to India. He started volunteering at places that used English to improve his language skills, and he took on more jobs for the money, working as a security guard and a cafeteria attendant in a large corporation. For a while, he even lived in the company's janitor's closet.

Eight years after he had started college, he finally had enough money saved to travel to India. He went on an exchange program to study at a Dalit Christian theology school, having learned that some 80 percent of Christians in India are Dalit. While there he reconnected with Caroline's father, who was in the midst of a burgeoning political career, simply showing up at his door one day. After Caroline's father recovered from the shock of seeing this young Japanese man arrive randomly on his doorstep, he threw Mizuno on the back of his motorcycle, gave him a tour of Dalit neighborhoods, and introduced him to key organizers within the broader community. He treated Mizuno as family, and Mizuno quickly became friends with his daughter, Caroline.

Twenty years later, Mizuno and Caroline remained close friends. Caroline had become a lawyer and the leader of the Chennai-based Dalit group, and Mizuno had become one of the core members of the Tokyo branch of the liberation league. They had each visited each other's homes multiple times and were actively engaged in each other's political movements. Mizuno had introduced Caroline to the head office of the BLL, whose members had invited her to speak at several of the organization's large gatherings in the late 1990s and 2000s, and Mizuno had spent months with Caroline's family in India. In 2004 the two decided to organize a study tour of Dalit communities in Chennai that would connect Caroline's political work more directly to Mizuno's, potentially channel funds from relatively wealthier Japanese organizations, and allow for the inspiration of cross-pollination.

LEARNING ENGLISH FOR DALIT SOLIDARITY

The 2006 tour was the second tour organized by the Toren, its research institute, and Caroline's partner organization. The first had occurred a year and a half earlier, and both trips shared very similar itineraries and participants. There had not, however, been any language preparation for the first trip. Rather, Mizuno had served as the interpreter for the Japanese participants, using his English picked up informally through years of friendship with Caroline and visiting her home. These participants had left the first tour in part frustrated with their lack of English-language skills. They hired me prior to their next trip to help prevent this experience the second time around.

The first meeting of our class was in early June 2006, five months before the scheduled study tour to India. Over those months we would meet on the first and third Mondays of each month in the Toren office building located in a neighborhood called "Imamiya," just north of Asakusa, Tokyo's iconic leather goods district. Participants would pay me ¥3,000 (approximately 30 U.S. dollars) per session, and it was incumbent upon me to decide what the group would study and then to prepare and teach accordingly. On the first day I started the course with a brief, generic introductory conversation that consisted of the greeting, "Hello. My name is Joe. What is your name? It is nice to meet you." After an hour of practicing this conversation, I ended the class by brainstorming collectively on the types of things students wished to learn over the next five months, to give me a clearer idea of what to prepare for classes.

As I explained previously, there were twelve students who regularly came to the class, between the ages of forty and eighty. Many were directly involved in some aspect of the Buraku political movement and had heard about the trip through that connection. Four people worked directly for the BLL at the Toren or at other branches, four were involved in either the leather or scrap metal industries and were active in their local BLL branches, and two were sanitation workers who were there with and through the financial support of their union. These two were very much interested in traveling to India to meet Dalit sanitation workers and exchange experiences. The final two of the group were representatives from different companies that belonged to the Buraku Industrial Federation.[11] They were participating in the partial fulfillment of the human rights requirements of their companies. Ten of these people were men, and two were women, both of whom worked for the liberation movement, one at the Toren, the other in a neighborhood branch of the BLL. All of the participants were almost complete newcomers to the English language. A very small handful could read the English alphabet and knew some stock phrases, but the majority knew next to nothing. The last time most of them had been in a classroom setting was decades earlier, in high school. Mizuno served as my assistant, there in case I got lost in Japanese explanations of English grammar.

On that first day, during our brainstorming session, we planned out the eleven classes prior to the study tour. As a group we decided to explore the following themes: introductions of self, family, and home; travel English; asking for help and clarification; explaining Buraku discrimination; and detailing one's job and activist work. We would use these themes for two purposes: one, to acquire basic conversational skills, and, two, to augment the creation of "my story," which we decided should be a self-introduction explaining one's background, political engagements, and how the student came to know if they were (if indeed they were) Buraku. There would be time in each session devoted to crafting this story, with the intention of having a polished blurb by the time of the study tour.

Within these classes and then further into the study tour, several key moments demonstrated the work entailed in achieving the "empowerment" of self and the commensuration of that self with a projected other in "solidarity." Five different moments in particular demonstrated the constraints and possibilities enlivened by this work. The first three moments I draw from the class itself; the last two follow the English class to India. They show the ways in which language, economics, and the pains of discrimination create both challenges and possibilities for the work of solidarity, the work of extending sympathy and in the process rewriting one's self, and the work of creating a multicultural Japan.

The demonstration of wounds here is key to this project of self-fashioning and solidarity. Since the work of the anticolonial thinker Franz Fanon,[12] many scholars on colonialism and its historical successors in liberal multiculturalism have commented on how the marginalized are more and more represented and evidenced through the figure of pain.[13] Instead of taking pain as a given category of experience, I am interested here in the work required for certain experiences to be felt as painful, and how actors respond to demands that they be wounded.[14] The transnational solidarity project between the Tokyo Buraku activists and the Chennai Dalit relies on a commensuration of the pain that each of these groups feels in the face of discrimination. This project requires each group to narrate and equilibrate pain, and in the process to create anew what might count as pain. In presuming a similarity with the visceral physical pains of the Dalit—the kidnappings, torture, murder, and rape—Buraku activists learned to orient themselves differently to their own pain of refused marriages or jobs. In becoming the "same pain," their own deeply personal experiences of pain were dramatically rewritten. The examples I pursue next hinge on the narration and back projection of a category called "pain," a prospect imperiled when those pains refuse to cooperatively line up.

"My Story" and the Crafting of Selves

"My story" was supposed to be a first-person narrative about the experience of being Buraku, the discrimination and potential difficulties that went along with that, and the kinds of antidiscrimination activities in which one was engaged. Most of the students wrote these narratives first in Japanese and then asked me to translate them in class, but some used our lessons and created their narratives in English from the outset. Each person practiced these narratives in class, in preparation for opportunities to say them in Chennai. The woman who broke down in tears in front of the class read to us this story:

> When I was in junior high school, I first learned that I was Burakumin when kids made fun of me. When I was in high school, some of my classmates refused to hang out with me or date me. Now I work with the Tokyo Liberation League.

This woman, whom I will call Kimiko, had prepared the narrative in English ahead of time. With some corrections from me, she presented the previous story to the class five weeks prior to our trip to India. She stumbled and choked on the words as they came out of her mouth. Her stumbles were not because of an unfamiliarity with the words. She had evidently practiced before she came to class. Instead, she was moved by the intensity of voicing these things, which she later told me she had almost never done.

In reading this story for the class, Kimiko is narrating her self. On the one hand, Kimiko is the "I" that is being narrated as she uses her newly learned English grammar to position herself in a time years ago and to describe the types of discrimination and emotional pain she faced then. This narrated Kimiko, hurt and saddened, is then placed in the now of the utterance to describe her work as a Buraku activist. On the other hand, Kimiko is also the "I" uttering these words, words that are spoken with more than one audience in mind. First, as she explained when I apologized for making her recite this in front of the class, these words are intended for an audience in India. The positioning of the narrated Kimiko in the past and present struggle is meant to describe an experience that will potentially allow her to bridge a gap with Dalit people in Chennai. For that, however, practice is necessary. Kimiko is also performing this narrative in the moment of utterance for the English class, with the intent of cultivating competency in narrating herself in a language she typically does not use. She is trying out new grammar, new words, and new deictics as a mode of articulating her self, and she is doing so under the potentially critical ears of her classmates and her teacher, who are at least as attentive to the content of her words as to the linguistic competence they index. This is a moment of self-creation that locates and consolidates all of these "I's" against the multiple, different "you's" that serve as possible audiences.[15] In subjecting herself to present linguistic critique, she is opening up the possibility of connecting herself to a future audience, and at the same time she is invoking and enacting the described pain of the past in the moment of the utterance, bringing the emotional state of the narrated "I" into the narrating frame.

The stories of the other students were similar to Kimiko's. Each served as a conduit both for the potential transference of information to a Dalit audience and for the rehearsal not just of English but of a self that was consolidated around a presumed sympathetic engagement with the Dalit, around the pains and triumphs of facing, and potentially overcoming, discrimination. These stories helped the class members establish a relationship with their own pain, articulated in relation to a possible connection to Dalit others.

Defining Discrimination

In the fifth through the eighth sessions of our class, we focused on defining and describing Buraku discrimination. I arrived at the fifth session with a pre-scripted definition of Buraku people as "a minority group who face discrimination in Japan." I put this definition and its Japanese translation on the board at the beginning of the class, explained it, and said that we would come back to practice it later in the class. First I wanted students to take a few minutes to write down a brief description of their activist work (*shakai katsudō*) in Japanese, which we would translate into English together. As the participants were working on this task, Mizuno came over to me and suggested that we "rethink the Buraku definition." He said, "People in India won't understand this definition well. They won't understand minority in the same way. Buraku people are not an ethnic group." As he explained this to me, in English and in Japanese, I noticed that one of the sanitation workers, a man who had gone to India the previous year, was listening in and nodding in agreement with Mizuno. I asked for a more appropriate definition, and Mizuno suggested: "Buraku discrimination is a form of caste-based discrimination." The sanitation worker nodded again at this, in seeming understanding and agreement.

When the students finished developing their descriptions of their activist work, I suggested that we collectively develop a definition of Buraku. One man, who had told the class he did not have a job but, rather, was an activist, guffawed at this suggestion, saying: *"Sore ha naka naka muzukashii. Nihon no dokutoku no mondai desu kara"* ("That is pretty difficult. This is a problem unique to Japan"). In other words, he was suggesting that perhaps no matter how the Buraku delegation expressed itself in India, a true recognition of the issues would never happen. I suggested to the class that we use Mizuno's definition rather than what I had prepared, and after some discussion, students agreed that it provided a sufficient description and that it would be better understood in an Indian context. One worry that was expressed, however, was that *"Nihon no Buraku tte chiiki to kankei aru sa. Indo de ha mibunseido ni motodzuku sabetsu ha sono kankei ga nai. Chotto chigau ime-ji wo ataeru to omou kedo . . . tabun daijōbu"* ("In Japan, 'Buraku' is related to space. Caste-based discrimination in India doesn't have the same connotation. We'll be giving them a slightly wrong impression . . . but I guess it is okay"). Most of the participants agreed with this assessment but also agreed that a slight misunderstanding was acceptable. The main points of similarity would be understood even if there were slippages around the specifics.

In this description and the discussion that generated it, then, similarity is created as dominant over difference. The class participants chose to downplay the potential differences between the two groups strategically in order to convey to their Dalit interlocutors the outstanding similarities between the groups. In creating this description, they simultaneously create the identities on which possible solidarity will be based. They establish themselves as an example of a group facing a particular type of discrimination, and that type is the same as the Dalit people face. Rather than constituting itself as a minority group, it instead relies on the terminology of "caste." This is a category of discrimination that the Japanese government has consistently refused to recognize domestically, and a category that the BLL rarely uses to describe its own type of discrimination. The situations in which the BLL does use this terminology (and these situations are on the increase) are ones precisely like these, when they assert similarity between themselves and South Asian groups. Here, then, as the possibility of similarity is constructed in this description, there is also a consolidation of this activity as a type of activity, namely, that of engaging in international solidarity. At times that solidarity means downplaying certain aspects of the Buraku experience, such as the connection to space, that are key in other situations, such as arguing for domestic pro-Buraku legislation.

Preparing for Economic Disparity

My third and fourth examples deal with an aspect of the relationship between the Dalit and the Buraku that the members of my English class anticipated would be divergent and potentially problematic from the outset, and that they strategized around prior to the trip. That aspect was one of economics. There was no doubt on the part of my English class that there was a vast economic difference between these two groups facing "caste-based discrimination," the Buraku and the Dalit, and that entrenched poverty continued to exacerbate in a very serious way the forms of pain and discrimination the Dalit faced. The whole study tour was set up as a fund-raising venture for Caroline's organization. Each person was paying, or having their parent organization pay, close to 3,000 U.S. dollars for the seven-day trip to India. This fee included airfare, hotel, and all meals but left over was a large amount to be donated. Furthermore, several members of the class had participated in the first study tour and had seen the vast economic disparities. One member of the first study tour, a relatively wealthy Japanese businessman who had recently been diagnosed with terminal cancer, had been so moved by the poverty that he encountered and so impressed by the work the Dalit organization was doing that he donated close to the equivalent of 20,000 U.S. dollars for the construction of a rural community center and a Dalit education program. The man was too sick to participate in the second study tour, but our group was to visit the community center that his donation had made possible.

The participants in the second study tour felt that the economic disparity that some of them had seen, along with the precedent set by the large donation the previous year, was going to put them in a situation where they would be asked for money—by people on the street and by members of the communities they would visit. In anticipation of these requests, they wanted to learn English sentences that would allow them to be polite in their refusal and instead reroute the conversation to other possibilities. They anticipated that they would be asked, "What will you do for us?" or "Can you give us money?" In response, they wanted to know the English for, "We came to learn how we can help each other best. We will go back to Japan and share what we learn. That is all we can do for now." These statements and their preparation reveal an anticipation of inequality and a desire to render the relationship one of mutual benefit rather than merely a relationship of charity or unidirectional contribution. "What will you do for us?" is transformed to "help each other best." Here the work of solidarity is created and presumed to be one of mutuality, even in circumstances of vast inequality that might otherwise hinder such an assertion.

It was in the context of these conversations that one member of the group, who had participated in the first study tour, explained to the members who had not yet been that what they would encounter was "like the Buraku situation of our grandparents, of seventy or so years ago," referring to small, squalid housing conditions and the physical brutality of the discrimination the group faced. Here he employed the logic of linear progress that I discussed in the previous chapter to make sense of the economic disparities that the group would encounter, but also to understand the differences in pain between the two groups. The presumption was that the intense physical wounds that the Dalit face—physical and sexual abuse, starvation, and disease, exacerbated by entrenched poverty—could be understood on the same grounds as the pain that the Buraku faced—the pain shown briefly in the stories that Buraku participants were preparing of refused marriage or employment, of harassment—with the use of time. Though around the turn of the previous century Buraku people had faced physical attack by people affronted by the suggestion that Buraku people were equal to them, those attacks were infrequent and typically came in the form of en masse riots. Individual acts of brutality had never been as chronic and systematic as the contemporary situation of Dalit people. However, this type of explanation, that is, that the Dalit are now where the Buraku were seventy years ago, was frequently one means of relating these two divergent experiences. Commensuration was achieved by inserting the Dalit into stories about "ourselves."

Encountering Economic Disparity

When we arrived in India, the economic disparities and poverties that previous participants warned about could not have been more evident. Most of our days in Tamil Nadu were filled with various meetings and tours, including tours of Dalit slums, meetings with people who had faced discrimination and "had their human rights violated," tours of a slaughterhouse and a leather tannery, meetings with sanitation workers, or "cleaning caste people," and a visit to the community center that the previous year's donations had made possible. The financial disparities between the group from Japan and the received group of Dalit activists were patent. For the time we were in Chennai, we stayed in a hotel that cost approximately 30 U.S. dollars a night, roughly equivalent to a month's earnings for many of the people we met during the week. I stayed in India two days longer than the rest of the group, and Caroline asked me if I would be willing to stay at her house rather than at the hotel for those two nights. She instead wanted me to donate that money toward the college expenses of a young Dalit man. Sixty dollars, she explained, would go a long way toward paying for his school expenses for the year.

In the middle of our week of tours and meetings, we had one "free" day. That day we were scheduled to go to Puducherry, a city some distance south of Chennai and originally a French colonial city. The city still maintained some of that colonial influence, which differentiated it from the surrounding towns and made it, Caroline argued, an interesting tourist destination. It was also, it turned out, a location that would render that much more palpable the economic differences between two groups cast as partners in solidarity.

After checking into our hotel, where rose petals floated in a marble swimming pool, we wandered out into the city. We happened upon some men of the "cleaning caste" and watched for a moment as they cleared out a sewer along one of the streets close to our hotel. These men were wearing nothing more than loincloths and had jumped into a backed-up and flooded sewage container. Their bodies were submerged in diluted human waste as they attempted to solve the problem. Here were people engaged in what "Discrimination Based on Work and Descent" might cast as similar forms of work, but the actual specifics of those works highlighted their profound differences. The Tokyo sanitation workers, eager as they were to establish a connection, were both interested in and taken aback by the labor performed by those who might be their comrades. As we stood watching, we noticed that no one else on the street was paying any attention to this situation, indicating perhaps that this was a common occurrence. Instead of sticking around and gawking in an awkward mix of identification and dissonance, the Tokyo group instead headed away and found a restaurant for lunch.

After eating, the seven of us set out again for a walk through the city before retiring to the hotel for a respite from the afternoon sun. On our walk, we met a street performer. He was an older man, who appeared to be in his sixties or seventies and who had a monkey with him. He would sing and play a keyboard instrument, and the monkey, who was dressed in a hat and a little suit coat, would jump and flip in time to the man's song. The man had collected some loose change from the passersby, approximately the equivalent of 20 U.S. cents.

The Buraku group was quite excited by the sight of this man performing with the monkey. One of the occupations of the "outcastes" of Tokugawa Japan was exactly this kind of performance: itinerant performers who traveled entertaining people with songs coordinated with dances by half-tamed monkeys.[16] Called *saru mawashi,* this activity had recently received much attention in eastern Japan, including Tokyo, as one of the "cultural activities" of the predecessors to the Buraku people. Four months prior I had been invited to attend a traditional *saru mawashi* by a sociology professor at Saitama University who worked on Buraku issues. That professor had invited his students, and followed the performance with a lecture on the historical connections between this type of performance and Buraku identity.

On the streets of Puducherry, the Buraku study tour immediately recognized this man, by virtue of his activities, as someone potentially like themselves. While they had watched the sewage cleaner workers earlier with a similar recognition, this performance by the man and his monkey was more easily recognizable as an expression of culture and identity. It was, moreover, more palatable to the senses and, by virtue of explicitly being a performance for audience consumption and enjoyment, was more amenable to staring, which is exactly what the Buraku group did.

After about three minutes of watching, the man finished a song, stopped, and looked expectantly at the group of Japanese people, all with cameras around their necks. A few members of the group reached into their pockets and dug out change to give to the man. One man, whom I will call Harada-san, in contrast, was so moved by the performance and its similarities to an identity that he held dear, that he was compelled to give more money than simple loose change. Instead of going for his coins, he pulled out a wad of bills. The monkey man's eyes gleamed in surprise when he saw the bundle of what looked to be the equivalent of several hundred U.S. dollars. People in Japan rarely use checks or debit cards; instead, they are more likely to carry large sums of cash, sometimes the equivalent of thousands of dollars. Despite the admonishments it would later be clear his wife had given him at the beginning of the trip, Harada-san was keeping with a similar custom there in India.

The wad of bills he pulled out amounted to several hundred U.S. dollars. As the monkey man watched, Harada-san peeled off the equivalent of 20 U.S. dollars, a huge sum, and leaned forward to hand the bills to the man. As he did so, however, an errant breeze caught the notes left in his other hand and sent the remaining money scattering across the pavement and down the street. Harada-san handed the $20 to the performer before turning to watch street children descend on the blowing bills. He watched calmly, expecting, he explained later, that the children would do what he hoped children would do in Tokyo: bring the bills back to him. This is not what happened. Rather, the children grabbed the bills and fled, taking the universal equivalent with them. A bit shocked at the sight of his money running down the street, Harada-san turned back to the group to meet the irritation of his wife and the silent, downcast gazes of the others. The street performer, watching this entire event, quickly packed up his stuff, perhaps embarrassed, perhaps disgusted, and walked away from the group of Buraku Japanese people. Harada-san's desire to make a connection with this man, based on a feeling of potential similarity, ended up with him alienating this man and driving him away. It also left him with empty pockets and an angry wife.

After this event, the group walked back to the hotel and back past the men covered in human sewage. This time no one stopped. When we reached the hotel, most people retired to their rooms to rest after this embarrassment. One of the Japanese sanitation workers and I, however, went to the marble pool to swim laps amidst the rose petals and to reflect on the extreme differences between these groups that we were all trying to stitch together.

Pained Commensuration

Following our visit to Puducherry, we returned to Chennai for a few remaining meetings before flying back to Japan. One of these meetings was with a prominent Dalit activist, and the encounter foregrounded the vast difference in the Dalit and Buraku experiences of discrimination, so much so that it threatened to overwhelm the entire solidarity project. On the first day of the tour, each group gave a presentation, with a slide show, about its history and experience of discrimination. Our daily activities quickly provided sometimes startling examples of the stark differences. One of the trip's planned tours, of a tannery, was canceled on the last day because Caroline had to rush to a small urban Dalit community that had just found two of its young men brutalized and murdered. The entire study tour group was with Caroline, on the way to the tannery, when she received the phone call, and we all accompanied her to the Dalit community where the young men's bodies were laid out.

To some degree the English class and the study tour participants had anticipated this stark difference, particularly those who had been to India on the first trip, and they had come prepared, perhaps attempting to think of the situations they were encountering as being akin to their grandparents' time. There were times, however, when this rubric was insufficient to explain the palpable differences with which the study tour group was presented. The meeting with the Dalit activist was exactly one such moment. It foregrounded the vast difference in the Dalit and Buraku experiences of discrimination, so much so that it surpassed the sympathetic possibilities of an idea of linear progress and threatened to undermine the entire solidarity project. We met this man on our second to last day in India. He was, Caroline explained to us, a leading force for the Dalit movement. We met him in the back of a shop that he owned in central Chennai. During our conversation, he called over two younger men, perhaps in their early twenties, whom he noticed wander into the shop, to introduce them to us as well. These younger men were members of the older man's Dalit organization and also regularly ran errands for him in his shop. They had recently been released from jail and found a lawyer sympathetic to their cause who helped with the legal proceedings. What we heard from them, however, was a far cry from the "my story" that each student in the English-language class had prepared.

I had been doing the interpreting during the meeting, providing some respite for Mizuno, who shouldered most of the English to Japanese interpretation for the trip. I continued interpreting as the young men introduced themselves in English. They were both from a rural Dalit community a short distance outside of Chennai. They had moved to the city several years earlier to join the Dalit group run by the older man at the table. For the first two years that they were in Chennai they were active in the group and worked odd jobs for the man's business. Three years earlier something terrible had happened to one of their sisters. She disappeared from the Dalit village, and eventually, four months later, wandered home, thin and bruised from lack of food and obvious beatings. She had been locked in a closet by the Brahmin man whose house she occasionally cleaned. She had been held there, raped and beaten repeatedly and fed only scraps from the man's table. One night she managed to force open the door and escape and then proceeded to walk home. When the young men heard about this, they, just as the rest of the family and community, were outraged. However, they did not dare go to the police because, they said, the Brahmin man had a lot of influence and connections with the police. Contacting the police, they argued, would probably do more to endanger than to help the woman. As a result, the family decided to do nothing.

At this point in the young mens' story, the Buraku contingent was shaking their heads partially in disbelief but also partially in recognition. This story was terrible, but it was not too far afield from other stories they had heard during their tour. These types of stories gave the Buraku group pause and changed the tenor of their own stories about discrimination. They said they found it more difficult after hearing these stories to share their experiences as something equivalent to what the Dalit people were experiencing. Their stance regarding their own pain shifted as it was placed alongside the pain of the Dalit people.

The men continued. The woman's older brother and his friend, against the opinion of the rest of the family, decided that action was necessary. They spent a few days watching the Brahmin man's house, and then one night, when they were sure he was alone, they broke in, beat the man, told them who they were and why they were there, and then beheaded him. They put his head in a sack and carried it back to their village, where they paraded it around in victory. Shortly thereafter, they were arrested on suspicion of murder. The families found a lawyer who agreed to work pro bono and managed to have the charges against the men dropped. In all, the men spent two years in police custody and were beaten and mistreated during that time, but now they were free. They explained that they thought what they had done, as well as what they had suffered, was worth it.

As they finished their story and as I finished the Japanese interpretation of it, one of the members of the study tour leaned over to me and, while the woman next to him shook her head in disbelief, said, "Joe, I think you misinterpreted that. They didn't actually kill that man, did they?" I turned to the young men and said that I wanted to make sure that I had understood him correctly, that they had actually killed the man. I received a fiercely proud, "Yes, Joe, they did. They put his head in a bag and brought it into the village and held it high. They could not go to the police so they took care of the problem themselves." Understanding this response before I could finish the Japanese interpretation, the other members of the study tour were visibly stunned. Even the sanitation worker who had been to India on the previous trip and had enjoyed appearing unflappable by the differences the group was encountering was visibly shaken. They still wanted to believe that it was a problem of mistranslation, and one participant murmured across to me, "Really, Joe? That is what they are saying?" Otherwise, the implications were stunning.

As I have mentioned, Japan, like India, lacks antidiscrimination legislation. If people face discrimination in Japan, they have no legal recourse to act against the discriminator. However, the discrimination in this case is typically that of being refused marriage, for instance. If someone were to be assaulted, on the basis of being Buraku, or for any reason, there are laws in place that would allow for the prosecution of the offender, and a legal system, including police, that would allow for that to happen. Furthermore, as I have discussed in other parts of this book, the Buraku liberation movement developed a response to discrimination early in its existence that did not include physical violence. While some of the original denunciation sessions involved physical clashes between Buraku and non-Buraku people, a physical attack was never the explicit objective of the session. Also, while some Buraku people might have had connections to larger organized criminal organizations (e.g., the Yakuza), whom they could have mobilized in response to a discriminatory attack, the accounts of individual Buraku people physically brutalizing or killing their offenders, at any point in the movement's history, are basically nonexistent.[17]

What the study tour participants heard from these young men defied their ability to use a metric of linear progression to commensurate the two sets of experiences and defied their ethical ability to approve of the situation and their political ability to desire solidarity. Solidarity here, and the sympathetic engagement they had nurtured over the week and the years, became, in a fashion, a threat. While the Buraku group saw itself as facing a similar form of discrimination, strained though that similarity might at times be, it had a much harder time asserting itself as being similar to a group that would so nonchalantly, with pride even, report the killing of another person. As the group sat stunned before the fierce intensity of these young men and our guide, there was a palpable drawing away; sentiments no longer beat in time. The study tour participants could not sanction the tactics used by the Dalit youth, and they did their best to deny the occurrence of those actions, first questioning the linguistic interpretation and then being forced to call into question the ability to commensurate the Dalit to Buraku experience—for if this were what they resembled, they were insufferable to themselves. As we retreated from the meeting, over the next few days up until the return to Japan the participants in the Buraku study tour left this incident unmentioned, preferring to let it sit in ignored silence than face the potential threatening implications. And there it sat after we returned to Japan as well. This anecdote was never mentioned again; it was never incorporated into the reports and presentations that followed the group's return. Instead, it sat as an unassimilable difference best shunned and ignored lest it undermine the entire project.

This description of the work entailed in *solidarity* and *empowerment* as forms of political engagement indicates the vast complexity of this work. This is a complexity that extends beyond any simple claims to radical equality or fundamentally "horizontal" "deep democracy." This work is itself a locus of strife and contestation as well. Only subsequently is it claimed—by Buraku activists or NGOs—as horizontality, or as a type of politics imbued with a range of possibilities contrasted with and better than other forms of politics. This kind of labeling can be eased or hindered by the work involved in achieving "solidarity," as my previous examples have demonstrated. Sometimes those attempts succeed, opening the passionate possibilities of a "fellow feeling" flowing between the groups. At other times this traffic of sympathy falters or even comes to a standstill. In either case, there are results—a reorientation to the possibilities of politics, and a reorientation to one's self or to the experience of pain. All of this is achieved in and through the sympathetic project of transnational solidarity.

What, then, comes of "my story"? The students in my English class spent weeks preparing and practicing these stories, creating themselves for their envisioned Dalit interlocutors, for the other participants in the class, and for themselves. However, not once over the five days that we were in India on the study tour did any students share their story. There were several reasons for this. First, as the class participants told me in our one follow-up class after the trip, the prospect of talking to someone and not being able to understand the response was extremely daunting. Though we had practiced in class, it was still difficult to transfer those skills to a "real-life" situation. Even equipped with a handful of English phrases, there was a fear that linguistic proximity would still not be achieved—or, worse, an embarrassingly muddled linguistic exchange would shame the parties further apart rather than foster a proximate sympathy. It was easier, and safer, to rely on an interpreter. Second, the majority of the Dalit people we encountered had little formal education and had never been taught English; they spoke Tamil. Even if the tour participants had been able to use the English they had learned, they most likely would not have been understood, except perhaps by our guide, who was already quite familiar with the Buraku situation and familiar to most of the tour participants.

It is perhaps tempting, then, to call "my story" a failure, a failure of the Buraku to bridge the difference separating them from the Dalit. Indeed, in our final feedback class, several class participants expressed frustration and disappointment in themselves over not trying to use their English more, and for not being willing to make mistakes. However, the aforementioned description provides an analytic other than a binary success or failure model through which to evaluate and ponder what happened in the creation of "my story," even if it was never performed in India to a Dalit audience. Here, as the category of labor is tested as a social identity appropriate for the building of a social movement, there were still interlocutors and effects of the preparation of this story and of the English class. This is a moment both of the creation of self and of the creation of a new potential locus of solidarity—one consolidated around an identity category of labor, and one that is subsequently available as evidence of Japan as multicultural.

Now, seven years after that trip, the Tokyo group is preparing for their ninth visit to India. They have gone there every year in the interim, always a group of ten or so people that includes some core members and some new ones. The rural Dalit community center has been completed and the Tokyo group, partnered with Caroline, has set up a foundation to direct funds to the education and employment of Dalit children and youth. Similarly, the Toren and its research institute continue to hold educational seminars about Dalit and Buraku solidarity issues to garner more interest and concern among people in Japan, primarily including, but not limited to, those who identify as Buraku.

This is a form of solidarity that extends beyond sympathetic engagement. The philosopher Gilles Deleuze, in his reading of Hume on sympathy, argues that sympathy is always about the tension between similarity and difference; it is about how to project a bridge of similarity across a gulf of difference.[18] The politics of sympathy, then, are centered around the problem of what Deleuze refers to as "extension": how to ever broaden the sweep of sympathetic imagination. This chapter and the previous one have shown this work, how it requires and bolsters standards like the UN category of "Discrimination Based on Work and Descent," how it ameliorates differences through the insertion of conceptual tools like an idea of linear progress, and even how it navigates moments of seemingly incommensurable challenge. Despite the risks, hesitations, and work that this project of solidarity entails and demands, the two different sets of actors continue to push for engagement.

This project, however, goes beyond a mere extension of sympathy between two otherwise disconnected groups. At the foundation of this political effort of care, support, and being with each other is an understanding of the Buraku and Dalit situations as fundamentally interconnected. As Mizuno put it to me in an e-mail conversation about these trips, "We start from a place of connection. The discrimination that the Buraku people face is tied to the discrimination Dalit face." This solidarity project does more than simply reach across a projected gulf. It recognizes Buraku and Dalit marginalization as interconnected; as, in the words of social theorist Elizabeth Povinelli, part of "a shared body."[19] Extending the sympathetic imagination to the Dalit serves more as an entry to understanding this connection and reworking this shared body than it does for an engagement of simple compassion or pity alone.[20] It also serves as a model for actors such as myself, an ethnographer from the United States, UN representatives, or delegates from the International Dalit Solidarity Network, whom I discussed in previous chapters, to engage in a similar politics of connection rather than a politics of sympathetic engagement, compassion, and indignation. It is in this call that I hear echoes of the challenge by anthropologist Rolph Trouillot that I introduced in the preface: the challenge to investigate how the geography of imagination and a geography of management are always intertwined.[21]

Buraku and Dalit actors continue to work in solidarity. This particular study tour is but one example of many such projects spearheaded by groups across Japan and in India and Nepal. It also serves as the basis for imagining beyond the bounds of just those two groups, out to other groups across the globe that are also caught up in similar transformations of economic and political assemblages. As Buraku actors respond to demands for representing a multicultural Japan, they do so in ways that exceed liberal empathy, and that move beyond the boundaries of the disciplines of multiculturalism, opening other potential, though by no means yet secure, ways of living.

Conclusion

THE DISCIPLINES OF MULTICULTURALISM

Across this book I have endeavored to show the labor that goes into producing a multicultural Japan. This labor is multiply productive: it calls on certain people and practices to serve as evidence in this argument, and it makes demands on the people, organizations, and nations who undertake it. It also opens up avenues of action that exceed its own demands. The first section of this book demonstrated the stakes in producing, or not, signs of Buraku difference. The second lingered on the particular ways in which Buraku difference is signaled and the work required to marshal an audience for that difference, elaborating a tension between individual authenticity and volition and the cultivation required to stage that authenticity. The final section turned to the transnational solidarity efforts of the Buraku political movement, examining how pain, as a sign of discrimination, is shaped in the negotiations to build new international standards of discrimination and remediation. All of this day-to-day labor, in factories and in nongovernmental organizations (NGOs), in domestic arenas, and across international venues, is labor required to build a multicultural Japan.

In the introduction I talked about multiculturalism as a particular mode of disciplining social difference. It is a particular way of creating and managing difference and its relation to unmarked populations in and across nation-states. It resides in the work that people do—in the demands foisted on them as they take up tools to forge evidence of multiculturalism in Japan. To close this book I delineate several characteristics of multiculturalism as they arise in the daily labor of Buraku people and of those who work in their name.

AN INCITEMENT TO MULTICULTURALISM

In chapter 4 I discussed a statement that the director of the Japanese Buddhist Federation made at the third World Conference of Religions for Peace in 1979. During the conference he was asked what the Japanese federation of religions was doing to combat discrimination against the Buraku people. The director responded:

> Presently, there is no Buraku issue in Japan . . . there is absolutely no discrimination in the country of Japan. This is why we need not include the issue of Buraku discrimination in our report. This is a matter of the honor of Japan.[1]

In chapter 4 I use this quote to characterize the history of domestic political activism around Buraku issues. As that chapter indicates, this quote figured at the center of a political push on the part of the Buraku Liberation League to address what it saw as structural discrimination against Buraku people within the religious establishment in Japan. Here, however, I would like to use this quote to address a different topic: that of the changing suitability of Buraku issues in representing Japan internationally. In some venues, Buraku issues have become not simply an appropriate but a necessary mode of internationally representing Japan. As a view of Japan as a multicultural nation-state has become more prominent and more expected, Buraku issues are being called on as proof of this status. In this process the category of labor has recently come to fulfill a key role. This change in suitability has progressively transformed the set of possibilities and challenges faced by purveyors of Buraku politics; in its suitability as representative of multicultural Japan, Buraku issues have changed. This is a point with which each of my chapters has dealt, in different ways. Here I bring together these separate points to outline an overarching argument about the project of multiculturalism in Japan and the role that labor and Buraku issues play in that project.

To return to the previous quote: for the director of the Japanese Buddhist Federation, speaking to an international audience in 1979, having Buraku issues not appear in the report is key to maintaining Japan's honor. It is so key in fact that it provoked the director into denying the existence of the problem altogether, despite the presence of ten-year-old Japanese legislation aimed at addressing Buraku economic and social marginalization. In this quote, Buraku issues themselves, whether past or present, are a source of threatening shame; they are not suitable for representing Japan internationally. This quote, however, was the statement of one person in 1979. Certainly some things have changed in the intervening years between then and the publication of this book—certainly there are other voices to be heard.

The color of my skin (white) and hair (red) and my height mark me as a very visible outsider to Japan. As a result, when I live in Japan, I am frequently asked what I am doing there. During fieldwork, I typically took this question as an opportunity to test out different explanations of my project. These explanations ranged from the hollowly vague, "I study internationalization and multiculturalism" to the academically inaccessible, "I study how two international circuits—that of multicultural discourse and that of labor and finance capital—effect the conditions of possibility for political action centered around Buraku issues," but the stock explanations also included the more provocative, "I study Buraku discrimination" and the more tantalizing (and perhaps more evasive), "I study the leather industry and the politics of defilement."

At one point during the first months of my fieldwork, I was on a train headed to an interview on the south side of Osaka when the woman next to me engaged me in exactly this kind of conversation. I played one of my response cards that included the word "Buraku," and the woman immediately went into action in a way that seemed to indicate that she had steeled herself for this eventuality. I was promptly told that my topic of study was an inappropriate one. Studying Buraku issues would not teach me anything about Japan. If I really wanted to learn about Japan, I should study *ikebana* or *shodō*. I ended the conversation by thanking her for her advice and later recounted this story to the leader in the Buraku liberation movement whom I was headed to interview. He shook his head at what he took to be the familiar and blatant continuation of anti-Buraku prejudice. And then we had some tea.

This incident, just one of many similar incidents I had during my fieldwork, conveys a sentiment similar to that of the statement by the director of the Japan Buddhist Federation in 1979: Buraku issues are not fit to represent Japan, particularly not internationally. Buraku issues are something either gone or on their way out, and, either way, they are certainly something shameful that might mar the honor of Japan. They stand at a distance from the true honor of Japan, which perhaps is located instead in *ikebana* or *shodō*, ironic though that might be.[2] The image of Japan here fit to occupy a space in international venues is one that does not include Buraku issues.

This anecdotal evidence, from the 1970s and more recently, mirrors the results evident in survey data. While no surveys explicitly track whether the general populace of Japan considers Buraku issues shameful or appropriate representatives of Japan internationally, some surveys track related information. As the sociologist Uchida Ryūshi shows, since the 1970s, when prefectural and municipal governments started to survey popular views of Buraku issues, a consistent majority of respondents claimed that the best response to Buraku discrimination was either to say nothing and simply let the issues disappear naturally, the *netako wo okosuna* ("wake not the sleeping child") mentality I discussed in chapter 2, or to have Buraku people assimilate into larger society, the *bunsanron* or "dispersal theory."[3] Working from surveys conducted in areas with high numbers of Buraku districts (e.g., Osaka, Fukuoka, Kitakyushu, and Kobe), Uchida traces the consistent prevalence of these mentalities since the 1970s. While neither of these approaches to Buraku issues, that is, *netako wo okosunaron* or *bunsanron,* indicates whether people are ashamed of Buraku issues per se, both approaches do indicate a preference for reticence when it comes to Buraku issues. In either case, Uchida argues, the prominence of these mind-sets reflects a consistent tendency to think of Buraku discrimination as wrong, a failing of Japanese society best not discussed.

Across the ethnographic anecdotes I offer, as well as in survey data, there is a consistent tendency for Buraku issues to be viewed as shameful or unmentionable. Despite this consistency, however, there have been identifiable changes in how Buraku issues are presented, particularly in international venues, across the same time period, some of which I have discussed at great length across this book. In these differences, we can read a change in the suitability of Buraku issues to represent Japan internationally. This is a change that my research, and the funding that made it possible, itself indexes, whether discussed informally on a train, seen in survey data, or, more widely, evidenced within academic and activist settings.

ENGLISH-LANGUAGE, ACADEMIC REPRESENTATIONS OF DIFFERENCE IN JAPAN

In 1979 only two books in English dealt with these "shameful" Buraku issues: the now-seminal 1966 *Japan's Invisible Race: Caste in Culture and Personality,* by de Vos and Wagatsuma, and the 1977 response to it, *The In-*

visible Visible Minority: Japan's Burakumin, by Yoshino and Murakoshi. Over the next fifteen years, these works were followed by a smattering of other texts, such as Upham's (1980) "Ten Years of Affirmative Action for Japanese Burakumin," Hane's (1982) *Peasants, Rebels, Women, and Outcastes: The Underside of Modern Japan,* Ohnuki-Tierney's (1987) *The Monkey as Mirror: Symbolic Transformations in Japanese History and Ritual,* and Neary's (1997) "Burakumin in Contemporary Japan." The more political of these works takes as its primary "enemy" the erasure of the Buraku, mediated variably through optical or auditory metaphors as either invisibility or silence. However, whether from more political, historical, or structural perspectives, each of these works focuses primarily on "outcaste" or Buraku issues, with elaborations of those specific contexts demanded by the perspective.

In 1983, however, one English-language work took a slightly different tack from this first line of inquiry and was published in a venue different from these academic texts. Seventeen years after the publication of de Vos and Wagatsuma's *Japan's Invisible Race,* de Vos and Wetherall published a report for the Britain-based Minority Rights Group, entitled *Japan's Minorities: Burakumin, Koreans, Ainu, and Okinawans.* This work set its investigation of "Burakumin" in a context of Japanese minorities, prompted by a recognition of the similarity between Japan and other countries: "[W]e are becoming more aware of how Japanese society resembles other societies in the manner that it supports discrimination against indigenous, aboriginal, and foreign minorities."[4] It also contained a smaller work by Norbeck (1967) that performed the same operation, entitled "Little-Known Minority Groups of Japan."

It was not until the mid-1990s that such a contextualization of Buraku issues as minority issues, similarly found in countries throughout the world, became widespread in the English-language academic literature. Harkening back across two decades to its namesake, Weiner's (1997) *Japan's Minorities: The Illusion of Homogeneity* is one of the hallmarks of this change. This work takes as its task not the elucidation of the situation of a particular population but, rather, "a historically contextualized analysis of 'otherness' in Japan with reference to its principal minority populations," which Weiner lists as "Ainu, Burakumin, Chinese, Koreans, Okinawans, and, of most recent origin, Nikkeijin."[5] "Otherness" is a central organizing category that allows for the creation and linkage of a variety of populations called, and conceptualized as, "minorities." Furthermore, in Weiner's work, the figure of "otherness" is taken to be manifestly inherent in Japan, a country that "[d]espite a master narrative of 'racial' and cultural homogeneity . . . is home to diverse populations."[6] What de Vos and Wetherall were beginning to assert in 1983, Weiner takes as a given in 1997. "Burakumin" are here contextualized as minorities in the same move that contextualizes Japan as a country with those minorities.

Additionally, Weiner's description projects a discursive and political enemy not present in de Vos and Wetherall's work: the figure of homogeneity. Not mentioned in the original *Japan's Minorities*, the figure of a homogenous Japanese nation-state becomes a central one in Weiner's work and in a similar work that follows. The several years following Weiner's *Japan's Minorities* saw the publication of Lie's (2001) *Multiethnic Japan* and Befu's (2001) *Hegemony of Homogeneity*, and the anticipated arrival of Fukuoka's *Minorities in Japan*. All of these works use a multicultural analytic framework in which different minority groups are offered together as evidence of an otherness capable of toppling the figure of homogeneity. Additionally, these works show a tendency to naturalize this framework of difference. For example, as I noted in the introduction, Lie goes so far as to say that "Japan has always been multiethnic," a statement that takes a present-day framework of thinking about difference in Japan, projects it back in time, and posits it as an ahistorical characteristic of Japan.[7] There are still monographs that focus on a specific Buraku population, for example, the recent ethnographies by Amos, Bondy, Davis, and McLauchlan,[8] but these works now too must locate that specific Buraku population within the context of other populations frequently recognized (and cast) as minorities.

In this academic arena, then, two changes are evident. The first is in the quantity of English-language materials on marginalized groups in Japan. There has been a marked increase in this type of research since 1997. The second change is in the way in which this information and these groups are presented. Rather than being treated as a stand-alone issue, Buraku issues are portrayed as evidence of the multicultural status of Japan, alongside other evidentiary populations, all of which are cast as "minorities" in a move to dethrone the specter of homogeneity. In this second moment, Buraku people, alongside their Korean, Okinawan, and other comrades, are able to represent Japan internationally. Their prominence within certain international venues is both the product of and creative of a Japan that is multicultural. These groups sit alongside each other in Japan in the same way that Japan, then, in these authors' descriptions, sits alongside other "multicultural" nation-states. These two changes within the academic arena—that of a multicultural tack and that of a proliferation of such literature—are not, I contend, unrelated.

RESEARCH FUNDING

A similar shift is discernible in the decisions of funding agencies that make such research possible. Take, for example, the Japan Foundation *(Nihon Kokusai Kōryū Kikin)*, which was established in 1972 as a special legal entity with the goal of undertaking international cultural exchange, making such an exchange possible with some of the most generous grants to foreign scholars doing research in Japan. Over the five years leading up to and including my fieldwork (2001–6), the Japan Foundation funded, on average, 175 graduate students, researchers, professors, and lecturers each year to do short- and long-term research in Japan. These recipients then go on to publish or present papers, teach, or lecture about Japan all over the world. In effect this foundation creates intellectual ambassadors and de facto helps decide the range of representably Japanese topics—whether they be ramen, radical art movements from the 1950s and 1960s, or Buraku politics, all of which were topics that received Japan Foundation funds the first year of my research.

I was fortunate enough to receive funding from the Japan Foundation for the first year of my fieldwork, and I used that connection to interview employees regarding the status of the foundation as bridge between Japan and other parts of the world. In discussions with different foundation employees, I encountered a firm belief that the Japan Foundation is not political in its funding decisions. As one employee put it, the foundation does not *represent* Japan, it merely *presents* Japan. The difference here hinged on assumptions that "representation" entails a change in the object of study in the process of representation, whereas "presentation" is an "objective" transference of knowledge. The former can have a political charge; the latter is merely an unmediated, objective act. Accordingly, the employees argued, the foundation grants money to those scholars who seem most likely to produce solid, objective academic work.

This belief in apolitical, objective academic excellence aside, some trends apparent in the Japan Foundation's funding history have political effects. According to the foundation's recipient database, which is available online and which covers all recipients back to the foundation's 1972 inception, none of the scholars mentioned earlier who work on Buraku issues received support from the foundation. In fact, of the thousands of scholars to receive aid from this foundation in its history of granting aid, only four research anything even remotely related to Buraku issues, and those four are all clustered in the five years leading up to my fieldwork. One 2001 recipient did research on ideas of pollution in medieval Japan, and two, in 2004 and 2005, respectively, did research on present-day multicultural education and city planning, which I imagine would have to consider Buraku issues. This tally, then, leaves me, the only person in the Japan Foundation's almost four-decade funding history, to receive money for graduate research directly on Buraku issues.

The lack of Buraku-studying Japan Foundation Fellows cannot be explained by a lack of Buraku-studying Japan Foundation applicants. It is more than likely, given this foundation's position as a major funder, that the people I previously mentioned applied for Japan Foundation aid. Furthermore, in an interview with a person who has sat on the foundation's fellowship board, I was told that there are always at least a couple of applicants a year whose projects address Buraku issues. At the beginning of my research, then, this situation prompted the following question for me: Why, now, has the Japan Foundation decided to fund a Buraku-focused research project? Japan Foundation employees explained to me in interviews that grants were given to scholars who showed signs of objective, academic excellence. While it might be personally appealing to believe this, it is hardly plausible that absolutely no applicant between 1972 and 2006 was qualified to research present-day Buraku issues. Furthermore, if we consider this funding decision within the context of the recent upsurge in studies of the "minorities" of Japan, and note that my project and the moderately Buraku-related projects from the past two years all use "multiculturalism" as part of their analytical framework, another plausible answer rises into view. Something has changed in the way in which Japan can be appropriately and effectively *presented* internationally. It has become appropriate and effective for even the supposedly apolitical, objective Japan Foundation to recognize and present a Japan that is multicultural. In so doing, it allows for the increased foreign study of Buraku issues and for the increased international portrayal of Japan as a multicultural nation-state.

I am not claiming that the Japan Foundation or its employees have consciously or strategically decided to advance the Buraku cause recently and allow for international representation. Nor am I claiming that either strategically blocked the representation of Buraku issues for the majority of the foundation's funding history. Instead, I take it as a given that politics can be and is done independent of volition. What I am calling a "shift" in funding tendencies by the foundation presupposes a social context in which the Buraku-inclusive "multicultural" representation of Japan is appropriate. This shift also entails such a social context, effecting a global view in which Buraku issues can in some fashion represent Japan on an international stage, a global view in which Buraku issues can be a boon and not merely shameful as it was for the director of the Japan Buddhist Federation. While the foundation's funding decisions might not be intentionally or strategically political, its decisions presume and create political possibilities, including, thankfully, the possibility of my own research. It also, however, creates new challenges.

My argument here, then, is that Buraku politics has become a proper object for representing Japan internationally to the extent that it arrive clothed in the garb of multiculturalism. In order to take on this garb, these politics—as articulated by activist, scholar, and funder alike—must conform to a set of demands in order to be recognized at all. As I argue in the introduction and throughout this book, we can productively think of multiculturalism as an immanent set of conventions governing the production of signs undergirding the recognition of populations of people. These immanent conventions, which come in the guise of merely recognizing that which already exists, function on the ground as demands. To be recognized as a minority group under multiculturalism, then, is an achievement of meeting those demands. This achievement is reliant on the production of particular signs of minority identity, an activity that takes work. It is this work to which I refer when talking about the "labor of multiculturalism," and it is a work that is multiply productive. Even as it achieves recognizable signs of multiculturalism, it also changes the set of conventions that will determine such appropriateness and effectiveness. In taking up a tool to work on an object, the worker transforms the object, the tool, and themself. Because multiculturalism, as a means of managing difference, serves as a tool in this work, it and its presumptions and effects are in constant motion, even as they maintain a recognizable form. Thus this means that multiculturalism, as this immanent set of conventions, has a history; it and its presumptions and effects are constantly changing, as these conventions are met, broken, or reordered.

Multiculturalism emerged as appropriate to the Japanese context in the last decade of the twentieth century and has created a new utility for Buraku stigma. It reconfigures Buraku issues and lands them on the international Japanese representational landscape precisely because of their stigma in other arenas and precisely because Buraku people are an object of discrimination. It does so by placing Buraku people alongside other groups, all labeled minorities, and by pitting them against the myth of national homogeneity, a myth that continues to haunt social and political interactions in Japan. It does so, however, by placing demands on various actors that work in the name of Buraku politics.

THE DISCIPLINES OF MULTICULTURAL REPRESENTATION: ENLISTMENT, EQUILIBRATION, AUTHENTICITY, AND VULNERABILITY

Multiculturalism—that is, a particular mode of managing social difference that presents minorities alongside each other as symptoms or evidence of the same thing—provides a vehicle for increased national and international recognition. It establishes conditions under which Buraku stigma can generate positive value. The sociolinguist Erving Goffman discusses this phenomenon in more general, and in more metaphorical, terms in his 1963 work *Stigma: Notes on the Management of Spoiled Identity*. He explains that while stigma can serve to limit the social authority of a stigmatized person, it also opens the possibility that that person might make a career out of their stigma. It can, given particular conditions, establish stigma as an enabling characteristic, a tool through which otherwise marginalized groups might achieve political solvency. In forming the basis for a career, argues Goffman, stigma gives a person the means to suddenly take what up until that point had been a liability and to "play golf with it."[9] However, in order to wield the club, the golfer must hold their hands and body in particular ways. Multiculturalism demands as much as it enables.

One of my informants, Kadooka Nobuhiko, who is born of Buraku parents and from a Buraku neighborhood in Japan's Hyōgo prefecture, currently makes his living as a freelance writer and lecturer on that which simultaneously stigmatizes him. He too has noted to me the irony in the situation that Goffman points out: "While I fight against Buraku discrimination and the marginalization of Buraku people, it is exactly this discrimination and marginalization that provides me with money to eat."[10] The Buraku population is still stigmatized in ways reminiscent of 1979, but the ways in which that stigma can be used to play golf have changed. While I would argue with Goffman that the terms of the game are immanent, staying with his metaphor, we can ask: What, then, are the terms of that golf game? Who can use Buraku stigma to play, in what venues can they do so, and how is that play regimented? In closing this book, I highlight four patterns in multiculturalism's demands, and the challenges and possibilities they open up. The demands on which I focus are enlistment, equilibration, authenticity, and vulnerability.

Enlistment

In all of these struggles for multicultural Japan, "the myth of homogeneity" is a primary target, and "otherness" is the primary tool to its dismantlement. The more that otherness can be identified and substantially characterized, the less chance this myth of homogeneity has of continuing to flourish, and the less chance it has of stifling aberrant forms of life. Minorities are thus "enlisted"—both enrolled and placed on a commensurating list—as evidence in this struggle.

Over the course of my research, I have had the opportunity to be part of the planning of two compendia of "minorities" in Japan. The first was a prospective project led by sociologist Fukuoka Yasunori of Saitama University. In 2004 he felt that the situation of minorities in Japan had yet to be correctly transmitted overseas and wanted to produce an English-language book to fill that gap. A team of five Japanese researchers would write essays on minority populations in Japan, and I would translate the work into English. The second project was one I was requested to do as part of my internship at the International Movement Against All Forms of Discrimination and Racism (IMADR). This project, though it did not come to fruition, was to be an English-language description of a pointedly nonacademic list of minorities in Japan: how it is, in the process of the building of the modern Japanese nation-state, that they came into being, and a description of their present situations—all done in collaboration with the described groups themselves.

In both of these projects, the organizers and I had conversations about who, which groups, to include, and who, given space and time constraints, not to include this time around. In the case of the project at IMADR, the line was drawn at groups that had a prominent relationship with the formation of the Japanese nation-state, which we decided were Buraku, Ainu, Koreans, and Ryūkyū-ans, and, potentially, late-coming migrants. Other populations then might be added, after this base is established. The former project with Professor Fukuoka extended beyond what he termed this *"kihon,"* or "base," and went on to include leprosy patients and people with mental and physical disabilities, along with similar plans for future projects treating other populations.

A comparable dilemma—who should be included and who should be excluded—motivated conversations behind the reconstruction of the Osaka Human Rights Museum, "Liberty Osaka." In November 2005 I visited its recently reopened exhibit with two representatives from the United Nations, leaders from Indian and African outcaste communities, and Buraku activist leaders from the Buraku Liberation and Human Rights Research Institute. We toured this hall of fame of Japanese minorities, on display for Japanese and foreigners alike, and with written explanations for literate Japanese and Anglophones alike. This new exhibit takes all of the aforementioned populations and adds to them victims of environmental disasters, sexual minorities, and atomic bomb survivors, with the same proviso of "more to come." Indeed, the issue of open-endedness pervades every instance, in academic or political fora, of the urge to wield "otherness" against the myth of homogeneity. The project is open-ended, and like the acronym describing sexual minorities in the United States, which now can be as long as "lgbtqq-itsa,"[11] or the general list of "minority groups," based on race, class, gender, religion, nationality, and so on, the lists get longer, and can never be quite enough.

There are benefits to this approach, including a constant search for additional minority populations that have perhaps been marginalized, a constant attention to the limits of liberal tolerance, and a desire to improve inclusion. In the realm of migration, for instance, as more immigrants come to Japan, they will find organizations conceptually ready to work with them and for them. Even more strongly, they will find groups desirous of working with them.

At the same time, however, this logic of enlistment entails challenges. Certainly for IMADR, and most likely for the Osaka Human Rights Museum and other organizations, the work and expenditures increase as the lists proliferate, and new forms of worry about discrimination or marginalization, this time by not including a group on one of these lists, appear. IMADR's now-requisite list of minority groups in Japan covers the basics: resident Koreans, the Buraku, Okinawans, Ainu, recent migrants, and sometimes women. However, to IMADR's own chagrin, and to other groups' umbrage, it does not include some other minority groups, such as sexual minorities. As the list of minorities expands, IMADR faces the threat of critique for noninclusiveness and finds itself having to strategize in response. Insofar as enlistment entails a constant push to include more groups, it also entails an attendant fear that some groups will always be excluded. Any representation of Japan as multicultural can always be assailed for being insufficiently inclusive and must always be on the lookout for new groups to summon to the role of minority.

Equilibration

Even as multicultural logic demands increasingly longer lists of minority populations, it also renders them equivalent under standards of "otherness" and human rights. Groups, the recognition of which has been intended to show diversity in Japan, are, ironically, being homogenized as "minorities." That equilibration entails an assumption that all of these groups rallied and maintained against the figure of homogeneity might sit nicely next to each other innocuously separated by commas. They may not be the same, but they are rendered commensurate under the umbrella of multiculturalism. At the same time that this pulling together of groups opens up possibilities, it also opens up arguments.

This enlistment and equilibration are evident in and provide for new venues for solidarity and networking among Japanese activist populations. Buraku youths are summoned to appear alongside Korean youths on minority panels; new friendships and political possibilities are envisioned where before there were struggle and competition. With the enactment of the Special Measures Law (SML) in 1969, municipal and national funds were directed to either registered Buraku neighborhoods or Buraku industries. As I have discussed throughout this book, some of the communities that registered themselves with the government to receive these funds have achieved major success in combating the intense poverty they faced. They have established welfare centers and centers for the care of the disabled and elderly. Occasionally, though, these funds have led to a so-called reverse discrimination, or *gyaku sabetsu,* where people in neighboring areas resent the funds flowing into Buraku areas and not into their own. When these neighbors have been Korean residents, for example, the tensions have frequently been cast along ethnic lines. This situation has contributed to tension between Buraku and Korean populations. However, successive iterations of the SML became less and less Buraku focused, opening the administrative window to other groups. With the end of the law in March 2002 came the end of Buraku-dedicated funds on a national level. Projects now operate under a broader umbrella of human rights, and Buraku people and Koreans, as well as whatever other groups might find themselves enlisted and equilibrated, are eligible for other benefits. This shift makes it easier for ongoing efforts to ameliorate the sometimes antagonist history of these two groups. Likewise, organizations such as IMADR host minority youth panels that include both Buraku and Korean youths.

At the same time that this pulling together of groups opens up possibilities, it also opens up arguments. The previous example shows why that might be the case. Indeed, while the resident Korean youths might now sit on a panel with Buraku youths, as testament to the newfound possibilities of solidarity, such a move is just as likely to horrify those youths' parents, who spent much of their lives in antagonistic relations with each other. Similarly, the possible inclusion of sexual minorities under the equilibrating umbrella of multiculturalism causes outright anger and consternation on the part of some activists focused on Buraku and resident Korean issues. For example, just before my fateful train ride down to the south side of Osaka to meet with the liberation leader, I was told by my friend Kadooka not to mention during my interview the fact that I am attracted to men. Kadooka explained that the leader was "of the old guard" and was likely to shut rather than open the door for me on account of an announced gayness. The intimations of similarity entailed in the enlisting and equilibrating moves of multiculturalism can, at times, be too unpalatable to be politically actionable. The leveling approach of human rights still does not always go down smoothly and can cause discomfort and outright dispute.

Authenticity

In various places throughout the book I have engaged with the work of Charles Taylor and Kurokawa Midori to examine how it is that the idea of an inner sense of self came about in contemporary Japan, and how that sense gains traction, or not, in the various political tactics of the Buraku movement. This sense of an authentic core identity is key not simply to the constitution of an individual but also characterizes demands placed on groups cast as minorities. The enlistment and equilibration of new minority populations are, in the hands of academics and activists, accompanied by the demand for demonstrability of groupness. At times the metric for this groupness is cultural and naturalized as part of that group identity. Under the examining gaze of several of the aforementioned academics, as well as UN representatives such as Doudou Diène, minority groups are assumed to have long-running group characteristics, called "culture." One of the rights of the minority group is to have that culture "recognized," which as I have argued is actually a form of demand to appear in a certain way but frequently is cast as merely recognizing natural cultural facts.[12] When the standard is culture, the fight for recognition appears in the guise of having a positive culture.

Take, for example, the indigenous Ainu. The indigenous Ainu population has its own traditional language, cuisine, and way of life. Historically, certainly during the process of the building of the Japanese modern nation-state, these characteristics were held in scorn and became the basis for widely held anti-Ainu prejudice. The fight against homogeneity and for multiculturalism includes a recognition of the value of these erstwhile scorned characteristics. Enlisted minorities, then, are summoned into having this culture, and it is best if that culture is something easily demonstrable or, even better, easily purchased—to be handed out at diversity fairs as food, sold as a garment, or performed as a dance. In the Buraku example, eating *motsu nabe* (tripe soup) and building *taiko* (drums) suddenly become "cultural" activities, whereas before they were simply things people did. In any case, this is culture not to be lived but culture to be displayed—or perhaps, more correctly, it is a new culture of display.

The remodeled Osaka Human Rights Museum presents exhibits with exactly this purpose of revaluing the cultures of minorities. The Ainu corner shows Ainu clothing and language; the Ryūkyū corner does the same, with patterns and sounds changed accordingly. Even the Buraku people, whose defining group characteristic is a relation to industries considered dirty, have a corner where leather tanning and drum making are put on display. This press for authenticity is not limited to international diversity fairs or museums. The benefits of international recognition are parceled out in accordance with the extent to which Japan's minority groups can present themselves to visiting UN and other guests as having a demonstrable culture. Visits by such actors frequently include tours of minority populations, their living situations, and their cultural artifacts. Such visits and such a demand for culture prompt conversations and worries on the part of domestic activist groups about how "best" to demonstrate Buraku-ness. Unlike the Ainu or the Koreans, the Buraku people are not an ethnic group. They have not been summoned to particular cultural traditions that function as a norm throughout their community. However, in order to appear as a minority in the face of the conventions of multiculturalism, they now face such summons. As a result, over the past twenty years, there has been a proliferation of Buraku foods and clothing marketed as culturally Buraku. This push has resulted in a backlash among some Buraku people and communities who feel as though these cultural artifacts bear no relation to their lives or histories.

As I argued in a different context in chapter 3, at the same time that this pressure for authenticity stimulates the need to demonstrate Burakuness, it also creates a foundation for pride in that identity. The Osaka Museum provides visitors, both members of the pictured groups and not, with concrete objects and images through which to positively value these identities. These practices lay the groundwork for positive aspects of identity politics.

In this context, the demand for authenticity summons into displayed being a pivot point for individuals to fight against whatever shame they might feel because of their minority status. It provides those identified as Buraku with the means to value their position. It also, on a personal note, opened the door for me, a white guy from a small town in West Texas that happens to produce cowhide that is later tanned in Japan, to step into fieldwork at a leather tannery in Tokyo. I could be seen as connected to Buraku issues because of a "cultural" overlap in the care of cattle. At the same time that it opens these doors, however, it also transforms a minority's culture into one of display, with the constant worry that perhaps the display is insufficient to prove authenticity. The culture of display is granted the status of a standard against which other instantiations of authentic identity can be gauged. The anticolonial thinker Franz Fanon said that under colonialism the destiny of the black man was the white man.[13] In this case we might follow the cultural theorist Elizabeth Povinelli and say that the destiny of the Buraku is the displayably authentic Buraku.[14] Each is equally unobtainable.

Vulnerability

There is another metric used to determine the qualities of a marginalized group. This metric is biopolitical, generated by statistics: an average of characteristics of a population set in contrast with data from society as a whole. These characteristics might be pulled from living situation, average income, or education level. They might also be about the experience of discrimination. As a statistical average, this yardstick creates an idea of "normal" against which the minority group can be judged different. Such statistics are attentive to the changes of history and context; however, as agglomerate numbers, they still produce an idea of the group "normal" that no one individual can ever be, and a social norm from which, in order to be a minority, a group must prove itself distant.[15] In multicultural characterizations of "the myth of homogeneity," the perniciousness of this myth lies in the fact that it erases—renders silent or invisible—the distance between a norm and its outliers. This erasure is both cast and experienced as social harm, and those who are erased, then, are understood, de facto, as wounded. "Otherness" becomes cast as wounded.

Such a presentation of woundedness can be seen in the displays at the Osaka Human Rights Museum, where contextualization is provided in terms of "violations" to rights. It can be seen in academic presentations of marginalization, and in the persistent desire for academics such as anthropologists to take suffering, marginalized populations as their objects of inquiry. It can also be seen in recent reconsiderations of Buraku identity and political issues, on which I would like to linger for a moment. As sociologists and cultural theorists Noguchi Michihiko and Uchida Ryūshi,[16] among others, have argued, the conditions that historically have given rise to Buraku discrimination have changed fundamentally in the past decades. Noguchi cites increased rates of marriage between Buraku and non-Buraku people, the movement of people in and out of historically Buraku neighborhoods, and changes in industries historically associated with Buraku stigma as changes that fundamentally challenge the until-now canonical definition of Buraku identity around blood, space, and occupational ties to stigma. Instead of this "Tripartite Theory," or *"San'i Ittai Ron,"* originally proposed by the historian Inoue Kiyoshi in 1950, Noguchi recommends a shift in how the Buraku category of person is defined. He proposes a definition based on "relational" categories of perception and discrimination: "Burakumin are those people who, thought to be Burakumin, are discriminated against, or those who have a strong chance of being discriminated against."[17] As Noguchi expands this argument, examining the definitions of the Buraku from the perspective of the government, the liberation movement, those who discriminate, and those who face discrimination, he relies consistently on discrimination being the basis for determining Buraku identity. While he focuses on a relation, he casts woundedness as characteristic of the Buraku category of person.

As I touched on in the previous chapter, a spate of scholarship has examined the ways in which liberal governance necessitates wounded subjects at its margins.[18] In order to define itself as tolerant, liberal multiculturalism needs to show an inclination and a capacity to improve itself and to always expand the inclusive circle of governance. It must demonstrate its concern. In order to do this, it must find (and enlist) groups that it has wronged. The self-corrective push of liberal, multicultural progressivism entails a commitment to seeing and understanding those on its margins as somehow wounded. The situation of marginalized groups in Japan, the Buraku among them, shows how this tendency unfolds in the practices of people summoned to perform it in ways that will always also exceed and transform those very disciplines that they enact.

The previous characteristic of authenticity would seem to provide an escape vector from this woundedness. The demands of authenticity establish a basis for a positively valued identity, based on a self-standing pride in group cohesion rather than solely on a relation of discrimination. Some Buraku people, for example, who are seen as Buraku, will never know personal discrimination nor necessarily suffer from institutional forms of marginalization but will know a sense of pride fostered at the hands of an activist social movement. Authenticity provides grounds for a pride that is the flip side of the woundedness demanded of the marginalized under multiculturalism. At the same time, however, this positive valuation based on an authenticity relies on woundedness as a fundamental starting point to the political project, which is then cast as a project of recuperation. While authenticity might provide an escape vector, complicated in the ways I previously described, it also will always have had suffering as a starting point. Indeed, frequently the authority of authenticity is achieved through displays of suffering.[19] And at other moments, the demands of this suffering authenticity arrive in a set of practices that link actors such as the Dalit and the Buraku, international NGO actors and foreign anthropologists, across the globe, pointing the way to new futures and possibilities of working together to transform these demands.

THE LABOR OF MULTICULTURALISM

These four characteristics provide some of the foundations for the ongoing struggle and challenge of achieving a politics of multiculturalism in Japan.

Buraku political actors must achieve a recognizable semblance of these characteristics in order to engage in the field of multicultural politics. The Buraku people are still stigmatized; they face discrimination in marriage and employment, and they are seen by some members of the Japanese population as inadequate candidates to represent the country internationally. However, under multiculturalism, the category of Buraku provides academics, activists, and even large cultural institutions such as the Japan Foundation with access to a new authority in international venues. That access, however, is structured by demands of an always-not-enough enlistment of minorities, equilibration of those minorities, and demands of provable authenticity and demonstrable wounds. The terms of this type of political engagement are, of course, conflicted. They entail both new possibilities as well as new complications. In the Buraku case, these complications are particularly salient, as Buraku political actors more and more mobilize the category of labor as the basis for arguing multicultural identity. In this formulation, labor, then, must bear the weight of indexing an authentic, locatable identity, even as this labor as a distinguishing group characteristic is on the wane.

While the terms of the game have changed, so too have changed those who can play. Certainly Buraku people themselves are called to the tee, but they are not the only ones. Any actor who might occupy a role with the authority to represent Japan can use the stigma of Buraku to demonstrate the "multicultural" dimension of Japan. And they can make their money to eat doing so. Not limited to Buraku activists, these actors include academics, particularly foreign ones such as myself, reporters, and major funding entities. The matter of being Buraku, then, is not just a matter for the minority, something that multiculturalism's focus on the marginalized and the marked too often obscures. It is a matter of Japan, in a way that now can prove, not only mar, the honor of that Japan. It is also a matter, as we have seen in the previous chapters, that extends to the concerns and motivations of UN and international NGO representatives, to ethnographers from the United States, and beyond. It is a matter deeply entangled in contemporary modes of creating and managing difference that are global in scope and effect.

Japan itself, immanent in the actors authorized to represent it in international venues, is making demands of stigmatized, shameful minorities to be visible now—and to be visible, as we have seen, in a very particular way that structures how one might, to one's own advantage and to the advantage of a multicultural country, play golf with stigma. A particular picture of the demands and possibilities of multiculturalism in Japan emerges from the aforementioned examples, which demonstrate how multiculturalism, present in the demands of enlistment, equilibration, authenticity, and woundedness, proffers political and social advantage insofar as it also disciplines the subjects that labor to be eligible for such a gain. This mode of managing difference is achieved in the practices of a diverse set of actors, set within globally circulating styles of political argumentation and representation.

This book is an exploration of the labor that goes into achieving such representations of the category of labor. Furthermore, it is an examination of the demands that this labor places on those who undertake it and who are taken up by it to achieve international recognition for the Buraku group and thereby recognition of Japan as multicultural. It is also an examination of the vast global scale crossed by these concerns and actors, in the constitution of a situation that simultaneously appears intrinsically Japanese. One of the moments of creativity entailed in the project of presenting Buraku issues internationally is the use of labor as the basis for a multicultural identity. The categories of race, ethnicity, class, and caste have all at times been taken up to understand and manage Buraku difference. The recent interplay between the Buraku political movement and the UN special rapporteur on racism is one such example. However, at the same time, these categories have also been judged insufficient. Contemporary Buraku difference is one ascribed and acted on on the basis of spatial, occupational, and hereditary characteristics, frequently mediated by speculation and rumor.

At the same time that the Buraku political movement has made renewed use of the category of race to describe itself internationally, "Discrimination Based on Work and Descent" has started to serve as a separate scaffolding for international recognition. Rather than using racial or ethnic identifiers that pair Buraku people with racial and ethnic groups, this new category uses the identifier of occupation as its defining characteristic and instead pairs the Buraku people with the "outcastes" of South Asia and beyond. Each of these modes of recognition has its own ideology and generic stipulations; however, taken together, they serve as a means of provoking the articulation of labor (in the form of "occupation" or "work") as the basis for Buraku identity within a multicultural field. In chapter 5 I discussed the ways in which this newly ratified UN category is connected to other political movements in Japan; chapter 6 examined some of the possibilities and challenges that this new category highlights in the lives of Buraku people and the ways in which it serves as a conduit to projects of interconnected solidarity.

Narrating Japan as multicultural is successful in two ways: to the extent that either race or ethnicity can be achieved as pertinent descriptors of the Buraku case, or to the extent that labor can be constructed as a valid category of multicultural identity. Both of these modes of representation are precarious, with unintended risks and benefits. *Working Skin* has been an extended examination of the work that goes into these achievements, the ways in which this work then positions Japan as a multicultural nation-state, and the ways in which this work both secures Buraku actors a place on international stages and simultaneously shows that they were already there, interconnected in the first place.

Epilogue

TEXAS TO JAPAN, AND BACK

In June 2005 Uchizawa Junko, the freelance illustrator and writer I mentioned in chapter 6, came to Lubbock, Texas, to tour ranching and slaughtering facilities. At the time I was a graduate student living in Chicago, finishing my oral exams and preparing for fieldwork. I had only corresponded with Junko via e-mail. We had been introduced electronically by a mutual friend, Kadooka Nobuhiko, another freelance journalist who makes occasional appearances throughout this book. Junko was working on a book detailing the meat production process in countries across the world. Her aim in this project was to provide a Japanese-reading audience with a detailed vision of the day-to-day activities of processing meat, to make less taboo and more approachable something that, for reasons tied to Buraku discrimination, received little attention in the Japanese public. She had visited close to twenty countries, including Korea, Indonesia, Nepal, Mongolia, and Czechoslovakia, touring slaughtering facilities, spending hours, days, or weeks in each, and sketching the different moments of labor and rest that go into producing meat. Perhaps most strikingly, she had also spent several weeks in the Shibaura Slaughtering Facility in Shinagawa, Tokyo, where she conducted interviews, sketched, and tried her hand at parts of the process. She had never had any interest in visiting the United States; actually, she had an active aversion to the United States, in response to the omnipresence of U.S. culture and influence throughout the world. However, she heard through her friend Kadooka that there was a researcher familiar with Buraku issues who was from West Texas and had connections to the cattle industry there. She contacted me asking if I would be willing to coordinate a tour for her.

Junko's first step into the United States was off a plane in Lubbock, Texas, where she was greeted by my mother holding a sign with her name on it. My flight from Chicago did not arrive for another several hours. With my mother amiably chatting along in a language Junko had a bare facility in, and with an accent that at times confounds native speakers of English, the two made it back to my family's house, where Junko was set up for a nap in the guest bedroom. There, much to my family's thrilled consternation, Junko chose the floor over the bed. Over the next few days, Junko and I, accompanied by Sally and Emily and sometimes Larry Hankins, toured a working ranch an hour east of Lubbock, the feedlots outside the city where my high school friend Reagan Anders worked, a dairy, Lubbock's ranching heritage center, Texas Tech University's school of animal husbandry, two small custom-kill slaughtering facilities, and a large meat center that processed some nine hundred head of cattle a day, all on an incredible whirlwind tour mostly set up by my mother. We did this in the midst of sweltering 112-degree heat and across a barren West Texas terrain that Junko provocatively likened to the countryside of Iraq. Two years later, when Junko returned to Texas for my sister Emily's wedding, we revisited the custom slaughterhouses and toured tanneries in the area, this time with my other sister, Katie, in the mix as well.

The current Buraku situation is characterized by a mobility that is global in scope. Journalists like Junko and academics like Sakurai Atsushi, who had visited Lubbock two years prior to Junko, travel the world researching Buraku issues; activists with organizations such as the International Movement Against All Forms of Discrimination and Racism (IMADR) or the Buraku Liberation League (BLL) travel domestically and globally to improve the Buraku situation and carve out solidarity projects with similar groups; UN representatives like Doudou Diène or Chinsung Chung travel the world investigating issues of racism and discrimination; hides from cattle raised on the ranch that Junko and my family toured make their way across the world to tanneries in Japan, or farther away, to China or India, to be turned into leather and perhaps then into the soles of shoes to be sold in China or back to the United States; characters like Ushimatsu from chapter 2 yearn to travel abroad and to escape Buraku stigma; the group of sanitation workers and activists from Tokyo go to India every year; and particular ways of thinking about and acting on social difference travel as well, in the practices of these people and in the movement of objects, from the United Nations to Japan, through the United States, and back. Even as these moves are global, however, that globalization only happens in concrete actions, personal affective attachments, and ethical orientations that

FIGURE 15. Cattle on a ranch in West Texas.

drive people's hopes and desires. Junko, driven to Texas because of the desire to demystify an industry obscured in taboo in Japan, has become a fixture in my family, who has actively and proudly tracked her rising success as a writer. Mizuno's friendship with Caroline is decades long. Other global encounters are more ephemeral, but no less material and concrete in their effects.

This mobility, however, is not evenly distributed. Not all of the actors who are touched by or propel the Buraku situation move globally or even domestically; some have no such desire. As I argued previously, only some have access to Buraku stigma as a potential boon, and it is a boon that pulls its user into new forms of mobility, both socially and geographically. The day before I traveled to Geneva with IMADR to meet with the UN high commissioner on human rights, I had dinner in Tokyo with a friend from the Buraku youth group who spent the entire meal, and many of our conversations, telling me how much he wanted to move to Italy and study to become a chef. The contrast in our situations was stark. Similarly, the man who very patiently trained me in the tannery told me time and again how much he would like to be a truck driver, not bound to a particular place but free to drive around and see the entire country. Mizuno labored for years, even living for a short time in a janitor's closet, to save up the money for his first trip to India. Other people, however, are unmoved personally by this mobility; they have no desire to move beyond the tannery at which they and their families have worked for generations, or to leave the neighborhoods in which they grew up. The contemporary Buraku situation, located at the intersection of two transnational circulations—of political argument and economic practice—is reliant on this uneven terrain of mobility.

The tension that has motivated my argument throughout this book—that multicultural forms of political argument that authorize labor as a category of Buraku marginalization are gaining traction at the precise moment the labor that renders people stigmatized as Buraku is disappearing—is characterized by this uneven mobility. Each moment, as I have shown throughout the chapters in this book, relies on and enables the other. The highly mobile figures of IMADR activists can only exist and fight for human rights and Buraku liberation to the extent that they have located forms of Buraku stigma to narrate as evidence of discrimination. The labor of multiculturalism hinges on and propagates this uneven terrain of mobility, bolstering a temporal break that locates Japan, as a multicultural nation-state in spite of itself, as modern.

NOTES

PREFACE

1. As this book describes and complicates, the Buraku people are a group stigmatized because of associations with occupations considered unclean, such as leather and meat production. The term *buraku* literally means "neighborhood" but is a euphemism for particular kinds of neighborhoods, those where the Buraku people have historically lived and worked.

2. Lubbock is famously home to many country-and-western singers, many of whom are not shy to note the lingering hold of that West Texas town, however bleak. See, for instance, Mac Davis's "Texas in My Rear View Mirror" (1980) or the Dixie Chicks' "Lubbock or Leave It" from their album *Taking the Long Way* (2006).

3. Here and throughout the book I use they/their/them as a gender-neutral singular pronoun.

4. The dynamics of liberalism are a central part of this book. Here I provide only the briefest gloss of tendencies on which I linger in later chapters.

5. Rorty 1991.

6. Trouillot 2003.

7. Trouillot 2003: 123.

8. Povinelli 2011: 5.

INTRODUCTION

1. Throughout the book I use only the names of public figures and of those who gave me permission. All other names are pseudonyms. Similarly, people, neighborhoods, and situations are typically composites rather than direct portrayals. I do this to protect the privacy of those with whom I work, particularly given the risks of being recognized as Buraku.

2. Though this term is used widely in English-language scholarly work on Buraku issues, it has a pejorative connotation in Japanese. Buraku people, particularly those active in the liberation movement, use the term, however, to describe themselves. In general, throughout the book I use the term "Buraku people," but I occasionally use "Burakumin" when I am voicing the term from the perspective of my informants.

3. Race and sex do not result from physical difference; rather, they are techniques of disciplining difference that call on physical qualities to substantiate themselves. Particular physical qualities are emphasized, scrutinized, and transformed in this process. Buraku difference relies on a divergent set of qualities to substantiate itself. Critical Race Theory has shown how processes of racialization recruit and highlight different characteristics to substantiate racial claims, in the process placing demands on those, sometimes physical or bodily, characteristics. The sizable literature on racial passing also demonstrates how being racially marked does not necessarily entail that the person in question knows that they are marked as such. Those situations overlap with Buraku experience.

4. Building on the work of Watanabe (1994), Kurokawa (2004) develops the concept of *shirushi* (marks) to trace how scientific technologies, such as anthropometrics and eugenics, call on physical characteristics to mark social difference, in the service of creating a normative Japanese citizen. I analyze registries, records, and gossip as epistemological technologies with a similar effect. My work here also draws on Goffman's (1963) canonical analysis of stigma. There he argues that stigmatization is a constant process of sorting people into stigmatized and nonstigmatized roles, a process that relies on and changes as the markers that serve as evidence of stigma, as well as people's knowledge of those links, shift. Membership is never set and is always a matter of debate, evidence, and competing authority.

5. The Tokugawa (or Edo) period (1603–1867) was characterized by a strict social order, including the management of people in distinct, hierarchical categories: at the top were the rulers, including the emperor, the shogun, and the daimyo or feudal lords; in the middle were the four Confucian classes: samurai, peasants, craftspeople, and merchants; finally, at the social bottom, were the "outcastes." This last category comprised *eta* (literally "full of filth," used to describe those who were firmly associated with death or defilement, frequently working in industries that involved the management of animal or human death) and *hinin* (literally "nonpersons," used to describe certain itinerant performers, fortune-tellers, beggars, and prostitutes, among others). The former of these classes was hereditary, the latter was not, but both were restricted in terms of where they could live or travel, and they were subjected to sumptuary laws that stipulated the types of clothing they could wear. These terms have very strong discriminatory overtones in contemporary Japanese. See Fujisawa (2013), Howell (2005), and Jansen (2002: 121) for more details on the Edo class system and the place of the *eta* and *hinin* within it.

6. Kondo 2011: 10–11.

7. Sekine (2000) provides a detailed discussion of different forms of multiculturalism. He argues that liberal multiculturalism permits diversity in the private

but not the public realm; that symbolic multiculturalism is little more than "lip service" to cultural diversity, fixated mostly on the enjoyment of ethnic foods or other cultural performances; and that corporate multiculturalism focuses on removed impediments to employment competition among individuals from minority groups. Yoneyama (2003) develops a notion of "critical multiculturalism." Kajita (1996) and Tai (1999) provide working definitions of pluralism as conceptualizing an array of social differences always in relation to a central, more dominant cultural reference. Takanori (2003) advances a multicultural approach to Japanese folklore studies.

8. The canonical texts in English on Buraku issues are de Vos and Wagatsuma's edited volume *Japan's Invisible Race: Caste in Culture and Personality* (1966), their compendium volume *Japan's Minorities: Burakumin, Koreans, Ainu, and Okinawans* (1983), Yoshino and Murakoshi's *The Invisible Visible Minority: Japan's Burakumin* (1977), and Hane's *Peasants, Rebels, Women, and Outcastes: The Underside of Modern Japan* (1982). These are complemented by more recent social-scientific texts on the Buraku situation: compare Amos 2011; Bondy 2005; Cangia 2013; Davis 2001; Gordon 2008; McLauchlan 2000; Neary 1989, 1997, 2010; Reber 1999; Upham 1993; also compare works that take multiethnic or multicultural Japan as their object of inquiry: Befu 2001; Lie 2001, 2004; McCormack 2001; Weiner 1997. McKnight's (2011) and Zimmerman's (2008) examinations of the writings of Buraku author Nakagami Kenji situate Buraku issues in practices of writing and state building. Morris-Suzuki (1998) provides a discussion of difference in Japan, particularly as canalized along lines of race, culture, or civilization, where she argues for understanding Meiji social structure not defined by a clear mark of racial exclusivity but, rather, as "an intricate galaxy of statuses spiraling outward from a center represented by the imperial court and Shogunal administration" (91).

9. Befu 2001, Lie 2004, Oguma 1995, and Yoneyama 2003 offer analyses of the myth of homogeneity in Japan.

10. Fujitani (2011) offers an analysis of how the management of populations through the category of race transformed in Japan and the United States during the Asia-Pacific War. He glosses this change as a shift from vulgar to polite racism.

11. Burgess 2007.

12. Here and throughout the book I distinguish between labor and work, where work is the form that the human power of labor takes under particular conditions of production.

13. The denunciation session, or *kyūdankai*, has served as the Buraku political movement's premier political engine. Developed in the 1920s, this tactic took redress for perceived discrimination into the hands of the Buraku people themselves, instead of relying on state intervention. I discuss this tactic, and its relationship to more recently developed tactics, such as human rights seminars, in chapter 4. For a critical engagement with the politics of anachronism, albeit in a different context, see Tambar 2011.

14. This edict was originally called the *Senminhaishirei*, or "Edict to Abolish the Abject Classes." It was later popularly referred to as the *Kaihōrei*, or "Emancipation

Edict." McKnight (2011: 40–41), drawing on the work of Hirota (1990), provides an excellent discussion of the ways in which this legal shift served as both an opportunity and impediment to Buraku liberation. She notes that despite the name "Emancipation Edict," the legal shift had nothing to do with slavery. Translating Hirota, she points out that the law reads that "the abjected names of *Eta* and *Hinin* should be abolished, and both *mibun* (status) and occupations should be the same as *heimin*," or commoners (Hirota 1990: 76–77, translated in McKnight 2011: 40).

15. Fujisawa 2001; Neary 1997; Upham 1993.

16. Inoue (1969) proposes what he calls *San'i Ittai Ron* (or Tripartite Theory) to understand the constitution of Buraku difference. Noguchi (2000) argues that the influence of these three vectors of contagion has decreased in recent years. Throughout the book I provide an ethnography of the ways in which these and other channels are marshaled as evidence of Buraku difference.

17. Deguchi 1999.

18. Neary 1997; Tomonaga 2005.

19. Morris-Suzuki argues that the Buraku situation highlights how "discrimination . . . produces difference as much as difference produces discrimination" (1998: 92). Noguchi, in his 2000 work, *Buraku Mondai no Paradaimu Tenkan (The Paradigm Shift in Buraku Issues),* offers a new, expansive definition of Burakumin as "those who are seen to be and discriminated against for being Burakumin, or, at least, those who stand the strong possibility of being seen and discriminated against as Burakumin" (16). These new definitions of Buraku prioritize the experience of discrimination as the basis of Buraku identity. Pride, similarly, even without experience of discrimination, can serve as the basis for some to claim a Buraku identity.

20. Kadooka 2003.

21. Kurokawa 1999.

22. Noguchi (2000: 22) argues that the challenge for Buraku political organizations is "to create people who, when told they are Buraku, say yes I am, so what of it," that is, to create people who claim a Buraku identity and yet see it as no impediment.

23. Tomonaga 2005.

24. Kelly 1998.

25. As I discuss later in this book, there has been a long-standing resistance within the Buraku political movement to using race (*jinshu*) to describe the Buraku situation. This resistance is born out of an insistence that Buraku people are as Japanese as any other Japanese person. However, in recent years they have developed a stronger constructivist analysis of race and in turn have become more willing to mobilize this category, and an analysis of racialization, to their advantage.

26. Similarly, folklore studies in Japan have recently taken up multiculturalism as a heading through which to understand Buraku issues. The founding figure of folklore studies (or *minzokugaku*), Yanagita Kunio (1875–1962), initially considered the issue of cultural diversity in Japan primarily centered on examinations of "mountain people" (*sanjin*) (1911–12, 1913a), wandering religious practitioners, and Burakumin (or "discriminated against villagers") (1913–14, 1914–15, 1913b). He contended

that these groups were all descended from aboriginal peoples ethnically distinct from the people of the lowland plains, and thus separate from "core" Japanese. He propounded the idea that cultural concepts radiated from one ideal center, his *shūken ron,* or "concentric theory." This entailed an idea of a pure center, which Yanagita characterized, in Japan's case, as sedentary and rice cultivating. Marginal groups were developed, in his estimation, primarily in relation to this ideal core. Folklore studies for the most part followed this focus, training their analytic gaze on this supposed center of sedentary rice producers. Some exceptions include those who incorporate groups such as the Buraku into their analysis: Orikuchi Shinobu (1887–1953), who brought the ethnography of marginalized groups into conversation with classical literature (1920, 1930); Akamatsu Keisuke (1909–2000), a Marxist who emphasized the importance of examining the lives of those at the bottom of the social hierarchy, including Burakumin (1991, 1995); Miyata Noboru, who gives a historical analysis of Buraku (1977); and a host of studies looking at agricultural Buraku (Nagano-ken Dōwa Kyōiku Suishin Kyōgikai 1982; Nakamura, Tsuboi, and Tada 1992; Buraku Kaihō Kenkyūjo 1995). Takanori (2003) provides a summary of folklorists' engagements and sets out a plan for a "multiculturalist approach" to folklore studies.

27. Marx 1992 [1867]: 284.

28. Graeber (2001) makes a strong argument for an always partial consciousness in this regard. Marx's own argument about the fetish underscores this point—what appears to be work on an object is actually work on a set of social relations.

29. See, for example, Bennett (2010) and her concept of "thing power"; Latour's (1996) concept of "interobjectivity" and his work on "actants" (2004: 75ff.); Braun (2005); Callon (2011); Kirsch and Mitchell (2004); Kohn (2013). This recent upswing in object-centered inquiry has coincided with an increasing concern about human/environmental relations, particularly as human action on the larger environment is more and more understood to have catastrophic effects. The English-language literature here is large: see, for example, Chakrabarty (2009); Connolly (2013); Descola (2013); Escobar (1999); Ingold (2011); Latour (2013); Morton (2013); also see the burgeoning literature on "infrastructure," for example, Anand (2011); Appel (2012); Fennell (2011). My primary conceptual framework here comes from Peircean semiotics (Peirce 1932) and those who have taken it up, for example, Chumley and Harkness (2013); Hull (2003); Inoue (2007); Keane (2008, 2009); Munn (1992 [1986]); Silverstein (2003a). This semiotic framework I find to be generalizeable beyond a focus on materiality per se; instead of starting with materiality or objects, it begins with sign relations as the site from which qualities arise. In this sense it precedes a judgment of whether something is material. Insofar as a thing is involved in sign relations, it is quality-laden, material, and symbolic. Matter does not have "vitality" until and unless in relation.

30. Latour 1996: 239ff.

31. Marx made it clear that social relations make different determining demands on things: "Hence we see that whether a use-value is to be regarded as raw material, as instrument of labor, or as product is determined entirely by its specific

function in the labour process, by the position it occupies there: as its position changes, so do its determining characteristics" (1992 [1867]: 289). At the same time, those objects make determining demands on those that wield or work on them.

32. For a more extensive discussion of bundling, see Keane (2003: 414) and Munn (1992 [1986]).

33. The substantial literature on the fetish takes up this line of inquiry. Beyond Marx and Freud, the works of Pietz (1985), Latour (2010), and Povinelli (1994) analyze the power of things, facts, and environments understood to have a will of their own.

34. Taylor (1994) provides a similar genealogy for the North Atlantic. Part of what this book offers is a consideration of liberalism told not from its purported roots in the West but from a location more contested.

35. "One thing to note is the vagueness of Hisabetsu Burakumin (discriminated-against Burakumin). More so than ethnicity or gender, it is dependent on the eye of the beholder. There are no definite characteristics that identify someone as Burakumin. Precisely because of this, our predecessors fighting for liberation have had constant difficulty when faced with the decision between 'dissimilation' and 'assimilation.' Even now, the argument continues. On the one hand, if one is perceived as different, it might provide the basis for exclusion and discrimination. Perhaps then there is benefit in ignoring difference and being subsumed in equality" (Kurokawa 1999: 18).

36. Taylor 1994: 26; compare Kurokawa 1999: 26–27.

37. Compare Fassin 2012.

38. I find particularly useful here Gal's (2003) argument regarding ongoing debates about the tensions between recognition and redistribution. For an analysis of multiculturalism, its relationship to recognition, and the binds it entails, compare Fraser 1995; Honneth 2001; see also Connolly 1991; Kymlicka 1995; Markell 2003; Povinelli 2002; Tambar 2014; Taylor 1994. Gal contends that "it is not the broad substance of demands that has changed in contemporary social movements. Rather, there has been a transformation in the social theories and categories through which movements justify themselves. Taken for granted terms such as 'class' 'economics' and 'exploitation' have largely given way to a vocabulary of 'identity' 'culture' and 'discrimination'" (2003: 93). Gal argues about the value of understanding the practices of social movements to unpack how they "create persuasive arguments and remake political subjectivities" (93). This tension is one manifestation of the tension this book traces and unpacks. I seek to understand how such frames are set up to contrast with each other, their temporal and gendered dimensions, and their ethical substance.

39. Compare Brown 1995; Robbins 2013; Trouillot 2003.

40. For example, de Vos and Wagatsuma 1966; Weiner 1997.

41. Compare Befu 2001; Oguma 1995.

42. For example, Fukuoka n.d.

43. See Lie 2001: 141, 170. To be fair, at another point in his writing, he asserts that "modern Japanese state-making made Japan multiethnic" (Lie 2004: 120).

44. One exception to this categorization is political scientist Ian Neary (1997), who deftly traces out the historical and legal conditions of possibility for different categorizations of the Burakumin and their political arguments over the past century. However, even while Neary demonstrates how, for example, the Special Measures Law of 1969 created and delimited a certain field of political argument and representation of the Burakumin, he teeters between characterizing these kinds of social practices as constituting the Burakumin as a category about which arguments can be made and characterizing them as merely affecting a preexisting category of person, whether it is called Burakumin, *eta*, or so on (compare Neary 1997: 52–53).

45. Markell (2003: 6) makes a similar point in noting "the 'politics of recognition' is not simply a framework through which some activists and scholars articulate demands for justice, but also a discourse through which some other academics and political actors have chosen to understand these demands, sometimes with suspicion and sometimes with sympathy."

46. "Dalit" refers to the outcastes of South Asia. The term is derived from the Sanskrit word for "crushed" or "ground to pieces."

47. As this book goes to press, the group is currently planning their ninth study tour to India.

48. For a more detailed elaboration of the work of commensuration, see Hankins and Yeh (2014).

49. Both Latour (1988) and Bernstein and Kockelman (2012) offer instructive analyses of the work involved in making meaning portable.

50. For example, Friedman 2008, 2009; Harvey 2005; Jameson 1991; Postone 1993; Trouillot 2003.

51. For example, Appadurai 1996; Bestor 2004; Kockelman 2005; Lee and LiPuma 2002; Pedersen 2008; Trouillot 2003; Tsing 2000, 2005.

52. Agha and Wortham 2005; Bauman and Briggs 1990, 1992; Gal 2003, 2007; Silverstein 2005.

53. Gal 2007: 2 (emphasis in the original).

54. Gal 2007: 4 (emphasis in the original).

55. My analysis here is indebted to the work of Hume (2000 [1740]) and Smith (2010 [1759]) on sympathetic transfers. I investigate the pedagogical projects that assert similarity across a bridge of difference, linking Buraku and Dalit in their own imaginaries, as well as in the imaginaries of UN representatives, even from a distance.

CHAPTER ONE

1. See, for example, Hardt (1999) and Graeber (2008) for a discussion of this distinction between material and immaterial labor. Hull (2003), Keane (1997, 2003), Miller (2005), Munn (1992 [1986]), and Povinelli (2002) all provide semiotically informed analyses of the productive powers of labor.

2. http://www.imadr.org/sayama/buraku.html, accessed August 23, 2007.

3. Compare Neary 1997.

4. While NGO work is chronically low paid, particularly compared to similar jobs in the United States, at the time IMADR provided some of the top-paying NGO positions in the country.

5. The area was renamed in 1966.

6. Japanese crows. These black birds clutter the tannery neighborhood of east Tokyo, cacophonously vying for the slightest bit of unattended raw flesh. Recently their clutter of the skies and building ramparts has increased. In late 2005 the governor of the Tokyo Metropolitan Area, Ishihara, passed a regulation enforcing the netted covering of trash throughout the city, effectively rendering unavailable what to that point had been a primary food source for the *karasu*. Forced to seek out other forms of sustenance, these massively beaked large birds have (1) turned to pigeonicide, eating pigeons out of the sky, and (2) stepped up their leather-focused vigilance, drawn in by the combination of empty stomach and the allure of succulent skin. See Kirby (2011) for a detailed examination of how these crows fit into a larger Japanese wastescape.

7. Such jobs are referred to in Japan as "*san K*" or "three K" jobs.

8. Deleuze 1992.

9. Deleuze 1992: 7.

CHAPTER TWO

1. Chapter 6 examines this study tour in more detail.

2. To be sure, this tendency to not communicate about family heritage across generational lines does not characterize all Buraku families, much less all Japanese families. Many families, particularly those deeply involved in the liberation movement in Kansai, frequently talk about Buraku issues across generational lines. However, the tendency to not have such conversations within families is, as this chapter traces out, common. Oguma-san's use of "Japanese" arises more from his contrast with my status as a U.S. citizen than as an accurate characterization of all Japanese citizens.

3. Goffman 1963.

4. This quote is from conversations with Tomonaga, but compare Tomonaga 1984.

5. See McKnight (2011) for a discussion of the role of confession in this process. See also Inoue (2006) on confessions more generally.

6. Noguchi 2003.

7. Yagi 2003.

8. Noguchi 2003.

9. It is from this novel that I take the title of this chapter. At the end of *The Broken Commandment*, Ushimatsu escapes Japan (and, he hopes, his stigma) by moving to Texas.

10. I find here the work of Gal and Irvine (2000) on scale and recursion instructive.

11. This development coincides with Taylor's (1994) analysis of the development of multiculturalism in Western settings. He contends that the lack of recognition or misrecognition confers a primary wound on those marginalized. I further discuss the politics and possibilities of woundedness in chapter 6. See also Kurokawa (1999).

12. Andersson 2000.

13. Kurokawa 1999. Again, Taylor (1994) offers a very similar analysis in a Western context.

14. Compare Inoue 1969; Noguchi 2003.

15. There is much scholarship disputing the codification of these "castes" and their articulation in different regions of Japan. Prominent here is the argument that it is anachronistic to discuss the myriad communities in the Japanese archipelago prior to 1868 as a unified "Japanese state." Modern conceptions of a unified nation-state were not born until after this restoration or, according to other analyses, not until after the Second World War. The point is to indicate that there was a tremendous amount of variation across the schematic that I so quickly gloss here. See Fujisawa (2013), Howell (2005), and Jansen (2002: 121) for more details on the Edo class system and the place of the *eta* and *hinin* within it.

16. Compare Fujisawa 2001.

17. Compare Yoshino and Murakoshi 1977.

18. Ohnuki-Tierney 1998: 41–42.

19. Compare Keene 2002; Tanaka 2004.

20. Compare Fujisawa 2001.

21. Amos (2011) makes an argument similar to the one I make in the introduction and throughout this book—that contemporary Buraku subjects are in no way determined by the caste system of the Edo period. My point in this section is that particular tensions, here between a principle of equality and a politics of difference, seeded with the Meiji Restoration, continue to haunt the Buraku political movement.

22. Amos (2011) demonstrates the ways in which this lineage is projected backward by current Buraku activists, scholars, and the Japanese government and general population.

23. See, for example, Lie 2001; Neary 1997; Ohnuki-Tierney 1987; Sakurai 2001.

24. Again, see Amos (2011) for a discussion of the ambiguities of this category of people.

25. Compare Kurokawa 1999.

26. Kurokawa 1999.

27. Neary 1997: 57.

28. Compare Robertson 1994.

29. Neary's (2010) masterful biography of Matsumoto Jiichiro provides a detailed chronicle of the outset of this organization.

30. Compare Lie 2004.

31. Data.gov, accessed July 20, 2008.

32. Compare Deguchi 1999; Japan Tanners Association 2007; Tokyo Leather Technology Center 2007.

33. Compare Deguchi 1999; Japan Tanners Association 2007; Tokyo Leather Technology Center 2007.

34. Compare Kinegawa Hikaku Shi Kenkyū Kai 2005; field notes.

35. Compare Sakurai 2001.

CHAPTER THREE

1. For example, Auyero and Switsun 2009; Checker 2005; Fortun 2001.

2. Kinegawa Hikaku Shi Kenkyū Kai 2005.

3. The government report read as follows: *"Hikaku kōjō, abura kōjō, kotsu kōjō hoka ni shite, iyō no ishūhana wo tuku, mizo, kawa he kawa no kudzu nagare warushi. Toku ni natsu ni wo te ha fu eisei nari."* See Kinegawa Hikaku Shi Kenkyū Kai 2005.

4. Suiheisha Declaration 1922.

5. Kinegawa Hikaku Shi Kenkyū Kai 2005.

6. Data.gov, accessed July 20, 2008.

7. Deguchi 1999: 12.

8. Goto 2009.

9. Goto 2009: 22.

10. I examine the possibilities opened up by this new category of discrimination in more detail in chapter 5.

11. My argument here is indebted to critical race studies work on the processes of racialization, for example, see Goldberg (1990) and Omi and Winant (1994).

12. Compare, for example, Fullwiley 2008; Moore, Kosek, Pandian 2003; Reardon 2004; Smedley 2007 [1999]; TallBear 2007; Wailoo 2007.

13. Compare Cornyetz 1994; Fujitani 2011; Russell 1998; de Vos and Wagatsuma 1966.

14. Compare Weiner 1997.

15. Compare Kita's (1968) rebuttal of the *i-minzoku* (different race) theory of Buraku difference.

16. Weiner 1997: 53.

17. I explore at greater length the qualities of this smell and its promiscuous relations with Buraku identity in a separate piece. See Hankins 2013.

18. Morii 2003.

19. Compare Inoue 1969; Noguchi 2003.

20. Yoshino and Murakoshi 1977.

21. Kadooka 2003.

22. Much of the information in the following paragraphs comes from Kadooka's (2005) work.

23. Kadooka 2005.

24. Compare Sassen 1998.

25. Kadooka 2005.
26. Maruyama 1961.
27. Povinelli 2006.

CHAPTER FOUR

1. Warner 2002: 86.
2. Habermas 1989 [1962].
3. Dewey 1954 [1927].
4. Habermas 1989 [1962]: 379.
5. Much has been said about the constitutive exclusions of the public sphere. Habermas (1989) was quite explicit that the public sphere is based on exclusions. Only property owners—and, by default, white men—were participants in the bourgeois sphere that he describes. Fraser (1992) and Warner (2002) have extended this conversation of the constitutive exclusions on which a public is based. My analysis, in complement to this literature, examines the disciplinary effects of inclusion.
6. Steger 2003.
7. Steger 2003: 183. In a similar analysis, Wolf-Meyer (2012: 183) discusses the fraught history of naps in the capitalist consolidation of sleep in the nineteenth and twentieth centuries in the United States.
8. See, for example: Inoue 1996, *Hirune no Susume (In Recommendation of Afternoon Naps);* Matsubara 1993, *Atama wo Yoku Suru Tanmin-hō (The Short-Sleep Method that Makes You Smart);* Sakai 1991, *Atama no Yoku naru Yojikan Suimin-hō (The Four-Hours Sleep Method to Become Smart);* Torii 1995, *Inemuri Ni-fun de Genki Ni-jiken—Desuku de Utatane Dekiru Sarariiman Hodo Shigoto ga Dekiru (Two Hours Fit with Two Minutes' Sleep: A Salaryman Who Can Sleep at His Desk Does a Better Job).*
9. For example, *Nemuri ha hyakuyaku no chō* (Sleep is the best of all remedies), and *Shokugo issue manbyōen* (A nap after a meal cures 10,000 illnesses).
10. Compare Steger 2003: 191.
11. Compare Le Blanc 2009.
12. Tomonaga 1984: 1–18.
13. Habermas 1989.
14. Warner 2002: 87.
15. Warner 2002: 87.
16. Warner 2002: 88.
17. Csordas 1993: 137.
18. Compare Parmentier 1994; Silverstein 1976.
19. Goffman 1966: 38.
20. Fraser 1992; Warner 2002.
21. Warner 2002: 89.
22. Goffman 1974.

23. Goffman 1974.

24. See Ober (2010), *Democracy and Knowledge,* for a discussion of the power of audience feedback. My thanks to Danielle Allen for directing me to this work.

25. Goffman 1981: 34.

26. Voloshinov 1973: 128ff.

27. Compare Bernstein and Kockelman 2012.

28. Mizoguchi 1995; Yoshida 1972; Ikegami 2005.

29. Compare Warner 2002.

30. Compare Gal and Woolard (2001) for an analysis of the interplay between these forms of authority.

31. Constitution of Japan, Article 14.

32. See www.bll.gr.jp/siryositu/s-sbet-nanika.html; also see Yagi (1976: 1).

33. Yagi 1976: 42.

34. Yagi 1976: 43.

35. Yagi 1976: 57.

36. My description here relies on Yagi (1976: 44–45).

37. Yagi 1976: 44.

38. Tomonaga 1984: 6.

39. Yagi 1976: 63–64.

40. Yagi 1976: 57.

41. Yagi 1976: 133.

42. Quoted in Chūō Riron Iinkai (1994: 107–8).

43. Uesugi 1988: 18.

44. Yagi 1976: 1.

45. http://www.bll.gr.jp/kaisetu-kydan.html.

46. http://www.bll.gr.jp/kaisetu-kydan.html

47. http://www.bll.gr.jp/kaisetu-kydan.html

48. Field 1993: 130.

49. Uesugi 1988: 333.

50. Uesugi 1988: 333.

51. http://www.bll.gr.jp/kaisetu-kydan.html.

52. Uesugi 1988: 21.

53. Uesugi 1988: 16–17.

54. Warner 2002: 88.

55. Habermas 1989 [1962]: 313.

56. Habermas 1989 [1962]: 313.

CHAPTER FIVE

1. Author's field notes.

2. Discussed in Simmel's (1997 [1909]) work, "Bridge and Door," is the constitutive tension between similarity and difference. A similar tension can be found in

the trans*queer rock opera *Hedwig,* when Hedwig sings, "There ain't much of a difference between a bridge and a wall" (Mitchell 1998).

3. In Japanese, the word *tōjisha* is used to refer to those directly involved.

4. See Reddy (2005) for a discussion of the relationship between caste- and descent-based discrimination in India. Reddy also examines the relationship of caste to the categories of race and ethnicity.

5. Hume 2000 [1740]; Smith 2010 [1759].

6. Rutherford 2009: 5.

7. I provided more details on this law in chapter 2.

8. Compare Kurokawa 1999; Neary 1997: 56.

9. Neary 1997: 57; compare Neary 1989.

10. Neary 1997: 57.

11. Suiheisha Declaration 1922.

12. Compare Neary 2010.

13. Asada 1969.

14. Asada 1969.

15. Neary 1997: 61; compare Neary 1986; Morooka 1981.

16. Neary 1997: 62.

17. Compare Morooka 1981; Neary 1989; Oga 1977.

18. Neary 1997: 62; compare Morooka 1981.

19. Compare Harada and Uesugi 1981; Neary 1986, 1997; Upham 1987.

20. Compare Neary 1997; Upham 1980.

21. Neary 1997: 68; Upham 1993: 330.

22. Upham 1993: 330–31.

23. Neary 1997: 75.

24. Fraser (1999) and Reddy (2005) examine similar shifts to the language of human rights within feminist and Dalit movements, respectively.

25. Compare Lee and LiPuma 2002.

26. Compare Bauman and Briggs 1990, 1992; Gal 2003, 2007; Silverstein 2005.

27. Compare Tsing 2005.

28. Gaonkar and Povinelli 2003: 395.

29. Compare Pedersen 2008.

30. Habermas 1989; Hull 2012; Warner 2002.

31. Hirschkind 2006.

32. Coleman 2009; Kelty 2008.

33. See also Keane 2003.

34. Lee and LiPuma 2002: 192.

35. Compare Espeland and Stevens 1998; Povinelli 2001, 2002.

36. Gal 2003: 94.

37. Compare Bauman and Briggs 1990, 1992.

38. Compare Gal 2003; Povinelli 2006: 16.

39. These words are both uncommon in Japanese. Seikei is rendered 世系, monchi as 門地.

40. Compare Tomonaga 2005.

41. Compare Inoue 1969; Yoda 2005: 22.
42. Lie 2001; Neary 1997.
43. Compare Chūō Jikkō Iinkai 2005.
44. Compare Goffman 1963.
45. Goffman 1963.
46. Kadooka (2005) offers a critique of the goal of marriage.
47. Trouillot 2003: 73–74.
48. Brown 1995: 66.
49. Taylor 1994: 26; compare Kurokawa 1999.
50. Povinelli 2001: 328.
51. Brown 1995: 27.

CHAPTER SIX

1. As I have discussed in other chapters, the Suiheisha was the original Buraku-proper political movement, founded in 1922.
2. http://imadr.org/about/, accessed February 21, 2009.
3. This was the case from IMADR's inception, in 1988, until 2010, when the BLL, due to financial constraints, moved to a less expensive building in another part of Tokyo. IMADR is now on the seventh floor of the new building.
4. Field notes.
5. Appadurai 2002.
6. Lionnet and Shih 2005.
7. Appadurai 2002.
8. Compare Neary 1997, in previous chapter.
9. Okiura, Teraki, and Tomonaga 2004.
10. Compare Uchizawa 2007: 325.
11. I discussed the history and function of this federation in greater detail in chapter 4.
12. Fanon 1952.
13. As I have discussed at several points throughout this book, Taylor (1994) argues that with the collapse of social hierarchies and the rise of liberalism and an internal, authentic self, it has become possible for those selves to be misrecognized, a process that inflicts grievous pain. Kurokawa (1999) makes a similar argument within the history of Japan and the Meiji Restoration. Taking up this train of thought, as I noted in the last chapter, Brown argues in *States of Injury* (1995) that liberalism brings with it an incitement to *ressentiment*—manifest in a pressure on those marginalized (here in multicultural terms of race, class, gender, sexuality, etc.) to present themselves as pained rather than to "conjure an imagined future of power to remake itself" (66).
14. See Kockelman (2005) for a discussion of the semiotically mediated experience of pain.

15. Compare Benveniste 1971 [1956]; Lee and Urban 1989.
16. Compare Ohnuki-Tierney 1987.
17. Compare Fujisawa 2001.
18. Deleuze 2001; compare Povinelli 2011, Rai 2002, and Simmel 1997 [1909].
19. Povinelli 2011: 5.
20. See Boltansky (1999) for a discussion of compassion, pity, and indignation.
21. Trouillot 2003.

CONCLUSION

1. Uesugi 1988: 21.
2. In line with recent literature that investigates the invention of tradition, contributors to *Mirror of Modernity: Invented Traditions of Modern Japan* (1998) make a convincing argument that the consolidation of Japan as a modern nation-state required a corresponding consolidation of a tradition stretching back centuries; such a tradition was a product of modernity. In that volume, Hashimoto Mitsuru in particular argues that this tradition included such arts as *ikebana* and *shodō* and cites Yanagita Kunio and his student Orikuchi Shinobu as key figures in this process (Vlastos 1998: 141).
3. Uchida 2008.
4. de Vos and Wetherall 1983: 3.
5. Weiner 1997: xiii.
6. Weiner 1997: xiii.
7. Lie 2001: 141, 170.
8. Amos 2011; Bondy 2005; Davis 2001; McLauchlan 2000.
9. Goffman 1963: 27.
10. Author's field notes.
11. Lesbian, gay, bisexual, transgendered, queer, questioning, intersexed, two-spirited, asexual.
12. Compare Markell 2003; Povinelli 2002; Tambar 2014.
13. Fanon 1967.
14. Povinelli 2002.
15. For a related analysis of how expressions of difference might reinscribe norms that they are intended to trouble, see Tambar (2010).
16. Noguchi 2000; Uchida 2008.
17. Inoue 1969; Noguchi 2000: 16.
18. For example, Brown 1995; Povinelli 2001; Rorty 1991.
19. See Ticktin (2011) for a related analysis.

REFERENCES

Agha, A., and S. Wortham, eds. 2005. "Special Issue: Discourse across Speech Events." *Journal of Linguistic Anthropology* 15:1.

Akamatsu, K. 1991. *Hijōmin no Sei Minzoku (Gender Folklore Studies of Abnormal Peoples)*. Tokyo: Akashi Shoten.

———. 1995. *Sabetsu no Minzokugaku (Folklore Studies of Discrimination)*. Tokyo: Akashi Shoten.

Allison, Anne. 2009. "The Cool Brand, Affective Activism and Japanese Youth." *Theory, Culture, and Society* 26 (2–3): 89–111.

Amos, T. 2011. *Embodying Difference: The Making of Burakumin in Modern Japan*. Honolulu: The University of Hawai'i Press.

Anand, N. 2011. "Pressure: The PoliTechnics of Water Supply in Mumbai." *Cultural Anthropology* 26 (4): 542–64.

Andersson, R. 2000. *Burakumin and Shimazaki Tōson's Hakai: Images of Discrimination in Japanese Literature*. Lund: Lund University, Department of East Asian Languages.

Appadurai, A. 1996. *Modernity at Large: Cultural Dimensions of Globalization*. Minneapolis: University of Minnesota Press.

———. 2002. "Deep Democracy." *Public Culture* 14 (1): 21–47.

Appel, H. 2012. "Offshore Work: Oil, Modularity, and the How of Capitalism in Equatorial Guinea." *American Ethnologist* 39 (4): 692–709.

Asada, Z. 1969. *Sabetsu to Tatakai Tsuzukete (The Struggle against Discrimination Continues)*. Tokyo: Asahi Shimbunsha.

Austin, J. L. 1962. *How to Do Things with Words*. Oxford: Clarendon.

Auyero, J., and D. Switsun. 2009. *Flammable: Environmental Suffering in an Argentine Shantytown*. London: Oxford University Press.

Bakhtin, M. 1981. "Discourse in the Novel." In *The Dialogic Imagination*, edited by M. Holquist, 259–422. Austin: University of Texas Press.

Bateson, G. 1972. *Steps to an Ecology of Mind*. New York: Chandler.

Bauman, R., and C. Briggs. 1990. "Poetics and Performance as Critical Perspectives on Language and Social Life." *Annual Review of Anthropology* 19:59–88.

———. 1992. "Genre, Intertextuality, and Social Power." *Journal of Linguistic Anthropology* 2 (2): 131–72.

Befu, H. 2001. *Hegemony of Homogeneity*. Melbourne: Trans Pacific Press.

Bennett, J. 2010. *Vibrant Matter: A Political Ecology of Things*. Durham, NC: Duke University Press.

Benveniste, E. 1971 [1956]. *Problems in General Linguistics*. Translated by M. E. Meek. Oxford, OH: Miami University Press.

Berlant, L. 1999. "The Subject of True Feeling: Pain, Privacy, and Politics." In *Cultural Pluralism, Identity Politics, and the Law*, edited by A. Sarat and T. Kearns, 42–62. Ann Arbor: University of Michigan Press.

Bernstein, A., and P. Kockelman. 2012. "Semiotic Technologies, Temporal Reckoning, and the Portability of Meaning. Or, Modern Modes of Temporality—Just How Abstract Are They?" *Anthropological Theory* 12 (3): 320–48.

Bestor, T. 2004. *Tsukiji: The Fish Market at the Center of the World*. Berkeley: University of California Press.

BLL. www.bll.gr.jp. Accessed January 8, 14, 20, 21, and 22, 2009.

Boltansky, L. 1999. *Distant Suffering: Morality, Media, and Politics*. Cambridge: Cambridge University Press.

Bondy, C. 2005. "Becoming Burakumin: Education, Identity and Social Awareness in Two Japanese Communities." PhD diss., University of Hawai'i.

Bourdieu, P. 1977. *Outline of a Theory of Practice*. Cambridge: Cambridge University Press.

Braun, B. 2005. "Writing a More-than-Human Urban Geography." *Progress in Human Geography* 29 (5): 635–50.

Braverman, W. 1998 [1974]. *Labor and Monopoly Capital: The Degradation of Work in the Twentieth Century*. New York: Monthly Review Press.

Brown, W. 1995. *States of Injury: Power and Freedom in Late Modernity*. Princeton, NJ: Princeton University Press.

Brysk, A., and G. Shafir, eds. 2004. *People Out of Place, Globalization, Human Rights, and the Citizenship Gap*. New York: Routledge.

Buraku Kaihō Kenkyūjo. 1995. *Hisabetsu Buraku no Minzoku Denshō (Folklore of Hisabetsu Buraku)*. Osaka: Kaihō Shuppansha.

Burgess, C. 2007. "Multicultural Japan? Discourse and the 'Myth' of 'Homogeneity.'" *Japan Focus*. www.japanfocus.org/-Chris-Burgess/2389. Accessed February 23, 2008.

Callon, M. 2011. *Acting in an Uncertain World: An Essay on Technical Democracy*. Cambridge, MA: MIT Press.

Cangia, F. 2013. *Performing the Buraku: Narratives on Culture and Everyday Life in Contemporary Japan*. Berlin: LIT Verlag.

Cattelino, J. 2008. *High Stakes: Florida Seminole Gaming and Sovereignty*. Durham, NC: Duke University Press.

Chakrabarty, D. 2009. "The Climate of History: Four Theses." *Critical Inquiry* 35 (2): 197–222.

Checker, M. 2005. *Polluted Promises: Environmental Racism and the Search for Justice in a Southern Town.* New York: New York University Press.

Chumley, L., and N. Harkness, eds. 2013. "Special Issue: Qualia." *Anthropological Theory* 13 (1/2): 3–11.

Chūō Jikkō Iinkai. 2005. *Zenkoku no Aitsugu Sabetsu Jiken (Annual Compendium of Nation-Wide Discrimination).* Osaka: Kaihō Shuppansha.

Chūō Riron Iinkai. 1994. *Aratana Kaihōriron no Kōzō ni Mukete (Toward a New Structure of Liberation Theory).* Osaka: Kaihō Shuppansha.

Coleman, G. 2009. "Code Is Speech: Legal Tinkering, Expertise, and Protest among Free and Open Source Software Developers." *Cultural Anthropology* 24 (3): 420–54.

Comaroff, J., and J. Comaroff. 2009. *Ethnicity, Inc.* Chicago: University of Chicago Press.

Connolly, W. 1991. *Identity/Difference: Democratic Negotiations of Political Paradox.* Ithaca, NY: Cornell University Press.

———. 2013. *The Fragility of Things: Self-Organizing Process, Neoliberal Fantasies, and Democratic Activism.* Durham, NC: Duke University Press.

Cornyetz, N. 1994. "Fetishized Blackness: Hip Hop and Racial Desire in Contemporary Japan." *Social Text* 41:113–39.

Csordas, T. 1993. "Somatic Modes of Attention." *Cultural Anthropology* 8 (2): 135–56.

Das, V. 2007. *Life and Words: Violence and the Descent into the Ordinary.* Berkeley: University of California Press.

Data.gov. www.data.gov. Accessed July 20, 2008.

Davis, J. 2001. "Challenging the State, Embracing the Nation: An Ethnographic Analysis of Human Rights in Japanese Society." PhD diss., Stanford University.

Davis, M. 1980. "Texas in My Rear View Mirror." Casablanca Records.

de Certeau, M. 1988. *The Practice of Everyday Life.* Berkeley: University of California Press.

Deguchi, K. 1999. *Hikaku a ra Karuto (Leather a la Carte).* Osaka: Kaihō Shuppansha.

Deleuze, G. 1992. "Postscript on the Societies of Control." *October* 59: 3–7.

———. 2001. *Empiricism and Subjectivity: An Essay on Hume's Theory of Human Nature.* New York: Columbia University Press.

Descola, P. 2013. *The Ecology of Others.* Translated by G. Godbout. Chicago: Prickly Paradigm Press.

de Vos, G., and H. Wagatsuma, eds. 1966. *Japan's Invisible Race: Caste in Culture and Personality.* Berkeley: University of California Press.

de Vos, G., and W. Wetherall. 1983. *Japan's Minorities: Burakumin, Koreans, Ainu, and Okinawans.* London: Minority Rights Group.

Dewey, J. 1954 [1927]. *The Public and Its Problems.* Columbus: Ohio University Press.

Douglass, M. 2003. *Japan and Global Migration: Foreign Workers and the Advent of a Multicultural Society*. Honolulu: University of Hawai'i Press.

Edelman, L. 2004. *No Future: Queer Politics and the Death Drive*. Durham, NC: Duke University Press.

Escobar, A. 1999. "After Nature: Steps to an Anti-essentialist Political Ecology." *Current Anthropology* 40 (1): 1–30.

Espeland, W., and M. Stevens. 1998. "Commensuration as a Social Process." *Annual Review of Sociology* 24: 313–43.

Fanon, F. 1952. *Black Skins, White Masks*. London: Grove Press.

Fassin, D. 2012. *Humanitarian Reason: A Moral History of the Present*. Berkeley: University of California Press.

Fennell, C. 2011. "'Project Heat' and Sensory Politics in Redeveloping Chicago Public Housing." *Ethnography* 12 (1): 140–64.

Field, N. 1993. *In the Realm of a Dying Emperor: Japan at Century's End*. New York: Random House, Vintage.

Fortun, K. 2001. *Advocacy after Bhopal: Environmentalism, Disasters, New Global Orders*. Chicago: University of Chicago Press.

Foucault, M. 1977. *Discipline and Punish*. London: Allen Lane.

———. 2003. "Society Must Be Defended": Lectures at the College de France 1978–79. Translated by D. Macey. New York: Picador.

Fraser, A. S. 1999. "Becoming Human: The Origins and Development of Women's Human Rights." *Human Rights Quarterly* 21 (4): 853–906.

Fraser, N. 1992. "Rethinking the Public Sphere: A Contribution to the Critique of Actually Existing Democracy." In *Habermas and the Public Sphere*, edited by C. Calhoun, 109–142. Cambridge, MA: MIT Press.

———. 1995. "From Redistribution to Recognition?" *The New Left Review* 212 (July–August): 68–93.

Friedman, J. 2008. *Modernities, Class, and the Contradictions of Globalization*. New York: Altamira Press.

———. 2009. *The Anthropology of Global Systems*. New York: Altamira Press.

Fujisawa, S. 2001. *Buraku no Reikishizō (Images of Buraku History)*. Tokyo: Kaihō Shuppansha.

———. 2013. *Buraku Sabetsu no Rekishi (A History of Buraku Discrimination)*. Osaka: Kaihō Shuppansha.

Fujitani, T. 2011. *Race for Empire: Koreans as Japanese and Japanese as Americans during World War II*. Berkeley: University of California Press.

Fukuoka, Y. n.d. *Minorities in Japan*. Oxford: Oxford University Press.

Fullwiley, D. 2008. "The Biologistical Construction of Race: 'Admixture' Medicine and the New Genetic Technology." *Social Studies of Science* 38 (5): 695–735.

Gal, S. 2002. "A Semiotics of the Public/Private Distinction." *differences: A Journal of Feminist Cultural Studies* 13 (1): 77–95.

———. 2003. "Movements of Feminism: The Circulation of Discourses about Women." In *Recognition Struggles and Social Movements*, edited by B. Hobson, 93–118. Cambridge: Cambridge University Press.

———. 2007. "Circulation in the 'New' Economy: Clasps and Copies." Paper presented at the American Anthropological Association meeting, Washington, D.C.

Gal, S., and J. Irvine. 1995. "The Boundaries of Languages and Disciplines: How Ideologies Construct Difference." *Social Research* (December 22): 967–1001.

———. 2000. "Language Ideology and Linguistic Differentiation." In *Regimes of Language: Ideologies, Polities, Identities,* edited by P. Kroskrity, 35–83. Santa Fe, NM: SAR Press.

Gal, S., and K. Woolard. 2001. "Constructing Languages and Publics: Authority and Representation." In *Languages and Publics: The Making of Authority,* edited by S. Gal and K. Woolard, 129–38. Manchester: St. Jerome Publishing.

Gaonkar, D., and E. Povinelli. 2003. "Technologies of Public Forms: Circulation, Transfiguration, Recognition." *Public Culture* 15 (3): 385–97.

Goffman, E. 1963. *Stigma: Notes on the Management of Spoiled Identity.* Englewood Cliffs, NJ: Prentice Hall.

———. 1966. *Behavior in Public Places: Notes on the Social Organization of Gatherings.* New York: The Free Press.

———. 1974. *Frame Analysis: An Essay in the Organization of Experience.* Boston, MA: Northeastern University Press.

———. 1979. "Footing." *Semiotica* 25 (1–2): 1–29.

———. 1981. *Forms of Talk.* Philadelphia: University of Pennsylvania Press.

Goldberg, D. T. 1990. "The Social Formation of Racist Discourse." In *Anatomy of Racism,* edited by T. Goldberg, 295–318. Minneapolis: University of Minnesota Press.

Gordon, J. 2006. "From Liberation to Human Rights: Challenges for Teachers of the Burakumin in Japan." *Race, Ethnicity, and Education* 9 (2): 183–202.

———. 2008. *Japan's Outcaste Youth: Education for Liberation.* Boulder, CO: Paradigm Press.

Goto, M. 2009. "Nihon-jin, Buraku-min: Portraits of Japan's Outcaste People." http://www.masarugoto.com/index.php#mi=2&pt=1&pi=10000&s=14&p=6 &a=0&at=0. Accessed February 18, 2009.

Graeber, D. 2001. *Toward an Anthropological Theory of Value.* New York: Palgrave Macmillan.

———. 2008. "The Sadness of Post-Workerism. Or, 'Art and Material Labor' Conference, a Sort of Review." Unpublished paper. http://libcom.org/library/sadness-post-workerism. Accessed December 10, 2013.

Habermas, J. 1989 [1962]. *The Structural Transformation of the Public Sphere: An Inquiry into a Category of Bourgeois Society.* Cambridge, MA: MIT University Press.

Hane, M. 1982. *Peasants, Rebels, Women, and Outcastes: The Underside of Modern Japan.* New York: Pantheon Press.

Hankins, J. 2013. "An Ecology of Sensibility: The Politics of Scents and Stigma in Japan." *Anthropological Theory* 13 (1–2): 49–66.

Hankins, J., and R. Yeh. 2014. "To Bind and to Bound: Commensuration Across Borders." *Anthropological Quarterly* (forthcoming).

Harada, T., and Uesugi, S. 1981. *Long Suffering Brothers and Sisters Unite!* Osaka: Buraku Liberation Research Institute.

Hardt, M. 1999. "Affective Labor." *boundary 2* 26 (2): 89–100.

Harvey, D. 2005. *A Brief History of Neoliberalism*. Oxford: Oxford University Press.

Hirota, M. 1990. *Sabetsu no Shosō (Aspects of Discrimination)*. Tokyo: Iwanami Shoten.

Hirschkind, C. 2006. *The Ethical Soundscape: Cassette Sermons and Islamic Counterpublics*. New York: Columbia University Press.

Honneth, Axel. 2001. "Recognition or Redistribution? Changing Perspectives on the Moral Order of Society." *Theory, Culture, and Society* 18 (2–3): 43–55.

Howell, D. 2005. *Geographies of Identity in Nineteenth-Century Japan*. Berkeley: University of California Press.

Hull, M. 2012. *Government of Paper: The Materiality of Bureaucracy in Urban Pakistan*. Berkeley: University of California Press.

Hume, D. 2000 [1740]. *A Treatise of Human Nature*. Oxford: Oxford University Press.

Ikegami, E. 2005. *Bonds of Civility: Aesthetic Networks and the Political Origins of Japanese Culture*. Cambridge: Cambridge University Press.

Ingold, T. 2011. *The Perception of the Environment: Essays on Livelihood, Dwelling, and Skill*. New York: Routledge.

Inoue, K. 1969. *Buraku no Rekishi to Kaihō Riron (Buraku History and Liberation Theory)*. Tokyo: Tahata Shoten.

Inoue, M. 2006. *Vicarious Language: Gender and Linguistic Modernity in Japan*. Berkeley: University of California Press.

———. 2007. "Things That Speak: Peirce, Benjamin, and the Kinesthetics of Commodity Advertisement in Japanese Women's Magazines, 1900s–1930s." *Positions: East Asia Cultures Critique* 15 (3): 511–52.

Inoue, S. 1996. *Hirune no Susume: Tanjikan Suimin no Fushigi (In Recommendation of Afternoon Naps. The Mysteries of Short Periods of Sleep)*. Tokyo: Ie no Kōkyōkai.

Ishida, H. 1989. "Class Structure and Status Hierarchies in Contemporary Japan." *European Social Review* 5 (1): 65–80.

Jakobson, R. 1985. *Selected Writings*. Vol. 7. Edited by Stephen Rudy. Berlin: Mouton.

———. 1990. *On Language*. Edited by L. Waugh and M. Monville-Burston. Cambridge, MA: Harvard University Press.

Jameson, F. 1991. *Postmodernism, or the Cultural Logic of Late Capitalism*. Durham, NC: Duke University Press.

Jansen, M. 2002. *The Making of Modern Japan*. Cambridge, MA: Belknap Press of Harvard University Press.

Japan Tanners Association. 2007. *Seikakugyō Jittai Chōsa Hōkoku Sho (Report on the Industry)*. Osaka: Japan Tanners Association.

Kadooka, N. 2003. *Hisabetsu Buraku no Seishun (Growing up Buraku)*. Tokyo: Kodansha.

———. 2005. *Hajimete no Buraku Mondai (Introduction to Buraku Issues)*. Tokyo: Bunshun Shinshō.

Kajita, T. 1996. *Kokusai no Shakaigaku no Pa-supekutibu: Ekkyō suru Bunka, Kaiki suru Bunka (Perspectives of International Sociology: Culture that Affects, Culture that Recurs)*. Tokyo: Tōkyō Daigaku Shuppankai.

Keane, W. 1997. *Signs of Recognition: Powers and Hazards of Recognition in an Indonesian Society*. Berkeley: University of California Press.

———. 2003. "Semiotics and the Social Analysis of Material Things." *Language and Communication* 23:409–25.

———. 2008. "The Evidence of the Senses and the Materiality of Religion." *Journal of the Royal Anthropological Institute* 14 (1): 110–27.

———. 2009. "On Multiple Ontologies and the Temporality of Things." *Material World* (July 7). http://www.materialworldblog.com/2009/07/on-multiple-ontologies-and-the-temporality-of-things/. Accessed December 20, 2013.

Keene, D. 2002. *Emperor of Japan: Meiji and His World (1852–1912)*. New York: Columbia University Press.

Kelly, J. 1998. "Aspiring to Minority and Other Tactics against Violence." In *Making Majorities: Constituting the Nation in Japan, Korea, China, Malaysia, Fiji, Turkey, and the United States*, edited by D. Gladney, 173–97. Palo Alto, CA: Stanford University Press.

Kelly, W. 1991. "Directions in the Anthropology of Contemporary Japan." *Annual Review of Anthropology* 20:395–431.

Kelty, C. 2008. *Two Bits: The Cultural Significance of Free Software*. Durham, NC: Duke University Press.

Kinegawa Hikaku Shi Kenkyū Kai. 2005. *Kinegawa Chiku no Ayumi—Sengo (A History of the Kinegawa Neighborhood—Postwar)*. Tokyo: Tokyo Buraku Kaihō Kenkyū Kai Shuppansha.

Kirby, P. W. 2011. *Troubled Natures: Waste, Environment, Japan*. Honolulu: University of Hawai'i Press.

Kirsch, S., and Mitchell, D. 2004. "The Nature of Things: Dead Labor, Nonhuman Actors, and the Persistence of Marxism." *Antipode* 36 (4): 687–705.

Kita, K. 1989. *Hōchi Sareta 1000 Buraku: Jigyō mijisetsu chiiki wo mite (1000 Neglected Buraku: A Look at Districts Where the Special Measures Were not Enacted)*. Tokyo: Kaihō Shuppansha.

Kita, S. 1968. *Tokushu Buraku Kenkyū (Studies of Tokushu Buraku)*. *Buraku Mondai Shiryō Bunken 5 (Papers on Buraku Issues 5)*. Tokyo: Sekai Bunko.

Kobayashi, T. 1993. *Kikai no Kaikyūsei (The Class Position of Machines)*. Tokyo: Shin Nihon Shuppan.

Kockelman, P. 2004. "Stance and Subjectivity." *Journal of Linguistic Anthropology* 14 (2): 127–50.

———. 2005. "The Semiotic Stance." *Semiotica* 157 (1/4): 233–304.

Kohn, E. 2013. *How Forests Think: Toward an Anthropology Beyond the Human*. Berkeley: University of California Press.

Kondo, A. 2011. "Migrant Immigration Policy in Japan." In *Grassroots Perspectives on Multiculturalism and Cohesion in Japan and the UK. Miejo Law Review* 61 (1): 3–30.

Kurokawa, M. 1999. *Ika to Dōka no Aida: Hisabetsu Buraku Ninshiki no Kiseki (Between Dissimilation and Assimilation: The Trajectory of Buraku Recognition)*. Tokyo: Aoki Shoten.

———. 2004. *Tsukurikaerareru Shirushi: Nihon Kindai Hisabetsu Buraku Mainoriti (Changing Marks: Modern Japan's Hisabetsu Buraku Minority)*. Osaka: Buraku Kaihō Jinken Kenkyūjo.

———, ed. 2007. *"Manazasareru Mono" no Kindai: Burakumin, Toshi Kasō, Hansenbyō, Esunishiti (The Modernity of 'People Beheld': Burakumin, Urban Poor, Leper Patients, Ethnicity)*. Osaka: Buraku Kaihō Jinken Kenkyūjo.

———. 2011. *Kindai Burakushi: Meiji kara Gendai made (Modern Buraku History: From the Meiji to the Present)*. Tokyo: Heibonsha.

Kurokawa, M., and Y. Fujino, eds. 2009. *Kin/Gendai Burakushi: Saihensareru Sabetsu no Kōzō (Post/modern Buraku History: The Revised Structure of Discrimination)*. Tokyo: Yūshisha.

Kymlicka, W. 1995. *Multicultural Citizenship*. Oxford: Oxford University Press.

Latour, B. 1988. *Science in Action: How to Follow Scientists and Engineers through Society*. Cambridge, MA: Harvard University Press.

———. 1996. "On Interobjectivity." *Mind, Culture, and Activity* 3 (4): 228–45.

———. 2004. *The Politics of Nature: How to Bring the Sciences into Democracy*. Translated by C. Porter. Cambridge, MA: Harvard University Press.

———. 2010. *On the Modern Cult of Factish Gods*. Durham, NC: Duke University Press.

———. 2013. *An Inquiry into Modes of Existence: An Anthropology of the Moderns*. Translated by C. Porter. Cambridge, MA: Harvard University Press.

Le Blanc, R. 2009. *The Art of the Gut: Manhood, Power, and Ethics in Japanese Politics*. Berkeley: University of California Press.

Lee, B. 1997. *Talking Heads: Language, Metalanguage, and the Semiotics of Subjectivity*. Durham, NC: Duke University Press.

Lee, B., and E. LiPuma. 2002. "Cultures of Circulation." *Public Culture* 14 (1): 191–213.

Lee, B., and G. Urban. 1989. *Semiotics, Self, and Society*. Berlin: Walter de Gruyter.

Lie, J. 2001. *Multiethnic Japan*. Cambridge, MA: Harvard University Press.

———. 2004. "The Politics of Recognition in Contemporary Japan." In *Democratization and Identity: Regimes and Ethnicity in East and Southeast Asia*, edited by S. Henders, 117–32. Lanham, MD: Lexington Books.

Link, B.G., and J.C. Phelan. 2001. "Conceptualizing Stigma." *Annual Review of Sociology* 27:363–85.

Lionnet, F., and S. Shih. 2005. "Introduction: Thinking the Minor, Transnationally." In *Minor Transnationalism*, edited by F. Lionnet and S. Shih, 1–26. Durham, NC: Duke University Press.

Markell, P. 2003. *Bound by Recognition*. Princeton, NJ: Princeton University Press.

Maruyama, M. 1961. *Nihon no Shisō (Japanese Thought)*. Tokyo: Iwanami Shoten.

Marx, K. 1992 [1867]. *Capital: Volume 1*. Translated by B. Fowkes. New York: Penguin Classics.

Massumi, B. 2002. *Parables for the Virtual*. Durham, NC: Duke University Press.

Matsubara, E. 1993. *Atama wo Yoku Suru Tanmin-hō (The Short-Sleep Method that Makes You Smart)*. Tokyo: Mikage Shobō.

McCormack, Gavan. 2001. *Multicultural Japan: Paleolithic to Postmodern*. Cambridge: Cambridge University Press.

McKean, M. 1989. "Equality." In *Democracy in Japan*, edited by T. Ishida and E. Krauss, 201–224. Pittsburgh, PA: University of Pittsburgh Press.

McKnight, A. 2011. *Nakagami, Japan: Buraku and the Writing of History*. Minneapolis: University of Minnesota Press.

McLauchlan, A. 2000. "The Current Circumstances of Japan's Burakumin." *New Zealand Journal of Asian Studies* 2 (1): 120–44.

Miller, D. 2005. *Materiality: Politics, History, and Culture*. Durham, NC: Duke University Press.

Mitchell, J. C. 1998. *Hedwig and the Angry Inch*. Directed by P. Askin. New York, Jane Street Theatre.

Miyata, N. 1977. "Hakusan Shinkō to Hisabetsu" ("Discrimination and the Worship of Hakusan"). In *Minzoku Shūkyōron no Kadai (Topics in Ethnic Religious Studies)*, edited by N. Miyata, 223–40. Tokyo: Miraishi.

Miyatake, T. 2007. "Hakai" Hyakunen Monogatari (One Hundred Years of "A Broken Commandment"). Tokyo: Kaihō Shuppansha.

Mizoguchi, Y. 1995. *Chūgoku no Kō to Shi (Public and Private in China)*. Tokyo: Kenbun Shuppan.

Moore, D., J. Kosek, and A. Pandian. 2003. *Race, Nature, and the Politics of Difference*. Durham, NC: Duke University Press.

Morii, T. 2003. "Mimoto Chōsa" ("Background Checks"). In *Buraku Mondai Jinken Jiten (Encyclopedia of Buraku Issues and Human Rights)*, edited by Buraku Liberation and Human Rights Research Institute. Tokyo: Kaihou Shuppansha.

Morooka, S. 1981. *Sengo Buraku Kaihou Ronsōshi (A Post-war History of Buraku Liberation Theory)*. Tokyo: Tsuge Shobō.

Morris-Suzuki, T. 1998. *Re-inventing Japan: Time, Space, Nation*. Armonk, NY: M. E. Sharpe.

Morton, T. 2013. *Hyperobjects: Philosophy and Ecology after the End of the World*. Minneapolis: University of Minnesota Press.

Munn, N. 1992 [1986]. *The Fame of Gawa: A Symbolic Study of Value Transformation in a Massim Society*. Durham, NC: Duke University Press.

Nagano-ken Dōwa Kyōiku Suishin Kyōgikai. 1982. *Arabori Chiku no Minzoku to Seikatsu (The People and the Lives of the Arabori District)*. Nagano, Japan.

Nakamura M., K. Tsuboi, and E. Tada. 1992. *Hisabetsu Buraku: Sono Seikatsu to Minzoku (Marginalized Buraku: Lives and People)*. Osaka: Kaihō Shuppansha.

Namihira, E. 1984. *Kegare no Kōzō (The Structure of Stigma)*. Tokyo: Seitsuchisha.

Neary, I. 1986. "Socialist and Communist Party Attitudes towards Discrimination against Japan's Burakumin." *Political Studies* 34:556–74.

——. 1989. *Political Protest and Social Control in Pre-War Japan: The Origins of Buraku Liberation.* Manchester: University of Manchester Press.

——. 1997. "Burakumin in Contemporary Japan." In *Japan's Minorities: The Illusion of Homogeneity*, edited by M. Weiner, 59–83. New York: Routledge.

——. 2010. *The Buraku Issue and Modern Japan: The Career of Matsumoto Jiichiro.* London: Routledge.

Nishimura, Y. 1990. *"Jōho Shakai ha Kaikyūka Suru" ("The Class Transformation of the Information Society").* Aestion 15:60–83.

Noguchi, M. 2000. *Buraku Mondai no Paradaimu Tenkan (The Paradigm Shift in Buraku Issues).* Tokyo: Akashi Shoten.

——. 2003. *"Dōwa Chiku" ("Dōwa Districts") and "Mishitei Chiku" ("Unregistered Districts").* In *Buraku Mondai Jinken Jiten (Encyclopedia of Buraku Issues and Human Rights)*, edited by Buraku Liberation and Human Rights Research Institute. Osaka: Kaihō Shuppansha.

Norbeck, E. 1967. "Little-Known Minority Groups of Japan." In *Japan's Invisible Race*, edited by G. de Vos and H. Wagatsuma, 183–99. Berkeley: University of California Press.

Ober, J. 2010. *Democracy and Knowledge: Innovation and Learning in Classical Athens.* Princeton, NJ: Princeton University Press.

Oga, M. 1977. *Buraku Kaihō Riron no Konpon Mondai: Nihon Kyōsanto no Seisaku, Riron Hihan (Fundamental Issues in Buraku Liberation Theory: A Critique of the Strategies and Theory of the Japanese Communist Party).* Osaka: Kaihō Shuppansha.

Oguma, E. 1995. *Tan'itsu Minzoku Shinwa no Kigen (The Origins of the Myth of Homogeneity).* Tokyo: Shinyōsha.

Ohnuki-Tierney, E. 1987. *The Monkey as Mirror: Symbolic Transformations in Japanese History and Ritual.* Princeton, NJ: Princeton University Press.

——. 1998. "A Conceptual Model for the Historical Relationship between the Self, and the Internal and External Others: The Agrarian Japanese, the Ainu, and the Special Status People." In *Making Majorities: Constituting the Nation in Japan, Korea, China, Malaysia, Fiji, Turkey, and the United States*, edited by D. Gladney, 31–51. Palo Alto, CA: Stanford University Press.

Okiura, W. 1999. *Kegare—Sabetsu Shisō no Shinsō (Stigma—Foundations of a Discriminatory Consciousness).* Osaka: Kaihō Shuppansha.

Okiura, W., N. Teraki, and K. Tomonaga. 2004. *Ajia no Mibunsei to Sabetsu (Discrimination and Asia's Caste System).* Osaka: Kaihō Shuppansha.

Omi, M., and H. Winant. 1994. *Racial Formation in the United States: From the 1960s to the 1980s*, Part II. New York: Routledge.

Orikuchi, S. 1920. *"Hahagakuni, Tokoyo e: Ikyō Ishiki no Kifuku" ("Motherland, to Tokoyo: Foreign Consciousness in Relief").* Kokugakuin zasshi 26 (5). Orikuchi Shinobu Zenshu 2: 3–15. Tokyo: Chūō Kōronsha.

———. 1930. *Kodai kenkyū Minzokugaku-hen (Classical Studies in Folkore)*. Tokyo: Okayama Shoten.

Ortner, S. 2006. *Anthropology and Social Theory: Culture, Power, and the Acting Subject*. Durham, NC: Duke University Press.

Parker, K. 1989. *The Continuity of Peirce's Thought*. Nashville, TN: Vanderbilt University Press.

Parmentier, R. J. 1994. *Signs in Society: Studies in Semiotic Anthropology*. Bloomington: Indiana University Press.

Pedersen, D. 2008. "A Brief Event: The Value of Getting to Value in the Era of 'Globalization.'" *Anthropological Theory* 8 (1): 57–77.

Peirce, C. S. 1932. *Collected Papers vol. II*. Edited by C. Hartshorne and P. Weiss. Cambridge, MA: Harvard University Press.

Pietz, W. 1985. "The Problem of the Fetish, I." *RES: Anthropology and Aesthetics* 9:5–17.

Postone, M. 1993. *Time, Labor, and Social Domination*. New York: Cambridge University Press.

Povinelli, E. 1994. *Labor's Lot: The Power, History, and Culture of Aboriginal Action*. Chicago: University of Chicago Press.

———. 2001. "Radical Worlds: The Anthropology of Incommensurability and Inconceivability." *Annual Review of Anthropology* 30:319–34.

———. 2002. *The Cunning of Recognition: Indigenous Alterities and the Making of Australian Multiculturalism*. Durham, NC: Duke University Press.

———. 2006. *The Empire of Love: Toward a Theory of Intimacy, Genealogy, and Carnality*. Durham, NC: Duke University Press.

———. 2011. *Economies of Abandonment: Social Belonging and Endurance in Late Liberalism*. Durham, NC: Duke University Press.

Rai, A. 2002. *Rule of Sympathy: Sentiment, Race, and Power 1750–1850*. New York: Palgrave Macmillan.

Reardon, J. 2004. "Decoding Race and Human Difference in a Genomic Age." *differences: A Journal of Feminist Cultural Studies* 15:3.

Reber, E. S-L. 1999. "Buraku Mondai in Japan." *Harvard Human Rights Journal* 12 (Spring): 297–359.

Reddy, D. 2005. "The Ethnicity of Caste." *Anthropological Quarterly* 78 (3): 543–84.

Robbins, J. 2013. "Beyond the Suffering Subject: Toward an Anthropology of the Good." *The Journal of the Royal Anthropological Institute* 19:447–62.

Robertson, J. 1994. *Native and Newcomer: Making and Remaking a Japanese City*. Berkeley: University of California Press.

Rorty, R. 1991. *Objectivity, Relativism and Truth*. Cambridge: Cambridge University Press.

Russell, J. 1998. "Consuming Passions: Spectacle, Self-Transformation, and the Commodification of Blackness in Japan." *Positions* 6 (1): 113–77.

Rutherford, D. 2002. *Raiding the Land of the Foreigners: The Limits of the Nation on an Indonesian Frontier*. Princeton, NJ: Princeton University Press.

———. 2009. "Sympathy, Statebuilding, and the Experience of Empire." *Cultural Anthropology* 24 (1): 1–32.

Sakai, Hiroshi. 1991. *Atama no Yoku naru Yojikan Suimin-hō (The Four-Hours Sleep Method to Become Smart)*. Tokyo: KK Rongusera-zu.

Sakurai, A. 2001. *Tojōbunka: Kataranakatta Sekai (The Culture of Slaughterhouses: An Untold World)*. Tokyo: Soudosha.

Salzinger, L. 2003. *Genders in Production: Making Workers in Mexico's Factory Labor*. Berkeley: University of California Press.

Sassen, S. 1998. *Globalization and Its Discontents*. New York: New Press.

Saussure, F. 1959. *Course in General Linguistics*. New York: Philosophical Library.

Sekine, M. 2000. *Tabunka Kyōsei Shakai no Tōrai (Advent of Multi-Cultural Society)*. Tokyo: Asahi Shinbun.

Silverstein, M. 1976. "Shifters, Linguistic Categories, and Cultural Description." In *Meaning in Anthropology*, edited by K. Basso and H. Selby, 187–221. Albuquerque: University of New Mexico Press.

———. 1993. "Metapragmatic Discourse and Metapragmatic Function." In *Reflexive Language*, edited by J. Lucy, 33–58. Cambridge: Cambridge University Press.

———. 1997. "The Improvisational Performance of Culture in Realtime Discursive Practice." In *Creativity in Performance*, edited by R. K. Sawyer, 265–312. Greenwich: Ablex Publishing.

———. 2003a. "Indexical Order and the Dialectics of Sociolinguistic Life." *Language and Communication* 23:193–229.

———. 2003b. "Translation, Transduction, Transformation." In *Translating Cultures*, edited by A. Rosman and P. Rubel, 75–105. New York: Berg.

———. 2005. "Axes of Evals: Token versus Type Interdiscursivity." *Journal of Linguistic Anthropology* 15 (1): 6–22.

Silverstein, M., and G. Urban. 1996. "The Natural History of Discourse." In *Natural Histories of Discourse*, edited by M. Silverstein and G. Urban, 1–17. Chicago: University of Chicago Press.

Simmel, G. 1997 [1909]. "Bridge and Door." In *Simmel on Culture: Selected Writings*, edited by D. Frisby and M. Featherstone, 170–74. London: Sage.

Smedley, A. 2007 [1999]. "Dismantling the Scientific Construction of Race: New Perspectives in Human Variation in Science." In *Race in North America: Origin and Evolution of a Worldview*, edited by A. Smedly and B. Smedly. Boulder, CO: Westview Press.

Smith, A. 2010 [1759]. *The Theory of Moral Sentiments*. New York: Penguin Classics.

Steger, B. 2003. "Getting *Away* with Sleep—Social and Cultural Aspects of Dozing in Parliament." *Social Science Japan Journal* 6 (2): 181–97.

Suiheisha Declaration. 1922. http://www.asahi-net.or.jp/~mg5s-hsgw/siryou/kiso/suiheisya_sengen.html. Accessed June 15, 2008.

Tai, E. 1999. *Tabunkashugi to Diasupora (Multiculturalism and Diaspora)*. Tokyo: Akashi Shoten.

Takanori, S. 2003. "Cultural Diversity and Folklore Studies in Japan, A Multiculturalist Approach." *Asian Folklore Studies* 62:195–225.

TallBear, Kimberly. 2007. "Narratives of Race and Indigeneity in the Genographic Project." *Journal of Law, Medicine & Ethics* 35 (3): 412–24.

Tambar, K. 2010. "The Aesthetics of Public Visibility: Alevi *Semah* and the Paradoxes of Pluralism in Turkey." *Comparative Studies in Society and History* 52 (3): 652–79.

———. 2011. "Iterations of Lament: Anachronism and Affect in Shi'i Islamic Revival in Turkey." *American Ethnologist* 38 (3): 484–500.

———. 2014. *The Reckoning of Pluralism: Political Belonging and the Demands of History in Turkey*. Palo Alto, CA: Stanford University Press.

Tanaka, S. 2004. *New Times in Modern Japan*. Princeton, NJ: Princeton University Press.

Taylor, C. 1994. "The Politics of Recognition." In *Multiculturalism,* edited by A. Gutmann and C. Taylor, 25–74. Princeton, NJ: Princeton University Press.

Ticktin, M. 2006. "Where Ethics and Politics Meet: The Violence of Humanitarianism in France." *American Ethnologist* 3 (1): 33–49.

———. 2011. *Causalties of Care: Immigration and the Politics of Humanitarianism in France*. Berkeley: University of California Press.

Tokyo Leather Technology Center. 2007. *Hikaku Tōkei Handobukku (Leather Statistics Handbook)*. Tokyo: Tokyo Leather Technology Center.

Tomonaga, K. 1984. *Heiwa, Jinken, Byōdō he no Michi (The Path to Peace, Human Rights, and Equality)*. Osaka: Kaihō Shuppansha.

———. 2005. *Nihon kara Sekai he no Hasshin: Shokugyō to Seikei ni Motodzuku Sabetsu (A Missive from Japan to the World: Discrimination Based on Work and Descent)*. Edited by Buraku Liberation and Human Rights Research Institute. Osaka: Kaihō Shuppansha.

Torii, S. 1995. *Inemuri Ni-fun de Genki Ni-jikan—Desuku de Utatane Dekiru Sarariiman Hodo Shigoto ga Dekiru (Two Hours Fit with Two Minutes' Sleep: A Salaryman Who Can Sleep at His Desk Does a Better Job)*. Tokyo: Goma Kenkō Books.

Trouillot, M. R. 1991. "Anthropology and the Savage Slot." In *Recapturing Anthropology: Working in the Present,* edited by R. Fox, 17–44. Santa Fe, NM: School of American Research Press.

———. 2003. *Global Transformations: Anthropology and the Modern World*. New York: Palgrave Macmillan.

Tsing, A. 2000. "The Global Situation." *Cultural Anthropology* 15 (3): 327–60.

———. 2005. *Friction: An Ethnography of Global Connection*. Princeton, NJ: Princeton University Press.

Tsujimoto, M. 1999. *Kegare Ishiki to Buraku Sabetsu wo Kangaeru (On Stigma and Buraku Discrimination)*. Osaka: Kaihō Shuppansha.

Tsuneyoshi, R., K. Okano, and S. Boocock. 2010. *Minorities and Education in Multicultural Japan: An Interactive Perspective*. London and New York: Routledge.

Uchida, R. 2008. "'*Bunsanron*' '*Netako wo Okusanaron*' *ni Kan suru Dōkō to Kadai*" ("Tendencies and Challenges in 'Dispersal Theory' and 'Wake not the Sleeping Child Mentality'"). In *Buraku Mondai ni Kan suru Ishiki no Hensen to Keihatsu no Kadai (Challenges in Enlightenment and Changing Awareness of Buraku Issues)*, edited by Buraku Liberation and Human Rights Research Institute, 101–10. Osaka: Buraku Kaihō Jinken Kenkyū Hōkokusho 10.

Uchizawa, J. 2007. *Sekai Tochiku Kikō (The World's Slaughterhouse Tour)*. Osaka: Kaihō Shuppansha.

Uesugi, S. 1988. *Sabetsu Hyōgen to Kyūdan (Discriminatory Language and Denunciation)*. Osaka: Kaihō Shuppansha.

Upham, F. 1980. "Ten Years of Affirmative Action for Japanese Burakumin: A Preliminary Report on the Law on Special Measures for Dowa Projects." *Law in Japan: An Annual* 20:39–87.

———. 1987. *Law and Social Change in Japan*. Cambridge, MA: Harvard University Press.

———. 1993. "Unplaced Persons and Movements for Place." In *Postwar Japan as History*, edited by A. Gordon, 325–346. Berkeley: University of California Press.

Urban, G. 1996. "Entextualization, Replication, Power." In *Natural Histories of Discourse*, edited by M. Silverstein and G. Urban, 21–44. Chicago: University of Chicago Press.

———. 2001. *Metaculture: How Culture Moves through the World*. Minneapolis: University of Minnesota Press.

Vlastos, S. 1998. *Mirror of Modernity: Invented Traditions of Modern Japan*. Berkeley: University of California Press.

Voloshinov, V. N. 1973. *Marxism and the Philosophy of Language*. Cambridge, MA: Harvard University Press.

Wailoo, Keith. 2007. "Inventing the Heterozygote: Molecular Biology, Racial Identity, and the Narratives of Sickle-Cell Disease, Tay-Sachs, and Cystic Fibrosis." In *Beyond the Body Proper: Reading the Anthropology of Material Life*, edited by J. Farquhar and M. Locke, 658–72. Durham, NC: Duke University Press.

Warner, M. 2002. *Publics and Counterpublics*. New York: Zone Books.

Watanabe, N. 1994. *Nihon Kindai Bungaku to "Sabetsu" (Japanese Modern Literature and "Discrimination")*. Tokyo: Ota Shuppansha.

Weiner, M., ed. 1997. *Japan's Minorities: The Illusion of Homogeneity*. London: Routledge.

Willis, P. 1981. *Learning to Labor*. New York: Columbia University Press.

Wolf-Meyer, M. 2012. *The Slumbering Masses: Sleep, Medicine, and Modern American Life*. Minneapolis: University of Minnesota Press.

Yagi, K. 1976. *Sabetsu Kyūdan: Sono Shisō to Rekishi (Denouncing Discrimination: Ideology and History)*. Tokyo: Shakai Hyōronsha.

———. 2003. *"Neta Ko wo Okosuna"* ("Wake not the Sleeping Child"). In *Buraku Mondai Jinken Jiten (Encyclopedia of Buraku Issues and Human Rights)*, edited by Buraku Liberation and Human Rights Research Institute. Tokyo: Kaihō Shuppansha.

Yanagita, K. 1911–12. *"Itaka oyobi Sanka." Jinruigaku zasshi,* September-November, 1911; February 1912. *Yanagita Kunio Zenshū* 4, 454–82. Tokyo: Chikuma Shobō.

————. 1913a. "Sanjin Gaiden Shiryō." *Kyodo Kenkyū,* March, April, August, September, 1913. *Yanagita Kunio Zenshū* 4, 385–418. Tokyo: Chikuma Shobō.

————. 1913b. "Iwayuru Tokushu Buraku no Shirui." *Kokka Gakkai Zasshi,* May 1913. *Yanagita Kunio Zenshū* 4, 483–506. Tokyo: Chikuma Shobō.

————. 1913–14. "Fujō Kō." *Kyōdo Kenkyū,* March 1913–February 1914. *Yanagita Kunio Zenshū* 11, 305–415. Tokyo: Chikuma Shobō.

————. 1914–15. "Kebōzu Kō." *Kyōdo Kenkyū,* March 1914–February 1915. *Yanagita Kunio Zenshū.* Tokyo: Chikuma Shobō.

Yang, L. H., et al. 2007. "Culture and Stigma: Adding Moral Experience to Stigma Theory." *Social Science and Medicine* 64 (7): 1524–35.

Yoda, H. 2005. *"Sabestu Kenkyū no Aratana Isō"* ("New Elements in Discrimination Research"). *Kaihō Shakai Gaku Kenkyū* (*Liberation Sociology Research*) 19:7–25.

Yoneyama, L. 2003. *Bōryoku, Sensō, Ridoresu: Tabunkashugi no Poritikusu (Violence, War, Redress: The Politics of Multiculturalism).* Tokyo: Iwanami Shoten.

Yoshida, T. 1972. *"Kōchi Kōmin ni Tsuite" (On the Kōchi Kōmin System).* In *Zoku Nihon Kodai Shi Ronshū Chūkan (Collection of Classical Japanese History),* edited by T. Sakamoto. Tokyo: Yoshikawa Kōbunkan.

Yoshino, R., and S. Murakoshi. 1977. *The Invisible Visible Minority: Japan's Burakumin.* Osaka: Osaka Liberation Institute.

Zimmerman, E. 2008. *Out of the Alleyway: Nakagami Kenji and the Poetics of Outcaste Fiction.* Cambridge, MA: Harvard University Press.

INDEX

affect, 27, 62, 66, 157, 238–39
agency, 20, 66, 137; and identity, 77–79, 81
All Romance Incident, 137–39, 161
anthropology: and the discourse of others,
    xiii–xiv; and the savage slot, xiv–xvi,
    231; and the suffering slot, xv
anxiety, 27, 62, 63–66, 88–89, 120
attention, 123, 130, 134; demanding, 141,
    143; and labor, 53; to minority groups,
    5, 15, 23; qualities of, 125, 129, 147–49;
    uptake of, 124, 129
attentiveness: and culpability, 143–44; and
    discipline, 48–49, 57–58, 128, 130, 148;
    and inattentiveness, 128; and publics, 22,
    124–25, 128–30, 134; and statistics, 231
authenticity, 9, 15, 22–23, 131, 133; and
    multicultural representation, 224–25,
    228–34

background checks, 1, 114–16, 144
biopolitics, 72, 230–31
body, 18, 20, 33, 52–56, 58–59, 179, 224;
    circulation of, 169; and embodiment,
    129; and sympathy, 157, 214
Brown, Wendy, 182
Buraku, 2–4, 34–36; ambiguity of, 2–4,
    108, 231, 244n19, 249n21; and folklore
    studies, 244n26; history of, 76–79,
    103–5, 249n15; and kinship, 115–16;
    and occupation, 85–86, 117–18; and
    race, 111–13, 242n3, 244n25; and space,
    116–17; and scent, 108–11, 113–14. See
    also Buraku Liberation and Human

Rights Research Institute (BLHRRI);
    Buraku Liberation League (BLL);
    Discrimination Based on Work and
    Descent; family; International
    Movement Against All Forms of
    Discrimination and Racism (IMADR);
    kinship; leather industry; Suiheisha
Buraku Liberation and Human Rights
    Research Institute (BLHRRI), 36, 37,
    38, 40, 68, 121, 126, 128, 132, 164–65,
    172, 175–76, 177, 189, 196, 226
Buraku Liberation League (BLL), 3,
    24, 238; and difficulty of cultivating
    membership, 8, 14, 63, 74, 88, 90; and
    defining Buraku, 3–4, 12, 13, 68–70,
    103, 112, 119, 203; and Dowa Special
    Measures, 70–73, 83–85, 87, 104, 158,
    163–64; and gender, 43; and the Liberal
    Democratic Party, 162, 163, 168; and
    relationship with Communist Party,
    36, 67, 161–62, 183. See also denunciation
    session; human rights seminar;
    International Movement Against All
    Forms of Discrimination and Racism
    (IMADR); Kumisaka, Shigeyuki;
    Ushimatsu

care, 16, 17, 34, 213; and the body, 55, 110;
    centers for, 227; ethics of, 45, 57, 58;
    immaterial labor of, 10, 33, 43; self-care,
    55, 187
Chennai, India, 194, 195, 198, 205, 209
circulation. See movement as analytic

human rights seminar, 10, 24, 123–27, 144, 147–49, 243n13
Hume, David, 157, 213, 247n55

inemuri, 125
International Dalit Solidarity Network (IDSN), 38, 121, 153
International Movement Against All Forms of Discrimination and Racism (IMADR), 7, 43–45; history, 31, 36, 37, 166, 188, 191–93; goals, 18–19, 32–33, 188–91; membership, 145–46. *See also* Buraku Liberation League (BLL); Discrimination Based on Work and Descent; labor
invisibility, 13, 82, 88, 189; and tracking, 108, 116; of variation, 231. *See also* Ushimatsu; visibility

Japan as project, 4–7, 10, 16, 19, 24, 183–84, 215–16, 222–23, 225, 227
Japanese Communist Party, 67, 83, 135, 160–63, 168, 183
Japanese Socialist Party, 160–62, 168

kanzen kaihō (total liberation), 67–68, 69, 124, 128
Kinegawa, 46, 47, 48, 97*fig.,* 101–2. *See also* Higashi Sumida
kinship, 11, 13, 24, 62, 70, 76, 88, 111–12, 115, 119, 176. *See also* family
knowing/unknowing people, 66–67, 70
koseki. See family: family registry system
Kumisaka, Shigeyuki, 41, 62, 68, 169, 179
Kurokawa, Midori, 21, 75, 82, 228, 242n4
kyūdankai. See denunciation session

labor, 19–21; of representation vs. work represented, xvii, 4, 6–7, 9–10, 16, 27–28, 38–59, 107, 224; and stigma, 2–3, 8, 11, 13, 35, 96, 99, 231, 241n1; and sympathy, 157, 214. *See also* body; multiculturalism, labor of; work
language: of discrimination, 102; and ideology of homogeneity, 5–6, 229;

language ideology, 132; for international audiences, 18, 23, 32, 37, 40–43, 168, 171, 253n23; preparation, 38, 186, 197–200, 201; use, 19, 39, 77, 209. *See also* publics
leather industry: historical statistics, 85–86, 97–100, 101–2; liberalization of, 9, 11–12, 85, 103–4, 108; and outsourcing of labor, 117. *See also* General Agreement on Tariffs and Trade; Special Measures Law
liberalism, 241n4, 246n34, 254n13; as product of framing, 27; and tension between freedom and constraint, 96, 119; and quest for progress, 182
Lubbock, Texas, xii–xiii, 48, 196, 237–38, 241n2

Marx, Karl, 19, 26, 246n33
Matsumoto, Jiichiro, 83, 160–61, 165, 169
Meiji restoration, 11, 35, 75–79, 100–101, 116, 119, 159, 243n8, 249n21, 254n13
mimoto chōsa. See background checks
Ministry of Economy, Trade, and Industry, 12
mobility: and discrimination, 176; and inability to escape stigma, 116; and shifting boundaries, 35, 77, 101, 117–18; uneven, 238–40. *See also* movement as analytic
movement as analytic, 16–17, 25–27; circulation as a form of, 168–71
multiculturalism, 4–6, 8, 15–16, 86, 215, 227–28, 242n7, 244n26, 246n38, 249n11; academic literature on, 23–24; as form of governance, 22, 94, 119–20, 224–25, 232; labor of, 6–7, 9–10, 17, 20–21, 26–27, 34, 148, 183–84, 223, 232–35. *See also* authenticity; Discrimination Based on Work and Descent; recognition; work

Nihon Dōwakai, 162–63

ooyake, 132, 141, 142. *See also* publics
other, the, xiii, xv; otherness, 219–20, 225–27, 231

pain, 54, 69, 254n13; approach to studying, 200; and commensuration, 25, 156–57, 195, 208–14; as projected into time, 179–83, 205; and self-narration, 186–87, 201–2. *See also* body

passing, 13, 21, 65–66, 242n3

political tactics. *See* denunciation session; human rights seminar

pollution: attention to, 96; and economic viability, 96, 98–99, 120; environmental critique of, 24, 86, 94–95, 104–5, 108; and identity, 108, 113, 120; legal standards for, 96, 98–100; relocation of, 101–2, 120. *See also* stigma

Povinelli, Elizabeth, xvi, 119, 169, 214, 230

private detectives, 1, 24, 94, 114–16, 118–19, 120, 144

privilege, xiii, xv, 61, 127, 168

progress, notion of temporal, xiv, 180–82, 205, 209, 211, 213

publics, 9, 22, 24, 123–25, 129–30, 132–34, 141–44, 148–49, 251n5. See also *ooyake; seken-sama*

qualities, 3, 20, 111, 112, 129, 230, 245n29; of attention, 143, 147–49; and sympathy, 157, 181–82

race, 3, 14, 24, 121, 159, 226, 234–35, 244n25; and descent, 167; and lack of legal protection, 135; and management of population, 5, 243nn8,10; and nature, 111–12, 242n3. *See also* homogeneity, myth of Japanese

recognition, 246n38; of Buraku, 3–4, 6, 23–24, 65, 77, 115, 118–19; and identity, 77–78, 207; international, 166–67, 234; labor of, 4, 6; misrecognition, xv, 22, 187, 249n11; multicultural, 14–15, 17, 38, 223, 229

representation. *See* work

seken-sama, 141–44. *See also* publics

signification, 26, 169

social justice, xiii, xix, 42, 45, 57, 247n45

Special Measures Law, 12, 70, 72, 83–85, 87, 89, 104, 116–17, 158, 162–64, 196, 227

standards: and commensurations, 4, 23, 25, 27, 94, 115–16, 156–57, 168, 171, 184, 188, 191, 213, 215, 230; environmental, 12, 96, 98–99; of living, 70, 72, 89, 177

statistics, 230–231

stigma, 3–4, 65–67, 242n4. *See also* passing; recognition

suffering, 22–23, 96, 172, 179, 210, 232. *See also* anthropology; pain

Suiheisha, 12, 75, 79, 82, 103, 134–37, 143, 160–61; declaration, 80–81, 83, 165, 191

sympathy, 24–25, 27, 157, 181–82, 184, 200, 212; and imagination, 157, 187, 192, 197, 213–14

tabunka kyōsei. See multiculturalism

Taylor, Charles, 22, 228, 246n34, 249n11

tōjisha, 42, 139, 178, 253n3. *See also* authenticity

Tokugawa period, 4, 8, 11, 34–35, 76–79, 119, 206, 242n5; family registry, 115–16; Tokugawa family, 136

Tokyo, registered Buraku districts in, 47, 70–71, 84, 94, 104

Tomonaga, Kenzō, 68–69, 121, 128, 130–31, 144, 158, 164–67, 169, 180

Trouillot, Michel Rolph, xiv–xvi, xviii, 214

United Nations, 14, 16, 25, 31, 37–38, 58, 68, 87, 107, 121–23, 127, 153–54, 156, 165–71, 178, 226; and the abstract human, 182; United Nations University, 126

Ushimatsu, xi, 21, 73–76, 82, 86–90, 107, 108, 238

U.S. occupation of Japan, 82, 83, 161

value, 19, 25, 33, 58, 75, 76, 136, 170, 245n31; stigma as generating, 224, 229–30, 232

visibility, 38, 53, 71, 77, 118; commitment to, 63, 82–83, 86; and project of Japan, 233; and racial and ethnic difference, 110–11, 217. *See also* invisibility; Ushimatsu

vulnerability, 18, 182, 224, 230

Warner, Michael, 123, 124, 129, 130, 148

willfulness of things, 17, 20